D1333056

MICHAEL,

NÉE

Laura

MICHAEL,
NÉE
Laura

LIZ HODGKINSON

COLUMBUS BOOKS
LONDON

Copyright ©1989 Liz Hodgkinson

First published in Great Britain in 1989 by
Columbus Books Limited
19–23 Ludgate Hill, London EC4M 7PD

British Library Cataloguing in Publication Data
Hodgkinson, Liz
    Michael, née Laura
    1. Great Britain. Transsexualism. Dillon,
    Michael
    I. Title
    616.85'83

ISBN 0 86287 872 1

Printed and bound by
Mackays of Chatham Limited

Contents

Introduction

D R Michael Dillon, ship's surgeon, finished dressing for dinner. He was 5 foot 9 inches in height, slightly stocky, with a naval-style beard. His uniform was brand new, tailor-made to fit him perfectly. At 37, he was mature, but still young enough to enjoy life. His hair had started to thin. This did not bother him: rather, it added to his general aura of masculine authority.

As he surveyed himself in the mirror, making sure every detail of his uniform was correct, he thought: can this really be me? Am I actually Michael Dillon? And am I really, at last, a man?

For Dr Dillon's masculinity seemed indisputable: his stance was manly, his voice was deep and his beard was full and heavy, after the manner of King George V. But contrary to appearances, Dillon was not a man. He had been born a biologically normal female. Until the age of 29, his name had been not Michael, but Laura.

In recent years, he had made every effort to conceal the fact that he had once been female. Now, surely, there were no longer any means by which his original sex could be discovered. He had erased every single trace of his female origins, arranged for his Oxford M.A. certificate to be issued with initials only, and even changed his entry in *Debrett's Peerage*, from 'Daughter living – Laura Maud' to 'Brother living – Laurence Michael' – and, coincidentally, had made himself heir presumptive to the baronetcy of Lismullen in southern Ireland.

The days when his gender was in doubt, when people stared at him in the street and openly questioned whether he was a man or a woman, were now over. No longer did he have to hide himself away taking menial jobs, despite his degree in Greats, to maintain his obscurity. Looking at him now, nobody could possibly have guessed his past or the traumas he had endured as the first person in the history of the world to undergo a surgical sex change.

Wonder of wonders, even his elderly maiden aunts, models of conventional respectability and Michael's substitute parents, had accepted him as their nephew rather than their niece. True, they had not been too happy about his joining the Merchant Navy, for in their view gentlemen joined the *Royal* Navy . . . but that was a minor consideration.

The only sadness was that his elder brother Bobby, Sir Robert Dillon, eighth baronet of Lismullen, barrister and landowner, would not acknowledge Michael in any way at all. At their last meeting, many years before, Bobby had pleaded with Michael never to admit to any kinship, even that of distant cousin. Still, this was a small price to pay for the feeling of liberation that had overcome Michael when he was at last able to change the gender on his birth certificate and declare himself legally male.

Whatever the years at sea might hold for him, they could not, he felt certain, bring any experience so terrible, so nightmarish, as that which Laura, knowing she could never live her life as a woman, had endured, mentally and physically, on her quest to cross the sexual divide. She had made a journey that no one had ever made before, a journey of unspeakable pain and suffering, in order to pass as an ordinary – male – human being.

Dr Dillon was more than content not to stand out from the crowd, and in the uniform of a Merchant Navy officer he looked, indeed, exactly like all the other officers on board ship: not more feminine, not conspicuously more masculine, just normal . . . and right.

That was all he asked – to be considered and treated as a normal man; not as a woman, not as a freak. It had been difficult at medical school, when he was still undergoing the surgery that would enable him to become male. He knew several students had wondered about him: whether he could be a hermaphrodite, or whether he was grossly underdeveloped. A few knew that he had been to a girls' school, but no one knew he had attended a women's college at Oxford. The medical students were aware that he had rowed for his Oxford college and been awarded a 'blue' – but he had discouraged closer questioning. In fact, Dillon had achieved the peculiar distinction of being the only person to row at university as both a man and a woman.

Now, all such difficulties were firmly in the past. Turning away from the mirror, Michael made his way to the ship's dining room. He could not help feeling a little self-conscious as he joined his fellow officers, but their behaviour was so open, friendly and normal that it was obvious he was accepted without question. He was just Michael Dillon, the ship's doctor.

'Hi, doc,' said one of them. 'What'll you have to drink?'

Wincing at the 'doc', Michael none the less heaved a huge sigh of relief. He was one of them. A man at last.

1

Nursery Days

MICHAEL, born Laura, Dillon belongs to that small class of talented and unusual people whose fate it was to be brought up by maiden aunts.

The roll-call of the aunt-reared includes such luminaries as Kipling, Saki (H.H. Monro) and Charlotte Bronte, all of whom wrote harrowing fiction on the theme of having an aunt as substitute parent. Michael Dillon was not to join the ranks of these literary giants, but he had in common with them a burning desire to make something of his life and not to accept the limitations of his class and upbringing. It was a yearning that could not be quenched, even by the most crass behaviour and insensitivity on the part of his aunts. The maiden aunts depicted in Victorian and Edwardian fiction were usually cruel, malicious and chronically bad-tempered, with a predilection for reminding their charges of their dependent status. The stories of Saki and Kipling often depict such women as fiendishly cruel, while Jane Eyre's aunt locks her into the Red Room and sends her to the terrifying Lowood School.

The three aunts – Maudie, Daisy and Toto – who brought up Michael Dillon and his older brother Bobby were not exactly cruel, but even so, they had little understanding of a sensitive and imaginative child's needs or feelings. After all, they were women who had decided, for one reason or another, that they did not want to marry and have children of their own. The Dillon aunts were all well into their forties and living a genteel life of leisure with their elderly parents in Folkestone when Laura, aged six weeks, and Bobby, fifteen months, were suddenly thrust into their care. The children's mother had died in childbirth and their father, who was then in his early fifties, had decided that he could not possibly take responsibility for two infants. Indeed, after Robert Dillon senior had delivered the two babies to their new home it seems that he did not even want to see them again; thereafter the children saw their father only once a year, in London.

Laura's father, Robert Arthur Dillon, belonged to a group of Edwardian gentlemen who were 'of no occupation'. On his wedding certificate he is described as being of independent means. He and his sisters came from an aristocratic family, descended from an ancient ruler of Ireland, O'Niall, King of Tara, who lived in the late sixth century. The family was granted large estates in the county of Roscommon, at one time known as 'Dillon country', and comprised mainly soldiers and farmers. Robert Arthur, only son of Lt. Col. Robert Dillon, joined the Royal Navy and became a midshipman on the *Britannia*, where his companion midshipmen were the future King George V, the Duke of Clarence; and the Duke of York. After rising to the rank of lieutenant Robert developed a drinking problem, which was to stay with him for the rest of his life. Thanks to the intervention of his father he narrowly escaped being cashiered. Afterwards, he returned quietly home, and it seems that he never did anything of consequence again, apart from writing a novel, *The Prince's Predicament*, which he had privately published. He was also quite a good amateur pianist and artist.

Robert was heir to the baronetcy of Lismullen, for the then holder, his cousin Sir John Fox Dillon, the seventh baronet, had no male children and the baronetcy could not pass to a female. The baronetcy had originally been conferred upon Sir John Dillon, an Irish MP, in 1801. He was descended from a common ancestor of the Lords Roscommon and Dillon, and the family seat was at Lismullen, County Meath.

Robert was a bachelor until the age of 47, when he met a young widow, Laura Maude Reese, who was 23 years his junior. Australian by birth, in her early twenties she had sailed to South Africa where she fell in love with and married a farmer. Not long after they were married, the farmer, whose name was McLiver, had a horrific and fatal accident when his horse caught its foot in a rabbit hole and threw its rider, rolling on top of him and killing him. Laura Maude, who was watching from the verandah, suffered a miscarriage and thereafter a long illness. Having made a very slow recovery, she left South Africa for England, where she met Robert Dillon in a London boarding-house. They fell in love at first sight and married as soon as possible, setting up home in a six-storey house in Westbourne Gardens, West London.

Instantly Laura became pregnant and, seven months after the wedding, gave birth to Robert William Charlier (Bobby), a delicate, sickly child. Long before she had properly recovered from Bobby's birth, Laura became pregnant again and on 1 May 1915 gave birth to a girl, a far more robust and healthy infant, in a Ladbroke Grove nursing home. Ten days later the young mother died, aged only 27, of puerperal fever.

The elderly father, so long a bachelor, was now left with two small babies to bring up. Distraught at the sudden death of his wife, he refused even to look at the new baby, whom he blamed for having caused his beloved Laura's death. In fact, the only thing he managed to do for his daughter, it seemed, was to give her a name – Laura Maud, after her mother. It was a name that the child was to hate all her life. The birth was registered six weeks late, on 3 June, by Jessie Emily Rhind, a nurse at the maternity hospital, who was present at the birth and also at the death of Dillon's mother. Robert Dillon could not even bring himself to register the birth, so unwilling was he to acknowledge the fact that he had another child.

There is nothing to suggest that the new arrival was anything other than a completely normal girl in the anatomical and biological sense. No ambiguity existed, nor was any mistake made at birth. The child was strong and thrived from the very start. Although in social terms Laura was born with a silver spoon in her mouth, she was never to know the love of either a mother or a father. The child was instantly rejected by her father, and as the mother was so ill after the birth, none of the 'bonding' which is now considered essential could take place.

Having decided that he could not take personal responsibility for the two children, Robert arranged with his favourite sister, Melita, who was just a year younger than him, to collect the babies and take them to Folkestone to live with her and her two spinster sisters. He would provide money for their upkeep and for a nanny, but he made it clear that he did not want to see them or play any part in their lives.

Although Robert was the only son of Lt. Col. Robert Dillon, there were six daughters, three of whom had married. At the time Bobby and Laura arrived at the Folkestone house, three aunts and the aged grandparents were in residence. Laura's grandfather, by this time in his nineties, died when she was a year old. Laura and Bobby were therefore brought up in an all-female house, without any male influence whatever. The three aunts who had married, and who all lived nearby, were widowed, so there were not even any uncles around. The maiden aunt called Melita – the name is the ancient one for Malta, where Laura's grandfather was for a time governor – took the prime responsibility for the children. By the time Laura and Bobby came to Folkestone, she had settled into a very strict, narrow and unvarying routine of shopping, church-going, resting in the afternoon and issuing her orders to the other members of the family. Melita, like the other five daughters, had been privately educated – which in their case meant not educated at all – and had never followed any kind of occupation or career. Melita had lived all her life with her parents and had never even considered marrying, being too 'nervous'. She was known as Tottie in the family, which Bobby and Laura soon converted to Toto, a name which stuck to her for the rest of her long life.

The second aunt, Daisy (real name Minna Marguerite), was four years younger than Toto and completely under her thumb. It seems that Daisy never learned to stand up for herself and did as Toto told her all her life. Maudie, the third maiden aunt in the Folkestone house, and an identical twin to another aunt, Evie, seemed to play little part in the children's life.

Although its inhabitants were far from ideal people to bring up children, the house itself was perfect. It was built on a square around public gardens in which it was perfectly safe for children to play. The square had six tennis courts and lots of bushes where, as Laura and Bobby grew older, they loved to amuse themselves. The house itself did not have a private garden, but because of the proximity of the square that did not matter.

For the first few years of Laura and Bobby's life in Folkestone their grandmother was still alive, although paralysed by a stroke and unable to walk. She was pushed around in a bath chair by Daisy, the aunt who devoted her life to looking after other people – first her mother, and then her older sister Toto. Daisy was consumed by a sense of duty, which led her always to put other people's wishes before her own. To modern eyes, the narrow life she led may seem to have been almost intolerable, but in a way she had chosen it.

There were no real intellectuals or scholars in the Dillon lineage, but Daisy came closest. Although not formally educated, she was fond of reading the classics in translation and was extremely musical. She was also a keen amateur photographer, with her own dark-room at the top of the house, and she submitted a lot of work to local exhibitions.

The first thing the aunts had to do when Laura and Bobby arrived was to get the baby christened, as it had not occurred to their father to do this. The next task was to fit out a nursery and hire a nanny: everything had to be done properly, and in the correct order. Although the aunts had never wished to bring up children, their own or anyone else's, they were determined to do what they considered correct, to bring Bobby up to be a gentleman and Laura a young lady. They wanted to be kind, but unfortunately for Laura the aunts were almost completely lacking in imagination or vision, and could not see that she was, in some indefinable way, 'different' from other little girls. To them, girls were brought up one way and boys another, and they were only interested in following current upper-class orthodoxy.

However, it must have soon become apparent even to the myopic and narrow-minded aunts that, of the two, Bobby was the more 'feminine' child and Laura the more 'masculine'. Bobby, of course, was to be given a proper gentleman's education; after all, he would one day inherit the baronetcy. Throughout their childhood the aunts tried to make Bobby more masculine in his behaviour while Laura was encouraged to be more like a conventional little girl – compliant, demure, neat, tidy and pretty. In fact, Laura soon turned into the typical tomboy and daredevil, much like Enid Blyton's George in the *Famous Five* books. From her earliest years Laura, like the fictional George, was extremely uncomfortable in the female role.

On the aunts' part there was certainly never any wish, conscious or unconscious, to pretend that Laura was a boy, or to treat her as male. Nothing was expected of Laura, and she was brought up, as most girls of her class were in those days, to be secondary, passive and kept in the background.

When Laura and Bobby were taken to Folkestone in the summer of 1915 the town was extremely respectable, indeed genteel, and aristocratic families such as the Dillons were by no means uncommon. In those days the place had an air of unhurried elegance and refinement.

The aunts knew plenty of their own kind living nearby. It was the sort of place where people lived by the rules, there being little tolerance of any deviation from them.

The aunts brought Laura and Bobby up much as they had been brought up themselves, with nursery teas, Sunday-best clothes, sedate walks and occasional treats. The first house they lived in, where some of the aunts had themselves been brought up, was one which had certain rooms for children and other rooms for the grown-ups. During their early years the children would eat separately from the grown-ups, being brought into the dining room only on special occasions. The house had both a drawing room and a sitting room, the former used for special guests and the latter for the less elevated visitors.

There were plenty of servants; apart from the nanny, a cook and two maids lived in, occupying rooms at the top of the house.

Bobby and Laura were taken for outings in a double pram by the current nanny and soon got to know other children of their age and class. They were of course completely segregated from any 'common' children, in case they picked up bad language or behaviour. From the start, their illustrious ancestry was drummed into them, and from an early age both Bobby and Laura knew their lineage off by heart.

If the aunts had been at all observant, they would have noticed that the infant Laura was not, perhaps, quite like other little girls, content with having ribbons put in her hair and playing with dolls. An early incident, ignored by the aunts, was a small pointer to what the future had in store. One morning, when the children were about five or six and Nanny was dressing them prior to a visit to the barber's, Laura announced that she wanted to have her hair cut 'just like Bobby's'. The nanny laughed and said, 'Don't be silly, you can't. You're a little girl and he's a little boy.' When they arrived at the barber's, the nanny then said to Laura: 'Now tell the barber what you said to me in the nursery.' Laura, having some sixth sense that she had said something wrong, became extremely embarrassed and refused to open her mouth, but the nanny insisted. Eventually she said that she wanted her hair cut just like Bobby's, which both the nanny and the barber found a huge joke. Of course, there was no question whatever of their complying with the request, and Laura's hair stayed in a girlish bob, with a slide or ribbon to keep it from falling over her face.

This incident had a curious effect on Bobby, who later demanded that he should have a ribbon in his hair, just like his sister. He cried and cried until one was put on him, and he wore it for the afternoon, although never again.

One evening, while they were both in the bath, Toto came into the bathroom and asked the children to get out quickly as their Daddy had come to see them. Laura could remember her father having been to the Folkestone house only once before, so far from being a fond parent was he. Even this time she retained no strong recollection of him, only a dim memory of a male figure in a dark suit who saw the children once they were in bed in the nursery. At this time Laura was aged about four and Bobby would have been five. Dillon says in his unpublished memoirs that the prime motivation for their father's visit must have been curiosity, to see how they were turning out, as he never showed any love or regard of any kind for his offspring. On this occasion, he vanished as soon as he saw them in bed.

It is something of a mystery how Robert Dillon senior occupied his time, as he had no job and no real interests. But perhaps his alcoholism, which was becoming quite serious by the time he was in his mid-fifties, served to blot out most of the days. For some reason, when Laura was about a year old, he bought an hotel, the Sorrento, which was in Tavistock Square (where the British Medical Association is now), and took up with a widow, Mrs Mary Hearne, who managed the hotel. Whether there was any sexual or emotional relationship is hard to establish, but Mrs Hearne managed to ingratiate herself so far into Robert Dillon's affections that she became a trustee for the children, and was eventually able to get her hands on quite a lot of his money.

As the children grew up and out of the nursery stage, the aunts entered more into their lives. The nanny was replaced by a nursery governess, who taught the children to read and write. Toto now took the children out shopping with her, and also to church. At church, class differences were strictly observed. Laura and Bobby were taken to the children's service on Sunday afternoons but were not allowed to go to the Sunday school, as that was for the children of tradesmen. At the children's service the tradesmen's offspring would sit on the left aisle while the elite, including Bobby and Laura, were seated on the right. The family was staunchly and conventionally Protestant and church-going constituted a major part of its social life.

The rigid upbringing which was standard for upper-class children of the day also incorporated codes of dress. In this, as everything else, the aunts were determined to be correct. For Sunday best the children wore sailor suits, with trousers for Bobby and a kilt for Laura. She did not mind about this distinction, but where coats were concerned Bobby came off best in Laura's eyes. He had a pilot coat, sporting brass buttons with anchors on them – a coat that Laura desperately envied. She badgered the aunts for one and eventually got her own way, wearing for the first time in her life a manly coat, as she thought.

Incidents of this sort built up Laura's moral strength and persistence, qualities which she would need in abundance in later life. At first, when she asked the aunts for something considered unsuitable for a child of her age, sex and class, it would be automatically refused. But early in life Laura learned that she could often wear them down by sustained effort, focusing all the time on what she wanted and refusing to take no for an answer. In the end the aunts, weary of her importuning, would accede to her demands. The other quality which enabled Laura to be so persistent was her clarity of purpose. From a very early age she knew what she wanted and refused to be deflected in her aims by the aunts' ideas of what was suitable or fitting.

Another lesson Laura learned from the aunts was how not to handle money. Although each of the aunts, like Robert Dillon, had sizeable private incomes, a fiction was maintained that they were very poor indeed and could afford nothing. As soon as they were old enough to be given pocket money, the children would be expected to save some of it in their money-boxes. Toto had a pathological attitude to money, and a mania, bordering on obsession, for saving everything she could. As she got older she grew increasingly miserly; at the age of 80, when she had to be taken to hospital for a fractured leg, she was thought to be a pauper, for she had no proper nightdress, dressing-gown or slippers. It seems that miserliness was a family trait, inherited from Laura's grandmother, who had passed her avarice on to her daughters. As small children Laura and Bobby thought that the family really was poor and grew frightened when they heard the grown-ups sigh and shake their heads over money. Yet when the aunts died they left over £20,000 each, a huge sum for the time. Laura was never in the least money-minded and had such a horror of accumulating capital to no purpose, like her aunts, that in adult life she gave as much of it as she could away, finally disposing of every single material asset while still alive.

As a small child Laura felt uneasy and never had a sense of belonging to her surroundings. It is impossible to guess whether these feelings were the early – as yet unsuspected – stirrings of transsexuality, whether they came about because she soon realized that the aunts' idiosyncrasies severely constricted the way they lived, or whether they related to her rejection by her father. But from her earliest years she had a sense of being an outsider, of watching what *other* people did, instead of joining in and feeling part of a society.

As she grew up, Laura began consciously to repudiate everything the aunts has instilled into her, except for speaking with what is generally known as 'received pronunciation'. This was a part of the aunts' upbringing which seemed to stick, as neither Laura nor Bobby were ever allowed to play with children who did not speak with acceptable accents. This 'elocution test' was the chief criterion employed by the aunts to decide whether a particular child was a suitable companion or playmate. One child who passed it was Tony Bentine, older brother of the comedian Michael, who became Laura's best friend in early childhood.

From Folkestone on a calm day the English Channel can be a particularly attractive prospect, especially when seen from The Leas, the main promenade in the town. The 'gentry' would parade on one side, and the 'town' on the other. The class barrier was implied by the second bandstand. That imaginary line lasted until the Second World War. Nowadays, when Folkestone has become a provincial town much like any other, with all the same chain stores, few will remember that Folkestone's residents once proclaimed their station each time they walked along The Leas. Laura was always fascinated by the sea, and loved it. She loved to swim, too, having been taught by her cousin Daphne (who also, in later life, broke away from the family, when she went to train as a singer in Italy).

When Laura was about six years old, a series of strange illnesses started that were to dog her throughout her life. There were occasions when she vomited spontaneously, without having felt in the least bit sick beforehand, and other occasions when she would show a strange allergy to sweets, cakes, strawberries and chocolate – all the things which most children love, and in which respect Laura was no exception. It seemed that the allergy was physical rather than psychological, for even one iced cake would be liable to produce an outbreak of spots and appalling itchiness. The itchiness was a forerunner of a crop of highly unpleasant blisters which spread all over her body. This meant that she could no longer eat sweets without suffering. Even the evening sweet – a 'treat' permitted by adults of the day, before it became common knowledge that sweet-eating causes dental decay – had to be given up. Later in life Dillon suffer fairly frequent hypoglycaemic (low blood sugar) blackouts, which were potentially dangerous.

In childhood there was clearly a blood sugar imbalance, which was not taken seriously until Laura was fifteen, when the family doctor was called. He took her off all forms of sugar except glucose. After that, she was able to eat anything she liked that did not contain sugar without either vomiting or having the rash, although the problem was not cured. But from her earliest years Laura suffered frequent bouts of ill-health and was also accident-prone. The illnesses may have indicated an underlying emotional malaise, but nobody thought anything of it at the time. Children's illnesses tended to be regarded as a nuisance, not a possible pointer to any kind of unhappiness or emotional problem.

Her allergic reaction to sweets and cakes was another characteristic that made Laura conscious of being an outsider, a feeling she was to retain all her life. At children's parties she had to stand and gaze while all the other children tucked into the tea-time spread. From a very early age she knew that if she were to succumb even to one tiny piece of birthday cake she would soon regret it. However, Dillon wrote later, having to exercise the discipline of self-denial was admirable practice for his later way of life.

Christmas for Bobby and Laura was, as for most children, a time of almost unbearable excitement, marred only by Toto not allowing them to play with their presents. Anything which was expensive or large had to be put away, because it was 'too good to play with and might get broken'. As a young child, Laura was given a doll one Christmas, but her guardians immediately put it away in a drawer. Forty years after this event, when Michael Dillon as a middle-aged man was clearing the house after Toto's death, he found the doll, still wrapped up in its paper and in pristine condition. When he asked Daisy to whom the doll belonged, Daisy replied that it had been a Christmas present to him (Laura), but was considered by Toto too good for her to play with. So it had been put away and Laura never saw it again. Laura probably did not experience any great disappointment over not being allowed to play with the doll, as she disliked dolls in general. However, the incident exemplified Toto's curious sense of values.

In that, she was probably typical of many maiden aunts and other childless women of her day. The mania for having 'best' china, 'best' clothes and 'best' cutlery – all of which were hardly used – was not confined to the upper classes. It signified, most probably, a longing for respectability, for standards to be maintained, a wish to separate the everyday from the special. It is a trait which in our present 'throwaway' society has now largely disappeared, and one which was, in any case, confined mainly to women who did not have much else to think about in their lives.

All the same, Christmas was usually a relatively merry time in the Dillon household, and it seems that the aunts tried to make the occasion the kind that children traditionally love. One Christmas, however, brought bitter disappointment. Laura was five years old. She and Bobby always looked forward to their cousin Daphne's presents, as her gifts tended to be the best of all. Daphne duly delivered her parcels, one wrapped in blue paper for Bobby and the other in pink for Laura. As soon as the presents arrived they were whisked out of sight until Christmas morning, when they took their place on the sofa with all the others, to be opened after breakfast. Bobby tore the wrapping from his and discovered inside a pair of men's hairbrushes. He seemed slightly disappointed, but made the best of it and muttered politely that they were very nice.

However, when Laura opened her parcel she found it contained a small blue leather jewel case, whereupon she burst into tears of rage and disappointment and threw it on the floor in disgust. Toto tried to comfort her, commenting that the case was very attractive and how much she would have liked something like that herself. Later that day, when the whole family, including Daphne, sat down to dinner, Daphne asked the children if they had liked their presents. Bobby, who all his life avoided causing upset, murmured, 'Yes' and 'Thank you very much', but Laura would not, or could not, dissemble. She said bluntly, 'No.' Everybody looked at her with horror and amazement. The 5-year-old girl had broken a cardinal social rule.

At once the aunts told Laura that she was a rude, ungrateful child and must apologize at once. This she refused to do, and remained in disgrace for the rest of the day. On any other occasion she would have been punished in the typical Edwardian manner – sent to her room without supper until she repented – but because it was Christmas she was allowed to stay downstairs. For her part, Daphne announced that never would she give the child another present unless she apologized.

Laura decided not to apologize as she did not feel sorry, but as her sixth birthday approached she relented and said she was sorry. Daphne never made the mistake of giving Laura a 'girl's' present again.

Although Bobby and Laura were as children invited to many parties, the aunts never gave a children's party in return. The main reason for this appears to have been because they begrudged the expense and moreover wanted to maintain the fiction that they were extremely poor. Another reason may have been that the aunts were getting on in years and did not relish the thought of having up to twenty young children in the house, screaming and shouting.

It became apparent that Bobby and Laura, who in their earliest years had been regarded as a unit, were to be treated very differently now that they were getting older. Bobby had to learn to take his place in the world, while Laura was to be kept at home, in readiness for looking after the aunts if and when infirmity should overcome them. When they were old enough, it was considered proper for them to be taken to London to meet their father once in a while. At first both children were taken once a year, but thereafter Bobby was taken more frequently while Laura stayed at home. It was thought essential for Bobby, as a boy, to see his father, but there was no corresponding need, in the aunts' eyes, for Laura to see him. In any case, Toto, who was always Laura's chaperone, had a strong aversion to going anywhere at all. (Bobby was accompanied by another aunt when he visited without his sister.) The outcome of this was that Laura saw her father, to her recollection, only three times before he died when she was ten.

Another reason why Toto may have been reluctant to take the children to meet him was because he was so often drunk and incapable. On one occasion Toto warned the children that they might find their father ill, and that he would not want to play with them or take them out anywhere. He never met the children at the station; they always travelled to Tavistock Square under their own steam. On arrival they would find their father, at all times of the day, sitting in a dressing-gown in the basement flat of his hotel. He was usually recovering from a hangover. By this time, it seems, alcoholism had set in and he was too far gone to be helped. Robert had suffered a drink problem from his youth; it had become markedly worse after his wife died, when he seemed to sink into a kind of permanent stupor of despair. The children served only to remind him of what he had lost, for which reason he could not bear to see them too often. He perhaps had a slight affection for his son, although he never showed this in any way, but he seemed to have no feelings whatever for Laura. Laura, however, could not feel sad, because she had never known her father, and therefore, at least at a conscious level, was not aware of any rejection. The aunts were the only 'parents' she had ever known.

Yet, despite Robert Dillon's strange behaviour, Laura enjoyed the rare, brief visits to her father's hotel, mainly because they gave her a chance to come into contact with men – a species she hardly ever encountered in her aunts' house. Several of the people in the hotel were regular guests, who took an interest in the children when they came to stay. One taught Laura to play chess when she was seven – a skill which was to prove useful in later life. The same guest, a young doctor, sometimes gave Bobby and Laura a rough-and-tumble, a childhood pleasure they could never otherwise experience, for lack of association with male grown-ups.

Laura remembers only two occasions when her father actually accompanied them outdoors: once, predictably, to Regent's Park Zoo, and once to a department store to buy Toto a new carpet. Here, the children were horribly embarrassed by the adult Dillons haggling over sixpence, until they piped up and said that they would pay it. The adults, they thought, must be terribly, terribly poor if they could not afford the extra sixpence for the carpet.

The aunts did not lead much of a social life, but they sometimes had visitors of their own class and kind. These functions would follow a strict routine. High-class visitors, as opposed to tea-party visitors, would arrive in the morning and stay to lunch. The children, who did not at that time partake of lunch with the grown-ups, would be brought in, having been told they had to be on their best behaviour, to say hello. One of these high-class visitors was 'Daisy Diz' – a great-niece of Benjamin Disraeli and a childhood friend of Toto.

Although the Dillons' early childhood may not have been a 'web of sunny air', as that of the Brontës was supposed to have been, the two children were quite close to each other in their nursery days. Now came a great change. Bobby returned from London one holiday wearing a brand-new suit of dark grey tweed with a white shirt, collar and tie. At the sight of her brother dressed thus, Laura burst into tears. It was thought that the tears were occasioned by Bobby's suit and the aunts carefully explained to Laura that she could not possibly be dressed in the same way. Perhaps even in those days they had some remote inkling that not all was quite as it should be with Laura, hence their alacrity in suppressing any indications in her of masculine attitudes or behaviour.

But for Laura there was a different reason for the tears. She perceived that these strange, smart new clothes signalled the passing of an era, an end to nursery days – cosy teas, governesses and being taught at home. The suit indicated that it was time for Bobby to go to school while she, Laura, would be left behind.

There were already signs that Laura would have liked to be a boy, for anybody astute enough to pick them up. The most perceptive adult in this instance was Mrs Hearne, the Irishwoman Robert Dillon had installed as manageress of his hotel. Once when Laura and Bobby were staying at the hotel Mrs Hearne suddenly said: 'We'll take you to the blacksmith's and have you made into a boy.'

Although Laura, aged six, had not previously expressed any longing to be a boy, she was overjoyed when she heard this as she believed it to be possible that the blacksmith really *could* effect such a miracle. But of course Mrs Hearne had only been joking. It was this remark, probably made in all innocence, as Mrs Hearne could have had no real idea of the depth of Laura's feelings, that made Laura hate the woman and regard her as evil. In fact, there was some justification for this view, as later events showed.

If her father had been any judge of character, he would never have let Mrs Hearne run the hotel, let alone appoint her the children's joint guardian, with Toto, in the event of his death. Neither was in any way fitted to her position of trust, according to Dillon when he analysed the peculiar circumstances of his childhood in later life. But by this time Robert Dillon's condition had probably deteriorated too far for him to be able to think clearly about the situation. He had never wanted to be bothered with the children and had arranged his life so that he never would be.

There was never any communication at all from Laura's mother's side of the family, the Reeses from Australia. Although the children were indoctrinated with Dillon history from their earliest years, no mention was ever made of their mother's family, so the picture they received of their background was completely one-sided.

The children were encouraged to be proud of their ancestry, but as she grew up Laura could not see any real reason for this family pride. So far as she could see, none of the Dillons had done anything at all remarkable or noteworthy. In fact, Laura was to be the only Dillon to make history.

As yet, however, while her nursery days drew to a close, there was no hint of an unusual future for the little girl. Daisy and Toto were doing their best to turn her into a young lady – one who would, in time, make a suitable marriage and settle down to an utterly conventional life.

2

Growing Up

IT was from this time, when Bobby first went to 'proper' school, a boys' school, that Laura began to realize that there was a profound difference between boys and girls – one which went far beyond mere anatomy. She was made painfully aware that boys and girls were not treated equally, and came to recognize that as the years progressed the chasm became ever wider. In some girls this discovery leads them in later life to become feminists, championing the cause and rights of women. Others eventually succumb to their stereotyped role and forget that there was ever a time when they despaired over the injustice of it all.

Laura's dissatisfaction was to take a different turn. She deeply envied Bobby for going to school, for learning Latin, mixing with other boys, and generally for moving in a world that she, too, would have liked to inhabit. Bobby was so lucky, merely by virtue of being male. He was not only allowed to travel up to London to see his father, in an environment that seemed much grander and more important than the narrow little Folkestone circle, he was bought a smart new suit and sent to a prep school. Worst of all, he now thought that playing with girls was sissy; he would no longer allow his sister to join in his games or be counted among his playmates. He already belonged to an all-male set, just as Laura was gradually learning that, through some biological error, she was to take her place in an all-female one.

She learned with growing misery that she was to be excluded from all boys' activities. While Bobby was at school, Laura remained at home with her governess, and in the afternoons, when

19

lessons were over, she would watch from the window and see the boys walking in a crocodile to play cricket or football. The school that Bobby attended was St George's, unofficially called the Pink-Cap School, in reference to the rather feminine-sounding pink caps embroidered with blue roses that the boys used to wear.

Laura envied the games and the lessons so much that one day when she saw Mr Darby, the headmaster, passing by outside the house, she ran out and told him she wanted to go to his school, too. He smiled and pointed out that the school took only boys, not little girls.

But why?, Laura wondered. What was the essence of this difference which so decisively divided the sexes? She was at least as clever as Bobby, at least as good at games, and certainly more courageous and determined. Why was he, as a male, singled out for special treatment while she was kept at home?

When Bobby brought friends home for tea on Saturday afternoons, Laura was rigorously excluded from the gathering and the games. The only compensation she had at this time was to listen to the stories that Bobby told of his days at school. Many of these stories concerned the exploits of a particularly mischievous little boy called Gibson, who was always in trouble. Many years later Laura discovered his first name, Guy, and realized that he was the same person who in the Second World War earned a VC as one of the famous 'Dam Busters'.

But schooldays were soon to dawn for Laura, too. True, she could not go to St George's, but she was sent to Brampton Down, the most exclusive girls' school in the area and the only one to which Toto and Daisy would consider sending her. All the other private schools in Folkestone admitted daughters of businessmen and even tradesmen, and there was no possibility of aristocratic Laura being allowed to mix with these low-class children. Brampton House, on the other hand, was established purely and exclusively for young ladies.

Laura was eight years old when she first went to school and had already learned to read and write at home with the various governesses. She loved the school and enjoyed being, for the first time in her life, among educated women. But at first she attended classes only in the mornings and came home in the afternoons, during which she would sit and wait for Bobby's return, when he could tell her of all the exciting things that had happened at his school.

Laura showed no inclination at all to behave like a 'young lady'. Daisy had hopefully taught her to sew and embroider, but the first thing Laura made with her newly acquired skills was a Red Indian outfit. She would put this on the minute she came home from school and crawl round the floor with a toy bow and arrow looking for 'palefaces'. These 'palefaces' were, of course, the aunts and granny, who all went for a ritual rest in the afternoons. Laura at this age also loved comics such as *Tiger Tim* and *Rainbow*, and was occasionally taken to see silent westerns at the local cinema.

After Laura had made herself the Red Indian outfit she refused ever to pick up a needle again. Instead, she became interested in fretwork – very much in vogue for boys at that time – and carpentry, neither of which pleased the conventionally-minded aunts.

Until now, the little girl's life had not been too unhappy. Bobby and Laura's childhood had at least been secure and the aunts were concerned to do their very best for the children. It was hardly their fault if Laura consistently refused to become ladylike and was forever tearing round the house in Red Indian tunic and trousers, scalping and killing palefaces. And the fact that the children's father played so small a part in their lives hardly mattered, as the Folkestone home offered security, plenty of servants and an ordered lifestyle.

Then came a series of events which were to alter the course of Bobby and Laura's lives for ever. The first was the death of their grandmother in 1924, when Laura was eight. Her passing had little impact in itself, as for many years she had been severely indisposed and, after her stroke, could hardly speak. Almost the only recollection of the period Laura retained was that her grandmother's bath chair was now empty.

In one respect Laura had cause to bless her bereavement. She had not done her geography homework and the teacher threatened to keep her in after school. Laura did not mind this too much in itself, but having been in such a situation before, she was in an agony of fear lest Toto found out that her niece had been given a detention. Laura knew that if she did, she would never hear the last of it. But when the teacher heard about the bereavement she relented, saying that she understood there had been too much disturbance in the house for the girl to be able to concentrate on her homework. Dillon said later: 'I marvelled at my undeserved luck and went on my way rejoicing.'

The other positive aspect of Granny's death was a very exciting ride in a horse and cab, following the hearse. The children both wore black armbands and noticed that everybody else was crying, but the ride was itself so thrilling that they could not feel any sorrow at all. In any case, they had had no real relationship with the old lady. Laura was impressed, too, on peering out of the curtain-covered windows of the cab, to see passers-by raising their hats as the funeral procession passed.

The major blows came after the funeral, and were set in motion by the sale of the large family house. Bobby became a weekly boarder at his school, while Maudie moved out to live at the local bridge club; as she was an addict of the game, and because she was supposed to be 'poor', she took on the job of hostess at the club, thus enabling herself to live there free. Being particularly good at bridge, she became a much-sought-after player and even made some money out of her new job.

From this point on, Laura lived an increasingly stifling and narrow life with just Daisy and Toto, who went to a set of rooms in a boarding house kept by a widow. The new accommodation was nothing like so comfortable as the huge family house and had the additional disadvantage that the three of them were thrown together to a far greater extent than before. There was, of course, no pressing need for Daisy to have gone to the boarding house with Toto, but she declared that her role in life was to look after her sister of four years' seniority, as Toto was supposed to be so delicate.

'Thereafter,' Dillon wrote, 'she came to lead a dog's life for the next thirty or more years. For Toto was extraordinarily difficult to live with as I, myself, was to find increasingly, as soon as I began to break away from her apron strings. Domineering, utterly selfish, quite incapable of imagining anyone else's feelings, and expressing her own freely without regard to the effect, and becoming more and more miserly, no one of the family but Daisy would eventually live with her. But Daisy developed a kind of cortical deafness, that is, a complete unawareness of what was going on or being said around or to her, and she lived in a little world of her own, the only possible solution to the situation.'

Like many younger sisters of the era, Daisy never stood up for herself but allowed herself to be completely dominated by Toto. The result for Laura was that life became steadily grimmer, more and more narrow, ever more penny-pinching. With increasing sensitivity, she became aware of this but for many years could do nothing, being in a peculiarly dependent position. The situation would have verged on intolerable even if she had not already been harbouring the as yet unexpressed conviction that she had been born into the wrong gender.

Bobby now came home only at weekends, which opened a rift between brother and sister that was never to close. As the children grew up they realized they had little in common and began to seek other friends. No amount of longing would bring back the cosy days in the nursery. Laura became more friendly with Tony Bentine and the two exchanged possessions, Laura giving up her bow and arrow in exchange for Tony's fairy-cycle, which angered the grown-ups so much that the children had to swap them back. Laura was always ready to get into a fight with boys, too. One of these was witnessed by Bobby and his classmates, and Bobby told his sister that her status was greatly enhanced by this set-to.

About eighteen months after their grandmother's death came news of another – that of the children's father. When Toto received the telegram she at first refused to open it, being in fear and loathing of telegrams, like many people who had lived through the First World War. When she saw Toto fingering the telegram, Laura had a sixth sense about the news it contained and wondered to herself whether it might be to announce her father's death.

On opening the telegram Toto burst into tears and then kissed her niece. Robert Dillon had apparently contracted pneumonia while on a short holiday in the Channel Islands with Mrs Hearne, the hotel manageress. (It seems very likely that she was his mistress.) Mrs Hearne had brought the body back to London and informed all the relatives. Bobby was quite upset when he heard the news as he had latterly been spending most of his holidays with his father, but Laura had seen him on so few occasions that she could neither feel sad nor experience the slightest sense of loss. As she got older, Laura had expressed a wish to see more of her father, but Toto, employing a form of moral blackmail, had always prevented this, saying: 'You wouldn't like to leave me, would you?'

At that age, Laura lacked the verbal skills with which to combat this sort of argument. Toto's method of getting her own way with her charges lay not in obvious cruelty, ill-treatment or neglect, but by subtly playing on their emotions. Although she had not particularly wanted to bring up children, she soon tried to make both Bobby and

Laura a part of her, stifling their natural wishes with her own desires. As she was a grown-up, it was for a time easy for her to impose her own inclinations. She would say to Laura, 'You can't really love me if you want to go away from me.' If ever Laura wanted to do anything, perhaps with the school or with a friend, Toto's typical response would be: 'You know I shall be worrying about you all the time, and that gives me one of my bad heads.' Likewise, her way of wheedling a favour out of somebody was to say: 'After all I have done for you, surely you can do this for me?' Daisy remained a victim to such pressures all her life, while Laura, in the fullness of time, learned how to foil her aunt's schemes once she realized what sort of game Toto was playing.

Robert Dillon died on 6 October 1925, aged 60. At the funeral in London Bobby and Laura saw their father's embalmed body; Bobby began to cry, and because he did Laura found herself weeping as well, though not out of sadness. Even so, the sight of the body awoke in Dillon a lifelong hatred of waxen images in churches and museums. Robert was buried in Kensal Green cemetery beside their mother, as requested in his will.

Having led such an unsatisfactory, unmotivated sort of life, Robert Dillon did not leave his children as much money as might have been expected. He had put all his money in rubber shares, which were then at their lowest ever, and his estate was worth just over £13,000. This was perhaps not a bad sum for 1925, and it gave both Laura and Bobby a little bit of independent income for when they were older. But it could have been much more. Robert did not distribute his money evenly between the children: he left Bobby three-fifths, and Laura two-fifths, of his estate. He also appointed Mrs Hearne and Toto their joint guardians, cousin Daphne to take over if they died before Bobby and Laura attained their majority.

Robert also stipulated in his will that the hotel was to be sold for the best price obtainable. He had bought it in Mrs Hearne's name and requested that the first £2000 from the purchase should go to her. Robert had made his will in May 1925, only a few months before his death. Probate was granted to Mrs Hearne and Toto on 30 December 1925.

Dillon does not comment on his father's unfairness in leaving more money to his son than to his daughter. In fact, bearing in mind how difficult it was in those days for girls, especially girls from aristocratic backgrounds, to earn a decent living, he should have bequeathed more to her. In every way, however, sons were considered more important. What bothered Laura far more was her father's choice of guardians. No worse people, Dillon commented later, could possibly have been chosen. Toto, for her part, was naive about money, for all her hoarding instincts, and she refused to take any responsibility for the children's inheritance. This task fell to Mrs Hearne, who had a good head for business but whose honesty was subsequently to be called into question.

Three weeks after Robert's death, Sir John Fox Dillon, the seventh baronet, also died. He had been the owner of the family estate in County Meath, Ireland. The Dillons' ancestral home, originally a fourteenth-century nunnery, had been burned down by Sinn Fein three years previously, when Sir John was in his eighties. The Sinn Feiners came in the night, gave Sir John, his wife and daughter Millicent just half an hour to pack a few belongings and then turned them out before setting the house ablaze. All the family treasures, including many paintings and priceless antiques, were destroyed with it. It was the last house burned down by Sinn Fein before it gave up the practice. After this, Sir John and his family went to live on their English country estate in Herefordshire.

Although Laura and Bobby had hardly known old Sir John, indeed, had hardly even heard of him, this event was to be truly momentous, for after Robert Dillon the next in line was Bobby, aged eleven, who was promptly named 'the baby baronet' at school. The aunts never ceased saying what a wonder it was that Sir John had lived just those three weeks longer than Daddy, otherwise Robert would have had the title and estate and become liable for death duties, which would probably have reduced the Dillons to genuine, rather than simply feigned, poverty.

Life now altered beyond recognition for Bobby, who was torn apart from Laura by the change in his fortunes. From this moment on Bobby and Laura were to be virtual strangers. The aunts now had a title in their immediate family, instead of far away in Ireland, and it was essential that the young nobleman should be educated in a manner appropriate to his new role. Having taken some advice, the aunts put Bobby's name down for a public school, Lancing College. This school was chosen, Dillon says, for two reasons: it was near Auntie Grace, one of the three sisters who had married, who lived in Worthing and could therefore have Bobby to stay with her at half term and keep an eye on him at other times;

also, perhaps more importantly, the school was slightly cheaper than Eton or Harrow.

There was also the question of what was to be done about the Irish estate, which had had nobody to attend to it since the Sinn Fein had burned down the house. Fortunately Mrs Hearne, the hotel manageress (who was herself Irish), offered to go to Ireland to see what was happening. The aunts were delighted at her offer, especially as they had little inclination to go there themselves.

While in Ireland, Mrs Hearne wrote to the aunts to say that although the old house was a complete ruin, the servants' quarters were still standing. She advocated building a new house, as the government would provide an appreciable sum of money for this, but only a tiny amount if the original house was to be restored. Mrs Hearne seemed kindness itself, offering to stay in the servants' quarters and supervise the arrangements. Daisy and Toto were only too happy to agree. Out of the estate, according to the terms of Sir John Dillon's will, £2000 per annum had to be paid to his widow during her lifetime. Finding this money was to prove in years to come a great strain for Bobby.

Nor was this the end of the upheaval. Toto decided that she, Daisy and Laura should leave the boarding house. They took up residence over a shop, probably because Toto felt that they were now genuinely poor: after all, Robert would no longer be paying for the children's education and upkeep and henceforth there would be £2000 a year to be paid to old Lady Dillon. During the holidays, the young heir was to go to Ireland and become acquainted with the estate and the local people. This was not something he enjoyed, being a shy, sensitive child and quite incapable of standing up to Mrs Hearne, who attempted to be a mother figure to him. He suffered in silence. When, in later years, she emerged in her true colours and tricked him out of his possessions, the aunts asked why he had never said anything about what was going on. His reply was that nobody would have believed him, which was true. The aunts were only too glad not to have to worry about the estate themselves. As they thought they were leaving it all in capable hands, it never occurred to them to enquire what was going on. Perhaps they did not really want to know.

In the meantime, however, one good effect was that Laura herself went, with Daisy and Toto, to the family estate in County Meath for the summer holidays. The estate was a marvellous place for children to play, as it had 360 acres of fields, a lake and a pond, a wood, and plenty of barns, stables and haylofts. Laura was taught by Mrs Hearne's grown-up son Tom to shoot and to fish. She went to Ireland each year from age ten to age fourteen, when the holidays abruptly stopped.

It was on the last of these, when Laura was fourteen, that she had yet another inkling that she may not be exactly the same as other adolescent girls. Although she was not generally 'musical', one day she sat at the piano picking out tunes and trying to play them. An old lady also staying there, Fanny Moody, who had been a famous opera singer in her day, heard the singing and asked who the 'man' was. As the only other 'man' in the place at the time was Bobby – whose voice did not break until he was seventeen – the singer had to be Laura. Fanny Moody would simply not believe it was a girl singing; she said she was certain she heard a man's voice. Laura had in fact been trying to deepen her singing voice by concentrating on the notes below middle C.

She still had no conscious longing to be a man, but when Laura returned to school the singing mistress recommended that she should no longer take part in singing lessons: Laura's deep new voice was anathema to her. However, the effect was marked only in singing – Laura's speaking voice continued to be that of an ordinary adolescent female.

By now adolescence was beginning to trouble the increasingly awkward girl. Laura attended an all-girls' school, and although she made firm friends with some of the girls she was beginning to find it difficult to identify in any way with them. However, the biggest problems at this time were probably physical. The unmistakable onset of puberty made it clear to Laura that she was truly female, whether she liked it or not. Menstruation started, but that was not the worst difficulty, as it could be hidden from others. What troubled her most of all was that her breasts were starting to develop. This caused Laura great anxiety and she wore a belt round them to flatten them. When a schoolfriend found out she told Laura, horrified, that she would be sure to get cancer if she continued this practice. So she reluctantly stopped, but this visible sign of womanhood made her very unhappy indeed.

Neither she nor anybody else had the slightest idea what, if anything, was wrong. All Laura knew at this time was that she was miserable. For a while she blamed her distress on her aunts, particularly Toto's continued strenuous control over her activities, and the shame of living above a shop.

Nobody liked Laura's hobby of carpentry: the shop owners, a draper and his wife, objected to the hammering, while Daisy and Toto did not consider that carpentry was a very suitable occupation for a young girl. Bobby having long ceased to be a companion, there seemed to be nobody in whom Laura could confide. She knew the aunts were restricting her in her activities and trying to make her as nervous and timid as they were themselves. In addition, the continued fiction that they were all poverty-stricken meant that Laura's life was limited in other ways. She was never allowed to learn to ride, as riding lessons cost 5 shillings (25p) an hour, which was considered far too expensive. Bobby, however, did learn, even though he hated it, because a doctor had recommended the exercise to strengthen a leg broken in childhood. For Laura, this was just another of life's injustices, her awareness of which was heightening as her body developed.

Laura was an extremely keen Girl Guide, and eventually won most of the proficiency badges on offer. Perhaps guiding was the most 'masculine' of the activities she could safely pursue. Even so, the aunts questioned every penny spent, on uniform, outings and items needed while working for particular badges. They would not allow her to go on camping holidays, which she longed to do, partly because they were 'poor' and could not afford it, and partly because they said they would worry about her all the time she was gone. Once, when the school was closed during a scarlet fever epidemic, Laura and two friends decided to try to collect all the Guide badges they could. Eventually, Laura had everything she needed for her Gold Cords – the highest Guide award at the time, equivalent of the later Queen's Guide and present-day Baden-Powell Trefoil award. But the aunts would not be prevailed upon to let her go for a week's camping to complete the Gold Cord work. In later life Dillon took many camping trips – perhaps to make up for the years when this type of holiday had been so rigorously denied by the aunts.

As the aunts got older, they became ever narrower in their outlook and ever more penny-pinching, creating an almost intolerable atmosphere for a sensitive adolescent. It was becoming apparent that Laura was both highly intelligent and scholarly. That, in the aunts' view, was no more fitting than that their niece should want to hammer nails into pieces of wood or learn to ride a horse.

They were content to pay for her schooling up to a point, but saw no point in further education for women. After all, Laura was being groomed to be a young lady, which meant sitting around at home until a suitable husband arrived on the scene.

When Laura was fifteen, however, her life improved a little. First, the aunts suddenly decided to move from their rooms above the draper's shop into a brand-new house in Bouverie Street West. Their change of heart came about only because of Laura's constant complaints about living over a shop and the pressure she put on the aunts for them all to go to live in a decent house. Laura, attending the smartest girls' school in the area, was desperately ashamed of where she lived and felt she could not invite her friends back home. Eventually the aunts had begun making enquiries about houses and decided on this one, built in the very grandest part of town on part of an estate owned by Lord Folkestone. The house, of which Daisy, Laura and Toto were the first occupants, was ideal, as it was spacious enough for Laura to get well away from the aunts. It is still standing – a large, detached house built (probably in 1929) in the typical style of the period, in its own grounds. The front door was shaped like a church steeple and there was a big square hall almost like a room in itself, with brick fireplace and parquet floor. Laura loved this new house but best of all she loved the huge garden, big enough for a tennis court – although, needless to say, there was no tennis court during Daisy and Toto's occupation. There was plenty of room for a garden shed, where Laura could do her carpentry without disturbing her aunts – even during the unalterable ritual of their afternoon rest.

The claustrophobic days of living above a shop were now over. Daisy and Toto were to live in the new house until the mid-1950s, when they became too infirm to run it on their own. The present owners found the building in a very bad state of repair after the aunts had left and its loft was crammed full of old furniture and junk.

Equally important for Laura was that she at last managed to emancipate herself from the emotional stranglehold of the aunts, particularly Toto. Daisy usually just took her lead from Toto and was in any case far fonder of Bobby than of Laura during those years. In later life her attitude was to change, but for the time being Bobby was her favourite. The event which released Laura from thralldom was trivial in itself, but it marked a significant turning point.

Laura used to love the annual school outing to Dymchurch, ten miles away from Folkestone. For a modern 15-year-old the prospect of going on a school trip to a place ten miles away would hold little charm, but Laura had hardly been anywhere in her life, especially without the aunts. Toto would never travel anywhere if she could help it, and generally would not let Laura go anywhere either. But the school outing was different, as it was to be closely supervised by the teachers.

The whole party had a wonderful time, playing cricket on the beach, bathing and, eventually, eating a magnificent tea. Then the bus which should have had everybody back by six o'clock failed to start. Sitting in the bus, Laura started to panic because she knew Toto would be sitting at home worrying if she were not back on time. Then a liberating thought struck her: how ridiculous it would be to worry all her life just because Toto might be worrying. If Toto wanted to worry, Laura decided, then let her! She, Laura, would not let it trouble her any more.

All his life Michael Dillon remembered this moment on the bus when he achieved emotional emancipation from the aunts. With this resolve, he wrote later, came a feeling of enormous relief. There was a simple way out, after all, from the prison cell of the aunts' confining and restricting attitudes – you just had to decide not to let it bother you.

Emotional emancipation was all very well, but Laura was of course still financially dependent upon the aunts. She had a little money of her own from her father's will but could not at that time touch it.

Having cut the Gordian knot which bound her so closely to the aunts, Laura's major problem was that she had absolutely nobody to confide in or turn to, for either comfort or advice. She had learned that it was useless to talk to the aunts about anything in the expectation that there might be some glimmer of understanding. Daisy and Toto evinced not the slightest interest in anything Laura did. The only thing that concerned them was that she should always be around, so that they knew exactly where she was.

If her woodworking hobby ever produced anything particularly good and she showed it, full of excitement, to Toto, the typical reply from the aged aunt would be: 'Yes, dear, very nice, but don't bother me now.' Nor did the aunts take the trouble any more to buy Laura Christmas or birthday presents. Toto would ask what she wanted and then give her the money to go and get it for herself. 'You get it, dear,' she would say. 'I can't be bothered.' Nor did Toto welcome being given presents, for all that she was an emotional blackmailer.

When Laura was fourteen, she decided to get a really special present for Toto, and for a shilling bought a little leather booklet containing a piece of chamois leather for wiping spectacles. Laura thought this would be ideal, and would please the aunt, because Toto was always complaining that her spectacles were dirty. After buying the present and wrapping it up in tissue paper, Laura could hardly wait for the next day, Toto's birthday. She would be so thrilled. But on receiving the present and opening it, she merely said: 'Thank you very much, dear, but I wish you wouldn't go spending your money on me.' A few months later, Laura was disappointed to find the present lying in Toto's desk, still wrapped up in its tissue paper. Such thoughtless behaviour on the part of the aunts – and they seemed to be much the same in this respect – intensified Laura's feelings of being lost and alone.

On one magnificent occasion, the aunts allowed Laura to go to stay with a schoolfriend whose grandmother Toto had known as a child. Laura was away for three weeks, a previously unheard-of concession, and came back full of excitement, eager to tell the aunts about her experiences. After all, she had nobody else to tell. On arriving home, Laura burst into the sitting room, eager to talk about all the wonderful things she had done, only to be confronted by Toto raising her hand to her head and saying, 'Don't make so much noise, I've got one of my headaches.' Laura felt her insides shrivel up, and she went to her bedroom to cry. Was there nobody she could talk to, nobody who would be interested in her? Laura decided there and then that this was the very last time she would try to tell Toto anything. For her part, however, Toto was always complaining that Laura never did tell her anything. Laura felt she couldn't win, and was becoming unhappier and more distressed all the time.

An additional factor in her frustrations was that no adult male had played any part in her life. Laura started to miss never having had a father in the usual sense, and felt that the aunts were a very poor substitute for proper parents; at least they would have taken a genuine interest in her. So she decided to make a 'father' of the new vicar, the Rev. C.S.T. Watkins, one of whose daughters was in Laura's form at Brampton Down School. The vicar was six feet tall, with fair hair, and seemed kindly and understanding. It was not long before Laura began hero-worshipping him and going to see him at every opportunity. She was also at this time becoming interested, as many clever adolescents are, in religion, and she read avidly to try to discover the meaning of life. She started to fantasize that this kindly vicar actually was her father. Mr Watkins, seemingly aware of what was going on, did his best to fill this post without making either his own family or the aunts jealous. It might be imagined that as Toto was so uninterested in Laura's doings the question of jealousy would not arise, but this was far from being the case. Possessive by nature, Toto hated Laura making any close friends at all and did all she could to discourage her niece from visiting friends in their homes, for tea or any other purpose. She would often say things like: 'No, you mustn't go round there again. You are only making a nuisance of yourself and they don't really want you.' Laura believed this, and so would often become cool towards people in the aunt-engendered belief that she was imposing herself on them.

The vicar's kindness extended to buying Laura a hockey stick when her old one broke and the aunts protested that they were far too poor to buy her another. To save embarrassment, Mr Watkins told the aunts that the hockey stick was an old one of his own for which he no longer had any use.

All her childhood Laura had been mollycoddled by the aunts. For some girls who did not like sport or outdoor activities, this may not have mattered too much, but Laura was a passionate sports enthusiast and loved being out of doors. She was always extremely athletic, which was probably something else the aunts could not understand, since they were not in the slightest so inclined themselves. As Laura had suffered from spontaneous vomiting and a mysterious allergy to sweet things when young, the aunts had the idea that she was delicate, had to be taken care of and should not exert herself too much.

Their views were no more or less than the conventional ones of the day: they believed that adolescent girls should not take part in violent or energetic sports as this might upset their menstrual cycles and lead to difficulties with conception or childbirth in later life. This doctrine is now so totally discredited that it is difficult to realize how firmly entrenched it was in the 1920s, when most sports for girls were very gentle. The aunts believed that hockey, for instance, was a highly dangerous sport and would not allow Laura to play it until she managed to persuade other girls' parents to make representations on her behalf.

The loneliness which was becoming ever more difficult to bear was particularly marked during school holidays. The aunts hardly ever went out now, apart from doing their shopping in the morning, and virtually never had visitors. As Laura was not encouraged to have schoolfriends to visit, or to go to their homes, she began to feel totally isolated and unloved. She hit on the idea of buying an animal, and purchased two white mice which she kept in Mr Watkins' garden. She did not think it prudent to tell the aunts about this purchase, but only a week after the mice had been bought Toto found out. She discovered Laura taking milk and crusts out of the kitchen and demanded to know why. On being told the reason, Toto insisted that Laura take the mice back to the shop. After that, however, Laura was at least allowed to take the vicar's little terrier out for walks.

Toto considered herself an animal lover, and always had a cat. The latest one, a neutered ginger stray, made its home in the new house shortly after they moved. Toto petted and cosseted it, claiming that it was highly nervous, and soon Laura realized that Toto was simply transferring to the cat all the affection she could no longer show to her niece. One day, Laura brought home a tortoise she had found in the road and put it in the garden. There it lived for the summer and in the autumn, of course, it hibernated. But Toto kept finding it and digging it up, believing that it would be smothered if it stayed underground. After Toto had dug the tortoise up twice, it died – not surprisingly. But nobody could explain to Toto that the animal was simply following its natural behaviour pattern.

To the average adolescent girl of today, Laura's life would seem little short of intolerable. But the aunts for their part must have been disappointed that their niece was not turning out to be the pretty, compliant young lady they had hoped she would be; instead she was becoming increasingly spiky, sullen, analytical and rude. A quality Dillon never developed, either as Laura or as Michael, was charm. Laura was straightforward, said what she thought, allowed all her emotions to show, and found herself constantly being hurt. Although she had by now developed coping strategies to deal with the sillinesses of the aunts, she was uneasy in any social context. This was probably because she was becoming uncomfortably aware that she would never, could never, fit into the female stereotype which society had ordained for her.

Laura passed the long, lonely hours by reading books, ever more voraciously. She continued to concentrate on theology, not only to justify her hero-worship of the vicar, but also to further her understanding of the purpose of life. It was becoming increasingly clear to her that the life the aunts led was completely purposeless. Why were people like Daisy and Toto put on earth? Why was Laura herself here? What was she going to do with herself? Why did she not seem to feel like other girls? What, if anything, was wrong with her? It was to be several years before she realized that she had been born into the wrong gender, but for the time being she sought the answer in theological and philosophical works. She read everything she could, and the depth of her reading was to stand her in good stead later when she thought of furthering her education.

Among the various thing they failed to do, the aunts never told Laura anything about sex. Perhaps they knew very little themselves; perhaps they simply did not wish, or know how, to raise the subject. At any rate, Laura was almost sixteen before she knew anything at all about the 'facts of life'. She did not, of course, have any idea that she was so ignorant. Then, one day, during a confirmation class, the vicar asked whether anybody had any questions to ask about anything they had read in the Bible that had puzzled them. Laura immediately knew which question to ask. A passage which had been bothering her a lot was the one in Exodus which states: 'He that lieth down with beasts shall be destroyed.' As Laura was fond of lying down by the fire beside the cat, she could not understand the reason for the prohibition. So, in all innocence, she asked the vicar, and instantly realized she had entered into dangerous territory. The vicar, confused, said he would answer that one later, but he never did. Instead, he asked Laura's headmistress at school to impart some knowledge to her pupil, which ended with Laura being not very much wiser.

In her early twenties Laura was to become an expert on sexual matters, particularly in the context of changing gender. But for now she decided that the subject did not apply to her. She put it to the back of her mind, preferring to concentrate on Greek and Latin instead.

She became an avid classical scholar, with help from the vicar. Here again, the aunts' professed poverty meant that she could not have proper lessons at school. Although Greek and Latin were taught at Laura's school, they were extras, and the aunts, who could see no point in them, refused to pay for the lessons.

In any case, Toto was now putting pressure on Laura to leave school. She had had quite enough education for a girl, in the aunts' opinion, and besides, the school was very expensive. Laura asked: what do you expect me to do with my life? Toto's answer was: you can help me carry the basket each morning when I go shopping and then try to find a nice husband with plenty of money. By this time, however, Laura had crystallized her ambition: she wanted to go to Oxford University. Furthermore, she *would* go, somehow. She had already passed School Certificate, the forerunner of O-levels, and, after much argument, was allowed to stay on at school for an extra term to take Greek.

In order to have any chance at all of getting to Oxford, Laura had to persuade Toto to let her stay on at school to take the Higher Certificate, the equivalent of A-levels. Toto at first said there was not enough money and she could not possibly afford it, although she had a balance of £1900 just in her current account, as Dillon discovered years later. The school fees at the time were £10 a term. Ever since she had attended this school, Laura had had to wear a secondhand uniform, as the aunts maintained they were too poor to buy the items new, and, although that was a minor consideration for a teenager who did not care in the slightest how she looked, it was indicative of the aunt's grudging attitude towards Laura's schooling. In the end, after much haggling, Toto agreed to let Laura stay on at school if she could go there free. The headmistress agreed, provided Laura earn her keep by helping out with the juniors. Thus the Higher Certificate was assured, although getting to Oxford was to herald another almighty battle.

By this age many of Laura's schoolfriends were becoming interested in boys. For Laura, there was no such interest, although she was dismayed to find that she was attracted to a maths mistress at the school. She made the mistake of admitting her love and was duly laughed at by the other girls, but for Laura this infatuation seemed perfectly normal and she could not understand why the others thought it odd. She later learned that her revelation – to one of the mistresses – that she was in love with Miss A caused much anxious speculation in the headmistress's office as to whether Laura Dillon was quite normal.

But the headmistress intervened with the aunts to allow Laura to take the Oxford entrance examination. She had no wish to see one of her prize pupils spending the rest of her youth carrying Toto's shopping basket around Folkestone every morning. This was all very well, but how would Laura ever be brought up to the required standard? And how, as the aunts seemed adamant about wanting to lay out any more money for education, could she possibly get a scholarship?

The vicar and an elderly Folkestone resident, Mr Whyte, who was a retired Latin teacher, made it possible for Laura to take the examination. As the Latin mistress at Brampton Down had fallen ill, some of the girls were farmed out to Mr Whyte for Latin coaching. As time went by, it became clear that Laura would never be able to attain scholarship standard in classics, but her wide reading in religious matters made a theology entrance possible. She was advised to try this and eventually travelled to Oxford for the entrance examination. Afterwards, she went down with a temperature of 104°F and was in bed for a week with strange ulcers on the mouth and face. A few weeks later, however, she heard that she had been awarded an entrance at both St Hugh's College and St Anne's College, the latter then known as the Oxford Home Students, as students at this college all lived in digs. There was, however, no scholarship, and for a time the aunts held out, claiming that they could not possibly afford to send Laura to Oxford.

The vicar, Mr Whyte and the headmistress joined forces to break down the aunts' resistance and at length they relented. Toto, Daisy and Maudie would pay the fees between them. This, when added to Laura's income of £120 a year, inherited from her father, would make it possible for her to accept the offer. St Anne's was chosen in preference to St Hugh's, for the simple reason that it was slightly cheaper, accommodation in digs being cheaper than living in college.

Laura's happiness, which should have been complete, was marred by a disturbing incident which had happened just before she took Oxford entrance; it was something she could not forget, and which was to have profound repercussions when she was installed at her women's college at university. She was eighteen, and technically a young woman, although, much to her aunts' distress, she showed no sign whatever of becoming womanly in appearance. This lack of womanliness arose not out of conscious rebellion but from a growing conviction that she was not really a woman at all. Laura was made to realize this in a shattering way when she was out for a walk one day with the vicar's 18-year-old nephew, who had himself recently gone up to Oxford.

They were pleasantly chatting away to each other while walking along the cliffs and came to a gate. Courteously, the young man stood aside to let Laura pass through first. Nobody had ever extended this courtesy to her before, but instead of being flattered, Laura was horrified. 'He thinks I'm a woman,' she thought to herself. She suddenly became aware that other people had an impression of her quite distinct from the one she herself had. For the rest of the walk she could not bring herself to speak to the young man, who must have wondered what was the matter.

'Life,' wrote Dillon, 'could never be the same again. People thought I was a woman. But I wasn't. I was just me. How could one live like that? With no one to ask I brooded long on this at night in bed, while still working hard all day.'

This terrifying sense of being in the wrong body, of being a different gender inside from the one proclaimed by the outside, was compounded by continual nagging from all her relations – Daisy, Toto and Maudie, together with cousins and other aunts – about her disinclination to look and dress like an elegant young lady. The Dillons, both old and young, had a very strong sense of how a woman of Laura's age and social standing should look. In particular, they were greatly embarrassed at anything which might 'show them up'. Instead of being an ally to his sister, Bobby – when she saw him – took the side of the aunts and grown-up cousins, urging Laura at least to *look* like a sister, rather than a pretend boy.

Pictures of Laura at the time show her to be a good-looking, though serious and unsmiling, young woman with short hair and clothes that are as masculine as possible for the time. In 1933 it was not 'done' for women to wear trousers, especially in Folkestone, although Coco Chanel and other French designers were now starting to show women's trousers. It was to be a long time before trousers for women became acceptable everyday wear.

But even if it had been possible for Laura to wear men's trousers and other male attire, that would not have solved the problem. Present-day female-to-male transsexuals can do this far more easily, but it does not diminish their desire to change sex. In particular, all transsexuals hate the outward manifestations, the secondary sexual characteristics which proclaim to others that they are members of the 'wrong' sex.

As yet Laura had no idea that she was transsexual. She just wondered why she did not feel in the least like a woman, and why the prospect of a man putting his arm round her, or worse, becoming romantically involved with her, caused untold anguish. She did not even know, at this stage, that there were such people as homosexuals and lesbians, so delicately and innocently had she been brought up.

Oxford was to clarify many uncertainties for Laura Dillon – not least of which was the knowledge that never, whatever happened, and however others saw her, could she be a woman like other women. Physically and anatomically she was a perfectly normal biological woman, 5 feet 6 inches in height, weighing just over nine stone, and with a slightly androgynous, athletic build and regular, clean-cut features. Mentally and emotionally she was male.

3

Oxford

ALTHOUGH Laura Dillon was thrilled to be going up to Oxford in the autumn of 1934, her happiness was marred by the now almost certain knowledge that something was seriously wrong. The incident with the vicar's nephew could not be forgotten, and she wondered why she could not be content to be a woman, as her aunts, cousins and schoolfriends all appeared to be. During her four years at Oxford, however, when it began to dawn on her that never, whatever happened, could she take her place in the world as an adult female, she was able to formulate a partial understanding of the problem.

It was not that Laura despised being female: there is no indication at all at this time that she wanted to be male because she thought women were inferior, or because she sensed that they got a rough deal in life. The dilemma went far deeper than that (although, when Laura became Michael, he did turn into something of a chauvinist).

For the time being, however, she was avid for the new experience of university, and it must have held the promise of heady freedom indeed for one who had led such a sheltered and restricted life. During the summer, before she went up, Mr Whyte continued to coach her, while Laura longed for the day of her departure. She almost burst with pride when any neighbours or acquaintances asked what she would be doing now that she had left school, and replied as casually as she could that she would be going up to Oxford in the autumn.

When the day dawned Toto – now nearly 70 – saw Laura off at the station, and put her into a ladies' carriage, 'for safety'. Laura extricated herself from it at the earliest possible moment, offering up as she did so a prayer for her wonderful deliverance from touting the shopping basket round Folkestone. Her years with the aunts had taught Laura that she could often get her own way by constant repetition of her requests, and a refusal to be budged. This obstinacy was to stand her in good stead when she later made enquiries about changing gender and living as a man.

At St Anne's College Laura soon had a lucky break. As a result of the classics don falling ill and all students being farmed out to other tutors until her return to work, Laura was sent to Jimmy McKie of Brasenose, who was to become a lifelong friend and was also to be instrumental in helping her to keep the secret of her sex change.

Although Laura loved Oxford from the start, and for the rest of her life was to look back on these four years with pleasure and pride, she soon found that the atmosphere and the social life made her even more keenly aware of her problems. Certain types of behaviour were expected of the female students, and Laura quickly discovered that she would not be able to live up to those expectations. She was determined not to attend any dance or other social event in case a male student should put an arm round her. Soon after going up to Oxford, Laura started to smoke a pipe, in the belief that no man would ever look at a woman with such a very masculine habit. It was an indulgence to which she would adhere for most of her life.

There was also the question of Laura's future career, since merely sitting around and waiting for a husband was out of the question. She would not have enough money to live by 'independent means', like her father and aunts, but would have to earn a living. She had been accepted to study theology, having some vague idea of becoming a deaconess, or perhaps a missionary, after graduating. To that end she was introduced to Canon Tom Pym, chaplain of Balliol, who was strongly against this idea, believing that Miss Dillon had chosen the career from completely wrong motives, negative rather than positive ones, and advised her to think harder about her academic work, suggesting initially a change to an Honours instead of a Pass course. The then principal of the college, Grace Hadow, agreed in theory to the change, but doubted whether Laura's command of the classics was good enough.

Apart from the actual theological content of the course, which comprised close study of Christian scriptures and doctrines, there was a large classical component. The Honours course required more than a working knowledge of Latin and Greek, and in the first five terms the set works included the whole of the *Iliad* and the *Odyssey,* also the *Aeneid*, the Georgics and the Eclogues of Virgil. These were seen as a kind of foundation for the rest of the course and the first examinations, known then as now as 'Moderations', were based on them. The reading included in addition Plato's philosophy, Aristophanes' comedies and a selection of 50 books in Greek and Latin, of which passages from eight had to be translated in the examination. Latin prose and two special subjects completed the course.

Somehow, however, Laura managed to persuade the authorities that she could, if she worked really hard, get at least a third-class honours degree, and was eventually granted permission to try. It was a major undertaking, since Laura's knowledge of Latin and Greek was nowhere near Honours standard, but during her first vacation Mr Whyte made a notable offer to Toto: he would coach Laura daily, free of charge, during the vacations. It was this offer, she said, which made possible the impossible.

Having settled the academic question for the time being, Laura had to turn her attention to other matters. Work would of course take up most of her time, as she would still have difficulty in achieving and maintaining the required standard, but what was she to do with her leisure time?

She considered the social world firmly closed to her. Not only was she finding it increasingly impossible to wear any kind of frock, but she could hardly bring herself to go to parties where she might meet young men.

The answer she hit on was exercise. All her life Laura had been athletic and loved strenuous physical exertion, despite Daisy and Toto's worries that it might be dangerous. So she took up rowing. Those university women who now take part in regattas and other boat races may not realize how much they owe to Laura Dillon. Before Laura went to Oxford, it was considered highly unfeminine and unsuitable for women to row, and for the usual reason: it was thought to ruin their chances of giving birth in later life. After Dillon qualified as a doctor, he was firmly of the opinion that rowing strengthened the development of the abdominal muscles and made childbirth easier rather than more difficult. Also, women were commonly regarded as too delicate to be able to wield an oar. During her years at Oxford Laura was to change all that, and she succeeded, after a lengthy struggle with the college authorities, in getting women's rowing accepted as a serious university sport. Many current students feel that women's rowing is still something of a joke in comparison with men's, and it certainly does not attract the razzmatazz and glamour associated with the male version of the sport. But at least nowadays women can row without being in fear of the wrath of the authorities.

In her second year Laura became a rowing blue and was elected president of the Oxford University Women's Boat Club. Her battle with the authorities was still not over, however. On 7 May 1937 the principal of St Anne's wrote a letter to Laura saying: 'The Principals are considering whether they think it desirable to encourage rowing among the girls or not.' After much haggling and to-ing and fro-ing, the principals of the women's colleges decided that one eight, and only one, could race. They sanctioned just one women's team, put together from all the female colleges combined.

When Laura first became interested in rowing, the male oarsmen used to stand and laugh at the efforts of the women. Women's boats were not allowed to race side by side initially: each had to be rowed by itself while someone timed it. The course itself, designed to be the gentlest possible, was only half a mile long and had to be rowed downstream. Moreover, as the oarswomen had no proper uniform, they looked rather a mess – 'absolutely pathetic', Dillon records. No wonder the men split their sides with laughter at the annual women's races against Cambridge and London Universities. The women's crews from these other universities were of course subject to the same restrictions as Oxford.

As soon as Laura was elected president, she set about getting the women's eight a good coach and a proper uniform. If rowing was to be regarded seriously, the girls could not turn out in any outfit they had available. Not only that, but a uniform helps crew members to regard themselves as a team. So Laura approached the firm of Bukta to produce a women's uniform: white vests and blue shorts, plus a proper peaked cap for the coxes, bearing the crossed oars and the letters OUWBC. She also managed to get blazers, scarves and sweaters designed, plus white trousers for the cox.

Through the type of dogged persistence which was to become her stock-in-trade, Laura obtained the services of a former Leander man called Danks, who worked as a crammer in the town, to be the crew's coach. In the following year, while still president of the Women's Boat

Club, the same persistence enabled Laura to get the course altered to a mile, instead of half a mile, and rowed upstream, thus making the event more of a challenge. Laura felt amply rewarded when the annual race, instead of being laughed at, was heartily applauded by spectators lining the river banks, and earned substantial good coverage in the Sunday papers. After this success Laura knew that never again would Oxford women's rowing be regarded as a puny attempt by the weak and feeble girls to ape the men.

Possibly without fully realizing it, when Laura created a women's rowing uniform she was making it permissible, via the boat club, for her to wear men's clothes. However, her first experience of wearing trousers in public was to have unlooked-for repercussions.

The Women's Boat Club had purchased a secondhand racing eight from Merton College and had to bring her up from the Lower River to its own boathouse. Some stretches of the river in that area were narrow and quite dangerous, so as the cox was new and not very experienced, Laura decided she would cox the boat herself. Laura had coxed on many previous occasions, in practice sessions.

She went down with the others wearing the cox's flannel trousers, blazer and cap while the rest of the crew wore their shorts. As it happened, the men's boat club was in training for the coming Oxford and Cambridge Boat Race, and a press photographer was standing by to take pictures. As the photographer saw the women getting into their boat, he quickly took a picture of Laura. She was completely unaware of it, but the next day was horrified to find a huge picture of herself sitting in the cox's seat in the *Daily Mirror*: it was captioned 'Man or Woman?'

After the initial shock had died down, Laura had to admit that anybody would have taken the picture to be that of a boy. Since coming up to Oxford, she had had her hair cut in an Eton crop, a style she would keep until the change-over, when she could go the whole way and have a real man's cut.

It was of course too much to hope that the aunts would not see it, or have their attention drawn to the picture, even though they did not take the *Daily Mirror* themselves. Instantly, Toto wrote to Laura asking why she felt she had to make such a freak of herself and excite attention in this way. Laura replied that she was simply wearing what female coxes on boats wear, and it was hardly her fault if she looked more like a boy than a girl. The aunts did not agree: they asked her to try to look more normal and not keep showing them up.

Laura's brother Bobby, who was turning into a deeply conventional young man, was now reading law at Trinity College, Dublin. He too was becoming desperately ashamed of his sister. In the first place, he hated the fact that she was a blue-stocking and that she was at Oxford at all. He could not see the point of girls being highly educated, and, along with the aunts, had opposed Laura's going to Oxford. Secondly, he could not bear her looking so masculine and being so tall. When both had stopped growing Laura, at 5 foot 9, was half an inch taller than Bobby, which hardly pleased him. The maiden-aunt upbringing had had a completely opposite effect on Bobby from what it had on Laura, in that it had made him a stickler for form, for what looked right, and for the conventions of society. Also, he took his position as eighth baronet of Lismullen very seriously.

Never a very masculine man, Bobby would have loved a pretty, feminine sister he could show off to his friends. Instead, he hardly felt he could admit to being Laura's brother, and relations were to become increasingly strained between the two from now on. As it was, they saw each other only once a year.

Towards the end of his life Michael Dillon found it in his heart to be charitable to Bobby, the brother who did not want to have anything at all to do with his sister when he realized she was more masculine than he was himself. 'Poor Bobby!' Dillon wrote. 'He needed a feminine frippery type of sister to offset his own lack of masculinity, for it had been said even in our nursery days that he should have been the girl and I the boy. He hated sports and although by no means could he be called effeminate, he enjoyed gardening, bridge parties, played the piano very well and could draw and paint, even as Daddy had been able to. His accomplishments would have been better suited to me as mine to him.' Nor did Bobby approve at all of the rowing, or of the way his sister kept getting into trouble with the college authorities over the status of the women's version of the sport.

During this time he, too, had had difficulties to sort out. Mrs Hearne, who had been appointed a guardian by Robert Dillon, had tried to keep Bobby completely under her thumb. Refusing to let him grow up properly, she had insisted on going everywhere with him, but as time went on she began to be excluded from the invitations Bobby received. This was probably because it was perceived that she was not of the same social class as her ward, and her conversation and attitudes were not suitable for the grand houses to which Bobby was now being invited. Spurned, Mrs Hearne now looked for revenge. She maintained that she had bought, out of her own money, a lot of furniture and fittings for the new house and once their relationship had deteriorated beyond redemption she made arrangements to auction the contents of the house immediately, prior to leaving Bobby and Ireland for good. The only articles she left were personal ones which had been bequeathed to Bobby by his father, and which she could not touch. Also, without Bobby's knowledge or consent, she sold a cow of his which the vet had condemned as tubercular. Bobby received a letter informing him of this while on his annual visit to Folkestone. The buyer apparently had no idea that the cow was diseased and Mrs Hearne congratulated herself on her deception.

It seems completely characteristic of Daisy and Toto that neither of them, or indeed any of the other aunts living round about, ever considered going over to Ireland to try to stop Mrs Hearne selling the contents of Bobby's house. They just let her do it, lamenting that they could not understand what had made her turn so nasty. Mrs Hearne went ahead with the auction and disappeared, leaving the house empty but for one partly furnished room. Bobby was at this time still having to pay old Lady Dillon £2000 annually from the estate. Mrs Hearne set up a hotel in Hertfordshire on the proceeds of the sale. Following the auction, Daisy went over to Ireland to help Bobby refurnish the house, and also sewed curtains for him. During the month she stayed with him, she became extremely close to her nephew. Indeed, she was to end her days on the Lismullen estate, looked after by Bobby and his wife Synolda.

In years to come, when Michael Dillon was a medical student at Trinity College, Dublin, he heard more about Mrs Hearne's misdeeds. Apparently the neighbours had known what was going on and had said that Bobby ought to be taken away from 'that evil woman'. But the aunts either did not know, or did not wish to know.

The *Daily Mirror* incident did nothing to diminish Laura's enthusiasm for rowing, and in her fourth and final year, 1938, the OUWBC won every race it entered – against Cambridge, London, King's, Bristol and Edinburgh. The crew also went to Europe with a four, to row in Amsterdam and Frankfurt, although with less success than at home. Laura felt that after she left Oxford the OUWBC fell into rapid decline. Years later, as Michael, Dillon thought back to those days and wondered whether the Women's Boat Club still survived. He would have been pleased to know that it not only survives in the late 'eighties, but is flourishing. Michael Dillon maintained that the most important attributes for a successful crew are a good coach and a uniform. These two aspects can, he said, make a crew out of eight individuals; and whereas a crew can win a race, eight individuals never could.

Amidst all the excitement and challenge of rowing, the academic work had to be kept up. Some students can meander through their years at university doing hardly any work, but this was not the case with Laura. She had to work hard to get an Honours degree at all. However, in her fifth term, she took Honours instead of Pass Moderations, and was awarded third-class honours, the most she could have hoped for. Her reward for this achievement was such severe eye strain that for the next term she was ordered not to do any reading at all. After her success in Part One, Laura asked the college authorities to let her change from theology to 'Greats', generally considered to be the stiffest of all university courses. They demurred at first, as Laura had been given a place for theology, but eventually she won her fight. The years of arguing and digging her heels in with the aunts were beginning to pay off.

The 'Greats' course necessitated intensive reading in logic and philosophy, two subjects which had always enthralled her. The philosophy course was a wide one, encompassing Western philosophical thought from AD 600 to the present, 1938. Laura blessed the fact that she had gone to St Anne's instead of one of the other women's colleges, for as St Anne's was non-collegiate in those days many students were farmed out to male tutors. Dillon wrote in 1962, 'Had I not gone to the non-collegiate Society I might have been confined to women tutors all my days.' The male chauvinism which was to be one of the more unattractive sides of Dillon's character was beginning to reveal itself. Laura was starting to align herself firmly with men and to consider herself one of them.

As it was, she managed to be taught by some of the most famous Oxford scholars of the day, such as Wade-Gery of Wadham, and enjoyed arguing with her tutors and lecturers about the finer points of Greek history and philosophy. Several tutors told her that she had the brains for a First, and this was probably true, but her eyes could not cope with the immense amount of reading required. She started to regret not having been able to go to a boys' public school, or at least one run on such lines, which would have given her the grounding necessary for university. As it was, she found huge gaps in her knowledge that would never have existed had she had a conventional classical education.

Work and rowing took up most of her time, and she was glad that these two activities left little space for a social life. But underneath the frenetic work and exercise her problems were becoming ever greater and more acute. Could she, perhaps, be homosexual? Laura confided in a college friend, saying that she did not like to dress up for parties and look like a woman, and what could be the explanation? The friend said that Laura must be lesbian, and so, for a time, it seemed.

The words 'homosexual' and 'lesbian' were both entirely new to Laura, who until then had had no idea that men and women could be sexually attracted to members of their own gender. Nothing like that had ever happened in Folkestone, to her knowledge. Then a former schoolfriend, now at Somerville, told Laura that she herself was lesbian. The Somerville friend advised Laura to find a girlfriend, and thus overcome her frustrations. Later on other friends, doctors and psychiatrists were to offer the same advice. Laura never took it. She did not feel that it would be right. She did not, in her heart, want a same-sex relationship.

Even though Laura did not see herself becoming an active lesbian, she fell madly in love with one of the coxes, a girl who looked exactly like Shirley Temple. Laura was shattered when this girl announced her engagement, though she kindly said that if Laura had been a real man she might have been the one chosen. 'That,' wrote Dillon, reflecting on the incident towards the end of his life, 'was some consolation.'

Now that Laura's clothes and hair put her firmly in the 'butch' category, she was subjected to a tirade of abuse from all her relations when she went home for the vacations. She would no longer wear any kind of dress, but opted for a skirt and blazer outfit – the nearest she could get to male attire.

Feeling desperate about the whole situation, she confided one day in her Aunt Evie, the twin of Maudie, who she thought might understand. The grounds for this belief were that Evie had always allowed her own two children, Leslie and Joan (Joan would be one of the few relatives to accept Dillon after the sex change), far more freedom than Laura herself had ever been allowed by Daisy and Toto.

Over tea at Aunt Evie's one afternoon, Laura took a deep breath and told her she feared she was homosexual: what could she do about it? Aunt Evie could not have been more unsympathetic. Dillon records that she instantly burst into loud, contemptuous laughter and said that everything would right itself as soon as Laura got married. Laura cycled away in despair, wondering whether there was anybody at all who could understand. She could not talk to Toto, and Daisy at the time was completely absorbed in Bobby and his activities.

Back at college, Laura formed a friendship with a young man in whom she felt able to confide. Without batting an eyelid he quietly took Laura to a men's outfitters, where she bought a sports coat and flannels. After this, she went with him in her men's clothes to Oxford University boxing matches, at which women were not allowed.

The other great friendship of Laura's university years was with another woman of her own inclination, and a 'brotherly' relationship developed between them. The two went on rowing holidays during vacations, and during term time, greatly daring, they took boxing lessons from the university's gymnastics instructor. He was an ex-Army sergeant and bemused by his two unusual pupils. Once, Laura went to the judo club for a bet, pretending to be a man (this was another place that was barred to women). Afterwards she confessed that she was female, only to hear the comment, 'Your voice doesn't give you away.' Laura in fact thought that her voice was deepening, although this was well before she began taking male hormones. At this time she had no idea that there was any kind of practical treatment available for her problem. But whether she was right about her voice getting deeper or whether this was simply wishful thinking can never be known.

Laura's 21st birthday, which occurred when she was in her second year at Oxford, occasioned some worries over finances. Legally the aunts were no longer responsible for her and could have refused, if they so chose, to pay her fees any more. However, they agreed to allow her to finish the course; her own £120 a year, even in those days, was not anything like enough to cover her living expenses. Her cousin Daphne, who had caused Laura so much heartache over the blue leather jewel case all those years ago, now presented Laura with a heavy gold signet ring bearing the family crest and, inside, the date of her birthday. This ring was to acquire an almost talismanic significance for Laura, who kept it through all the later vicissitudes to remind her of what she really was, a member of the Anglo-Irish aristocracy.

Masculinity was now asserting itself ever more strongly in Laura. Towards the end of her university career she bought herself a motorcycle, a light 2-stroke Coventry-Eagle which cost £17. She decided it would be prudent not to inform the aunts in her letters home that she had bought the motorbike, as they would almost certainly tell her it was dangerous and that she must sell it instantly. So she decided to say nothing, but to ride home from Oxford to Folkestone on it at the end of term, thus proving to the aunts that it was, in fact, perfectly safe.

Laura's four years at Oxford seemed to pass in a flash. In the summer of 1938 she came down, with only her degree result to wait for. On her very last afternoon she decided to cycle round all the famous landmarks to impress them on her memory once and for all. She had no idea what the future would hold, but knew that the personal problems which had dogged her during those years were far from over. If anything, they had become even more acute. To some extent, academic work and rowing had acted as displacement activities, stopping her from having to think too deeply about what she was, or might be. But before long the problem of her sexual identity would have to be faced if she were to be able to take her place in the world at large. Oxford had enabled her to emancipate herself finally from Daisy and Toto, to learn that she had powers of persuasion and could win arguments, and it had also allowed her to face the painful truth that she was in no way a 'normal' woman. Liberation from enforced and alien womanhood was still many years away, and so it was a very confused and disoriented young woman who returned home to Bouverie Street West once her Oxford career was over.

She had to wait some time to hear the results of her examinations, and heard eventually that she had, as predicted, achieved third-class honours. This was the best, she considered, that she could have done under the circumstances, but it was not, of course, good enough for her to follow an academic career, which would in many ways have suited her perfectly. For although she was stared at and thought odd in Oxford there is at least a tradition of eccentrics in ancient university towns.

It appears that Laura *did* cause some kind of stir during her time there, for looking impossibly masculine and behaving like a man. She was something of a talking point in academic drawing rooms. Mrs Mary Moore, now the principal of St Hilda's College, recalls having heard of the case of Laura Dillon when she was a small girl growing up in an academic household in Oxford during the 1930s.

But nobody, it seemed, understood her predicament. Laura had by this time gone so far along the path of masculinity that she neither would nor could turn back and attempt to be a conventional young woman. Now aged 23, she was aware that she had somehow to try to understand exactly what she was.

Laura was quite a good-looking young woman, with a clear skin, straight eyebrows and a steady, intelligent gaze. Facially, she did not look exactly like a boy, but there was something androgynous about her. She weighed about nine stone four at this time and, whenever she could, wore a collar and tie. She probably looked what we might call today 'dykey' or 'butch' – never any make-up, not the slightest suggestion of jewellery, and no concessions to feminine frippery at all. She did not much care what she looked like; contemporary photographs of her show her in crumpled clothes – old, worn jackets and creased shirts. The lack of attention to dress was indicative of an inner malaise which no one could have suspected. She was simply urged by the aunts, and by her brother, to try to smarten herself up a bit and to look happier and less sullen.

Sometimes she managed a smile for Daisy's camera on returning to Folkestone, but inside she harboured despair and desperation. Whatever was the matter? What could she do to resolve her difficulties? Was there, in fact, any solution at all?

4

Garage Hand

LAURA Dillon's four years at Oxford had been a largely pleasant interlude which enabled her to indulge her two passions of rowing and philosophical discussion. While at university she had also been able to dress in a mannish way without exciting too much attention. There were other women at Oxford who dressed similarly and the indulgence of harmless eccentricity worried no one.

Once she left, however, her life quickly became more difficult. Her appearance was now a major problem. Increasingly, people could not tell whether she was supposed to be a man or a woman, and she found that wherever she went she occasioned ribald comments, rude stares and hurtful remarks. She endured, in reverse, what the writer Quentin Crisp had put up with in the same era when as a young man he deliberately dressed as an effeminate homosexual so that no one could make any mistake about what he was. But Mr Crisp always had the ability to carry off his bizarre (for the time) appearance with confidence and humour. Even when he was beaten up, he managed to walk away with a camply amusing comment. 'I seem to have annoyed you gentlemen in some way,' he remarked to a gang of thugs who attacked him in the street late at night.

Laura had no such confidence in herself, and although she now felt she had no choice but to wear masculine clothes, underneath the poker face and the off-putting sullen expression she endured agonies of embarrassment and self-consciousness. If she ate out in a café, people would remark when she got up to leave (in tones loud enough for her to hear), 'Oh, I thought that was a man,' for the rigid dress code of the 1930s forbade women to wear trousers in public.

51

Laura Dillon was not, of course, the first woman to look deliberately butch. The literary world had seen several examples, including Radclyffe Hall, author of *The Well of Loneliness,* and Naomi Jacob, while in medical circles the case of Dr James (Miranda) Barrie caused considerable controversy. In the main, British women who wished to live and look like men had to go abroad, to France or Italy, where their eccentricities were supposedly tolerated. There was certainly no place for somebody like Laura Dillon in genteel Folkestone, where the gentry walked on a different side of the street from the tradesmen and other members of the working class.

During her immediate post-university days, Laura had to listen to people on buses openly discussing whether she was male or female, and to hear children call out after her in the street. She was an object of curiosity and fear. It was not until 1949, five years after Dillon officially became Michael on his birth certificate, that a surgical operation on a female-to-male transsexual was described in medical literature, and it was another four years before the first article on the phenomenon of transsexuality was published, by an American psychiatrist, Dr Harry Benjamin, who coined the word 'transsexual'. At the time Laura tried to change, hardly any doctors in the world had heard of such a notion.

Later in his life Michael Dillon addressed the question of why he should have felt the need to dress up in men's clothes and have his hair in an Eton crop while still a woman. The answer he gives in his unpublished memoirs is that there was simply no choice in the matter. The only time, he says, that he felt right was when he was dressed in male clothes. In female attire, he felt all wrong – as if he were in drag. In fact, while still Laura, Dillon felt as out of place in a woman's dress as any ordinary biological man would have done. Undoubtedly, one of the reasons why Laura embraced rowing so enthusiastically at Oxford is that it gave her a valid excuse for wearing men's clothes as often as possible. Earlier in her life, the Girl Guide's uniform had been another fairly masculine outfit. It is indeed fairly common for female-to-male transsexuals to take up jobs and activities which require a uniform, for this removes all personal responsibility for dress.

After Oxford, Laura quickly found a laboratory post researching a subject which had recently begun to interest her: pre- and post-mortem brains, which she examined to try to discover the links between mind and matter. After her four years of philosophy, she felt it was time that she learned something of the physical structure of the brain, which, she believed, philosophers had consistently ignored over the centuries. Laura had an inkling, perhaps deriving from her own experience, that the links between mind and body might be closer than are generally supposed. At any rate, they should not be ignored and separated, she felt. This interest, which was to become a consuming one, formed the basis of Michael Dillon's first book, *Self*, which was published in 1946, two years after the sex change.

Laura felt there should be a bridge between the two disciplines of philosophy and biological science. In the 1930s and 1940s, their respective groups of adherents each considered their own discipline superior to the other and wished to keep them well apart. Laura also had a growing conviction that it was possible to make a bridge between the sexes. She had for a long time been feeling that the two sexes were far too rigidly compartmentalized, each with its own seemingly unbreakable set of rules and behavioural patterns. She felt like a man – or, at least, not like a woman – yet society decreed that she had to act as women were stereotypically supposed to act, and she was finding this increasingly impossible. More than that, there seemed to be no good reason why it should not be possible to straddle the demarcation lines to some extent. After all, not every single woman who is equipped with the organs for childbirth wants to marry and have children.

Laura was coming to believe that men and women appeared so very different in their thinking and attitudes mainly because of centuries of conditioning, rather than because of innate differences. The supposed dissimilarities – apart from anatomical ones – were, she now considered, more artificial than real. In the same way, entrenched differences in branches of learning were often more artificial than real.

Laura had a growing conviction that keeping the sexes rigidly separate, and by analogy, keeping academic disciplines apart from each other, was contributing to lack of understanding and sympathy between the two. Men and women were innately suspicious of each other, philosophers and biologists similarly mistrusted each other – and yet each would have much to gain by sharing their knowledge and experience.

As the laboratory was near Bristol, Laura had to find digs, where she came into contact for the first time in her life with members of the working class. Her aunts had always forbidden her to associate with the lower orders; now Laura realized how great the gap was between her upbringing and theirs. Table manners were one external reflection of this difference. In the aunts' house those at table would politely ask for the salt or pepper to be passed, and would always serve other people before themselves. While in digs Laura learned that the working class did just the opposite – they helped themselves first, by simply reaching for things rather than asking. She was considered to have 'airs' because of her more refined table manners, which she found rather strange and unsettling.

But bad table manners were not the only aspect of working-class life that made Laura cringe. She was convinced – rightly or wrongly – that the working classes were less honest than her own class, and that their brains were less efficient. She probably felt this particularly strongly because as a child the aunts had not allowed her to mix with, or even speak to, any working-class children, including the children of cooks, housekeepers and cleaners employed by the Dillon family, in case she picked up their bad habits and way of talking.

Laura spoke with an upper-crust, plummy accent all her life; she cringed when she heard impure vowel sounds, and could not help attributing both lower moral standards and lower brain power to those who did not speak well. In later life, Michael Dillon tried to shake some of this snobbery off, but found it was even more deeply ingrained than the conviction that he was a man in a woman's body.

Laura did not feel that she was snobbish, nor did she wish to be thought of as a snob. Later, indeed, as Michael, Dillon was to make firm friends among working-class people, in a deliberate attempt to shake off the Daisy and Toto influence, although as he was to reflect in journals and letters, it was not that easy to do so. The 'English aristocrat' background was a taint that would not be removed. If anything, Dillon found it was easier to turn from a woman into a man than to shrug off this upbringing.

Laura's one comfort at this time was her motorcycle, on which she would tear round the countryside, trying to escape her growing mental agony. She also quickly got in touch with Bristol University Women's Boat Club and offered to coach them, with the result that in their next regatta they beat Oxford – previously their victors during the period when Laura Dillon had been the Oxford stroke.

Ever more miserable in her working-class digs and with her life in general, she began to wonder whether there was any possibility that she could physically change her sex. She had no idea whether such a thing had ever been done before, nor did she know whom to ask. In the meantime she was regarded as a curiosity by her workmates, who were friendly but distant and could not begin to understand what her problem was.

When war broke out in 1939, Laura joined the WAAF territorials and waited to be called up for full-time service. She became a despatch rider and was always automatically taken for a boy in her overalls, astride a motorcycle. She was excited about doing war work full time, but only a week after she had been called up the Commandant told Laura that she did not seem to be suited to a women's corps and pointed out that when army accommodation was eventually provided she would have to sleep in a dormitory full of women. Laura soon decided that that would be impossible. She abandoned the WAAF and returned to work in the laboratory, where she became post-mortem assistant and radiographer.

In deadly secret, Laura sought the advice of a doctor who was supposed to be an expert on sex problems. She hardly knew how to explain her dilemma, so she simply said she felt that she was far more male than female and had completely the wrong kind of body. Was there, she asked, anything at all that could be done? The doctor, George Foss, was intrigued and said he would like to help but insisted that a psychiatrist friend of his should know about it. Laura readily agreed to go to the psychiatrist, glad that at last something was being done. Nowadays, of course, the first stage of treatment for pre-operative transsexuals is psychiatric assessment. However, the next time she visited Dr Foss he had become nervous and said that he could not help after all; he was in any case expecting his call-up papers and would not like to have to leave his patient in a worse state than before, maybe half-finished. Laura went back to her digs in deep gloom.

Many years later Michael Dillon wrote in a letter to a correspondent who had asked for advice on how to change sex:

> I have a very good idea of how you feel. In 1939 I felt the same but at that time it was a false expectation; the doctor let me down and it was not till 1942 that I was able to get going and not till '45 that I met G [Sir Harold Gillies] so I know *just* how you feel. You have all my sympathy but I can't help saying I think it is a pity as I liked you the way you are. Still, people said that to me!

But Dr Foss had not entirely Dillon down, in fact. He had given the unhappy 24-year-old woman some male hormone pills, saying, 'See what they can do.'

The male hormone pills were testosterone, which, along with the female hormone oestrogen, had just been isolated and made available in tablet form. Laura began taking them, with the result that her voice deepened, she ceased menstruating and hair began to grow on her face. It is not known whether any biological female before Laura Dillon had ever used these male hormone pills; no previous cases are described in medical literature. The pills were normally prescribed to try to make underdeveloped biological males more masculine, and at this time, before the creation of the National Health Service, all treatment and medication were paid for by the patient.

The medical consultation, which the sensitive young woman found agonizing, had a nasty outcome. Some time after Laura had been given her first hormone tablets the psychiatrist who had been called in for advice described her case to some of his cronies, one of whom was a doctor in the laboratory where Laura worked. This doctor thought it was a huge joke and related the story to all his colleagues, exclaiming, 'What do you think? Miss Dillon wants to become a man!' Now she was not merely a curiosity, but a laughing-stock as well.

Laura felt she could not stay on at the laboratory after this. She resigned and joined instead the First Aid Nursing Yeomanry, or FANYs, a women's service of unpaid volunteers whose job it was to drive ambulances. American ambulances were now stationed in a suburb of Bristol, and the drivers were accommodated in a luxury hotel nearby. Laura suggested it might be more sensible to have the drivers camping at the ambulance station but was advised that ladies could hardly be expected to endure such conditions. Soon afterwards, she had a bad motorbike accident and could not walk for a month, and at this point decided to resign from the FANYs, who she felt were not putting in a proper war effort. Above all Laura longed to be able to join up as a real man to do 'real' war work, rather than doing comparatively unimportant jobs on the periphery. The need to earn money had also now become pressing, so she looked for something else to do.

As she was going home to her new digs on the bus, she saw an advertisement for a petrol pump attendant in a garage and immediately got off the bus and applied for the job. She already had a full driving licence, as she had passed her test (these had been introduced in

1935) in her first year at Oxford. The garage proprietor looked at her strangely, for although she looked so masculine she still wore a skirt. He accepted her on the spot, however: so many young men had now been called up that labour was hard to find. 'And so,' wrote Dillon, 'began my career in the garage, which was to last for four miserable years.'

Unable to go to Folkestone now because of her appearance, to say nothing of her abject misery, she spent Christmas alone in the garage on firewatching duty. As time went on, air raids were to be very heavy indeed in Bristol and few people wanted the dangerous job of firewatcher.

Laura felt she was at rock bottom. She had descended so far from her aristocratic upbringing that she now felt lucky to have been given a job in a garage – a job considered in those days to be very low indeed. She had very little money, hardly enough to live on, no friends and could not get proper medical help. Yet the garage years were not unrelieved misery, nor were they wasted. They enabled Laura to make a close and lifelong friend of another garage hand, Gilbert Barrow, and also allowed her to 'disappear' while she effected the change-over from female to male. It was during her time in the garage that Laura decided to call herself Michael. She dispensed entirely with Laura – a name she had always hated, and which she felt was ridiculously feminine. [*Author's note: Dillon will henceforth be referred to as 'he'.*]

Gilbert Barrow, now in his sixties and still living in Bristol, was a fair-haired youth of seventeen when he first met Dillon.

Like Michael, he was an orphan. He had been brought up in Muller's Orphanage in Bristol, a place which to Dillon sounded like the worst sort of Dickensian institution. The conditions had been so brutal that Gilbert had been unable to obtain an education, and, underfed and overbeaten, he removed himself as soon as he could to Wales, where he lived with a woman he called his mother. Although he and Dillon were from opposite ends of the social scale, they appeared to have something in common. And, young as he was, Gilbert championed Michael, and had the courage to stand up for him against the others in the garage.

As soon as Gilbert Barrow arrived there, the other men took him aside and said, 'You see that fellow over there? Well, he's not a man, he's a girl!' When Michael mentioned that every newcomer was given the same story, Gilbert replied: 'Yes, they told me that on my first day, but I said I would knock the block off anybody who tried to be funny about you. I also said that you really were a man and that had them puzzled. They didn't know what know what to believe then.'

From that time on, Michael felt that he owed Gilbert something which could never be repaid, although, as he wrote, he did his best in later years. This 'best' included sending Gilbert's son to public school.

Gilbert Barrow recently recalled the early stages of their friendship:

I first met Michael when staying in Bristol for a few months prior to call-up during the war. I took a temporary job in a garage where he was working . . . This threw us together and as we were from widely separated backgrounds enjoyed many a discussion on a range of subjects and became very good friends. He tried to explain why Miss Dillon was known as Michael, but I gave little thought to it, saying, 'You're a bloke as far as I'm concerned.'

After the first blitz on Bristol, Gilbert joined Michael as a fire-watcher, and both decided to live at the garage, bedding down there at night. Michael felt that it would make sense to make his home there, since he had been in dirty, unsatisfactory digs to which he would return at night only to be woken up for air raids. He arranged to live at the garage for 10 shillings a week.

Gilbert Barrow has paid tribute to Michael's extreme bravery as a firewatcher: 'We had some heavy raids during the period [while working in the garage] and he showed little regard for his own safety. I never met anyone in later events in the Navy or the Far East who showed such bravery, or in retrospect such lack of a fear of dying.' One of the reasons for his fearlessness was of course that Michael felt his life was not worth living, and that a bomb would have given him 'honourable discharge' from a life he had grown to loathe.

He felt himself extremely lucky to have found such a friend as Gilbert; and as for Gilbert, although the young boy could not really follow the Oxford graduate's philosophical arguments, he said that the discussions made him think for the first time in his life. None of the other garage workers would have been any kind of friend for Michael, not least because they were extremely dishonest – and proud of it. Daisy and Toto had brought Michael up to possess the highest standards of integrity, and at first he could not believe that there were other people with lower ones.

After Michael had been dispensing petrol for about two weeks, one of the boys in the workshop said casually that he expected Michael was making quite a bit of money on the side from the pumps. Michael, amazed, asked him what he meant, and was even more astonished at the answer.

'When the meat lorries come in,' the wide-boy explained, 'you pay the driver a bob [5p] to sign for thirteen gallons when he has had only twelve, and then you have one in hand to sell for double that.' Michael saw that the advice was kindly meant, and equally kindly pointed out that he could not condone such dishonest behaviour, whether he would be found out or not. The workshop boy backed away in disbelief, and Michael realized that his code of conduct and that of the garage hands was planets apart.

'During the next three years,' he wrote in his memoirs, 'I was at constant loggerheads simply by trying to keep to my own moral ideas. And the boss reproached me for quarrelling with my mates.' Later, Michael was promoted to tyre chief and breakdown driver and was also deployed to fetch and deliver customers' cars because he 'spoke nicely'. At first, the boss referred to Michael as Miss Dillon, which mystified the customers as they were certain they were dealing with a young man. After a time, the boss instructed his staff to refer to Michael as 'he' on all occasions.

All this time Michael was continuing to take the hormone pills, which were having a marked effect. His muscles were becoming tougher, his outline more male and his beard growth made it necessary for him to shave three times a week. Best of all, from his point of view, was the fact that menstruation had stopped, although nothing as yet could be done about the breasts. All the male hormone in the world will not shrink them once they have developed. The breasts were a continuing source of anguish, and made Michael fearful of taking off his overalls in public. Also, of course, he had no male organs as such, although the testosterone had the effect of making the clitoris grow into something resembling a tiny penis.

The raids on Bristol grew more frequent, and the wave of bombings during 1940 and 1941 was so heavy that the garage hands could hardly leave the building in safety, even for a few minutes. But Dillon was to look back on that time when Gilbert was his close companion and friend as relatively happy, and dreaded the day when the young boy would have to go. The moment came in the autumn of 1941, when Gilbert joined the Navy. Michael did not see him again until Boxing Day, when he turned up in Navy uniform with a bit of Christmas turkey hidden underneath his coat. On the train from Plymouth to

Bristol, however, Gilbert had felt so hungry he had had a nibble every now and again, until by the time he reached the garage there was hardly anything left. Nevertheless, Michael devoured the skin and sucked the bone – it was his only bit of Christmas cheer that year.

During this time Michael was not at all well, being troubled by recurrent bouts of hypoglaecemia, or low blood sugar, which on several occasions caused him to pass out. Hypoglycaemia was to plague him for the rest of his life. He passed out one day in the street in Weston-super-Mare, where he had gone for a rest after being given a weekend off work. By this time he had abandoned all pretence at female dress and wore a sports coat and flannels when not in garage overalls.

He looked completely like a man and also now spoke like one. He was shaving thrice weekly and beginning to acquire a man's shape. So the doctors at the hospital where he was taken were astonished beyond belief when they asked the patient for his name and were told 'Laura Maud Dillon'. Assuming that Michael's mind was wandering because of the fact that he was still semi-conscious, they asked for some identity as they could not believe their ears. Michael fished in his pocket and found his old FANY identity card, complete with photo. The photo showed a young person who was clearly a woman, although a rather masculine-looking one.

Nevertheless, Michael was admitted to a man's ward as the doctors still thought there must be a mistake and that he was really a man. He simply did not look like a woman, despite still having female breasts and no male organs.

On the first night that Michael spent in hospital there was a major blitz. He sat up in his hospital bed watching the flashes, the parachute flares, incendiaries and tracer bullets flying everywhere. There were many serious injuries and his ward quickly filled to overflowing with wounded men. Michael watched all this happening as if from a cinema seat; he felt it was all a million miles away from his own reality, his own private hell. Many times during the war he felt that it would be a blessed release if one of the bombs came and carried him off, which was why he took so few safety precautions on his own behalf.

The following morning the hospital was evacuated. The wounded and ill were moved by ambulance to a temporary hospital in Combe Down, Bath, which was housed in Nissen huts. Michael was still kept with the men. He stayed in the hospital for five weeks while tests were carried out to determine the nature of his illness. Nothing was said or done about his sex change during this hospital stay.

The doctors in the hospital decided that Michael was a true male, although for some genetic reason grossly underdeveloped, but paid him little attention as they were already overstretched attending to those wounded by the blitz.

As he had nowhere to convalesce, Michael had to go straight back to the garage and resume his work as a motor mechanic and firewatcher.

Six months after this incident he passed out again (it is possible that the massive doses of male hormone he was taking may have contributed to these attacks) and was taken to Bristol Royal Infirmary. He remained there for two weeks, during which he confided his story to the house surgeon. Dillon does not record whether he was admitted to a male or a female ward on this occasion, but his stay in hospital was to have fortunate repercussions for him. A plastic surgeon at the hospital said that he would remove the breasts with a bilateral mastectomy and then put Michael in touch with a well-known plastic surgeon who might be able to construct some semblance of male organs. The plastic surgeon also suggested that Dillon should re-register with the state as a male and get his birth certificate changed.

This was the first hopeful sign that the terrible dilemma of being neither one sex nor the other could be practically resolved.

'It was,' Dillon wrote, 'as if a sudden tiny gleam of light had appeared showing a possible line of escape from what had been a prison of darkness. Whichever way I had turned, I had seemed to be hemmed in by my birth certificate, identity cards, driving licences and my mail as it was addressed to me. If I tried to change my job or if I were to start in a new town, it would be the same. Everyone would know at once and everyone would tell everyone else. Re-registration? Was it possible?'

Michael soon realized that, with two serious blackouts behind him, it would not be difficult to get leave from the garage to have the chest operation. As it was, he had yet another blackout on the very morning he was admitted for the mastectomy. As soon as the operation had been completed and Michael came round, he vomited non-stop for 24 hours. This was the pattern for all future operations. Always after a general anaesthetic he vomited for hours; it was to become a considerable problem, for between the years of 1945 and 1949 he had several operations every year.

Michael was more delighted with the mastectomy operation than with almost anything in his life, a feeling commonly experienced by female-to-male transsexuals, who feel that breast removal gives them their greatest emancipation from the bondage of their bodies. Breasts, the chief outward sign of being female, cannot easily be hidden, even when the woman in question, like the young Laura Dillon, is slightly built.

Mastectomy was quite a common operation even in those days, and was mostly carried out to remove tumours supposed to be malignant. Michael's operation was more like cosmetic breast reduction – nowadays quite frequently performed, on women who feel their breasts are uncomfortably large. It consisted of making incisions round the nipples and areolae then removing the underlying fat and breast tissue. The operation, then as now, left noticeable triangular scars where the incisions had been made. Michael was to explain these away in later years by saying they were war wounds.

His main problem on this occasion was recovering from the anaesthetic. After a week, the stitches were removed and the scars remained red and livid for about six months. The mastectomy completed, the Bristol surgeons advised a laparotomy (an incision through the abdominal wall) to see if a tumour of the pancreas might be causing the low blood sugar and subsequent blackouts. The operation revealed nothing, although the surgeon did remove Dillon's appendix. Dillon wished later they had given him a hysterectomy – now a standard form of treatment for female-to-male transsexuals – but nobody thought of it at the time. So all his life Dillon had ovaries, although they would have atrophied considerably over the years under the onslaught of the male hormone.

The mastectomy took place in 1942. In the same year he received his M.A. (Oxford M.A.s may be bought, for a small fee, seven years after graduation) and, later, so he said, his name was entered in the records of Brasenose College, to save him the embarrassment of having to admit to a women's college when asked which Oxford college he had attended. The Oxford University Information Service confirmed in 1988 that Michael Dillon had indeed been taken on to the books of Brasenose, where his lifelong friend Jimmy McKie was a tutor, but the present principal of Brasenose, Barry Nicholas, has claimed that he is unable to find any trace of someone by the name of Dillon and indeed asserts that there is an 'inherent impossibility' about Dillon having migrated from St Anne's to Brasenose after taking his M.A. Whether the transfer was in fact informal, and never ratified by Brasenose, remains unclear.

Somewhat more important to Michael's future was his discovery that individuals could get their birth certificates changed if it could be shown that they belonged more to the opposite sex than to the one in which they had been born. Since 1970, however, it has been impossible for transsexuals to get their birth certificates altered unless it can be proved that a genuine mistake was made at birth. This does sometimes happen, or did in the days before chromosome and other sex tests were available, but in Michael Dillon's case there had been no mistake. His anatomical and biological sex was unequivocally female. The only respect in which he was originally male was psychological. But slowly Michael was becoming what is today called a female-to-constructed-male transsexual.

Michael discovered that there was a doctor in Bath, John Cooper, who would sign a medical certificate saying that he was far more male than female and wished to adopt that sex once and for all. But in order for re-registration to take place the registrar of births, marriages and deaths would also need a certificate from a member of the family. Michael knew that this would be impossible: neither his brother, the eighth baronet, nor the aunts could ever be persuaded to sign any such document. So he wrote to a little-known cousin, Maude Eileen Beauchamp (called Minnie), who was the daughter of his Aunt Grace, Daisy and Toto's sister. Minnie was much older than Michael; indeed, she had a son, Charles, who was Michael's contemporary. But Michael reasoned that this cousin was perhaps a little more 'modern' than the other relatives. After Minnie had written back to say she would sign the certificate, Michael sent off the application to Somerset House. It was accepted, and in 1944 Laura Dillon officially became Laurence Michael. However, the 'Laurence' was dropped instantly as it was too near the original 'Laura', which he had always hated.

Michael Dillon's birth certificate is amended by a marginal note which reads:

> In entry no 54, col 2, for Laura Maud read Laurence Michael and in col 3 for 'girl' read 'boy'. Corrected on 14th April 1944 by C.E. Weston, Supt Registrar on production of a statutory declaration.

Laura became Michael officially a fortnight before his 29th birthday. Two massive hurdles were now overcome: the mastectomy and the re-registration. Nobody would now mistake Dillon for a woman, or wonder what he was. The days of being a freak were over.

But two enormous obstacles remained. One was to break the news to the aunts and to Bobby, and the other was to acquire, somehow, a semblance of male organs – a penis and scrotum instead of the existing vagina and uterus.

The aunts had been evacuated from Folkestone after Dunkirk and had gone to stay at Mrs Hearne's hotel in Hertfordshire – somewhat surprisingly in view of the way this woman had mistreated their beloved nephew Bobby. Michael simply did not know how to break the news, so he asked a woman doctor who was also staying at the hotel to do it for him.

The aunts' reaction was predictable. Toto said that as far as she knew, 'Male and female created He them.' Daisy said she had never heard of anything like it in her life, but that if it *could* happen then Laura was the most likely person to change sex. Maudie, who was with her sisters again, having been evacuated from the bridge club, just snorted. But the worst was over. From now on, the aunts began to be able to accept Michael. They probably had no idea themselves whether he was truly male or truly female, or neither. Both aunts were now in their seventies. They had lived all their lives in a world of their own, and they knew little of what went out outside it. Nor did they want to know.

The reaction from brother Bobby was less positive. When Laura changed sex, the two had not met for about seven years. Sir Robert now lived permanently in Ireland, managing the family estates, and had been called to the Irish bar. However, he does not appear to have practised much, if at all, as a barrister. Michael met his brother in Dublin and told him, in the restaurant of the Savoy cinema, what had happened to him. Then he asked if Bobby could ever accept him as a brother. The answer, accompanied by a shudder of disbelief and horror, was an emphatic no. Robert never accepted Michael, either then or for the rest of his life. Even after Michael had died Robert would not own him. At the restaurant meeting Robert realized he had no choice but to accept the fact of Michael's re-registration, but he asked that Michael's name should never be coupled with his. He would neither admit to any kinship nor would he ever welcome Michael as a visitor to the house. Lady Dillon, Robert's wife, claims to have met Michael on only two occasions, amd has said that her husband never mentioned him at all. Robert simply cut Michael out of his life and his consciousness, thus ending their relationship.

Michael wondered if they could not regard each other more distantly, as cousins, but Robert said this was not possible. He had been horribly embarrassed by having Michael as a sister, and was never to own him as a brother. As he saw it, Michael had done the most outrageous thing a human being could do, by not accepting the sex into which he was born and by committing the outrage of having himself changed, hormonally and surgically, into a pseudo-male. Robert was fully aware that Michael could never be a 'real' man.

There was also another factor to be considered: having changed sex, Michael was now heir presumptive to the baronetcy. Although Robert married in 1947, no children resulted from the marriage, which left Michael directly in line. If he were to outlive Robert, he would become, quite legally, the ninth baronet of Lismullen. That was also probably something which Robert's conventional and unimaginative mind could not accept. As a female Laura could not have succeeded to the baronetcy. In Robert's eyes, Laura had turned herself into a usurper. As a sister she had always been more masculine than he; now she was to all intents and purposes a man, with a birth certificate to prove it. This made her heir to the title that would otherwise have gone to Robert's (male) offspring. Laura was also taking her place in the masculine world. For Robert this was all too much to take. He remained desperately ashamed of Michael and all his activities until the day he died, in 1983. Even now, when transsexualism is far more widely discussed and far better understood, the remaining members of Michael's family are reluctant to talk about the matter, or formally to acknowledge it.

When Michael went to the labour exchange (the National Insurance Office) to get a new identity card, which everyone had to have in those days, he had an unexpected reaction to his request. The man behind the counter said, 'We have had quite a lot of those applications lately' and made out a new card without evincing any surprise or curiosity. After that Michael received call-up papers but was predictably turned down when the army medical officer learned the truth – and saw for himself that Michael was still not a real man.

Michael returned to the garage, but by now the years of living in obscurity, the 'disappearance', had served their purpose. There was no need at all to take a menial job any more. What was more, the war was coming to an end.

But what could he do instead? Alison Macbeth, the woman doctor who had told Daisy and Toto about the sex change, now suggested that Michael should himself become a doctor. At first he was not interested, but on thinking about it he began to wonder if it might not be such a bad idea – if a medical school would accept him. This was by no means a foregone conclusion. He had become very interested in the links between mind and body, between hormones, personality and sexual orientation, and had just started putting some material together for a book on the subject. This book, *Self: A Study in Endocrinology and Ethics,* was probably the very first printed document to address the subject of sex change.

The main stumbling block to getting into medical school was that Michael had no knowledge of physics, chemistry, zoology or botany – all of which would be required for the pre-medical examination. However, he obtained permission from his boss at the garage to attend the Merchant Venturers' Technical College on day-release. Michael was very pleased about this, because it meant that for the first time in his life he would be among people who knew nothing whatever of his history and could simply accept him as a mature student. 'The relief,' he wrote, 'was indescribable.'

However, not having male organs preyed on his mind. Michael had no wish to be a half-man. He wrote to Sir Harold Gillies, at that time the most famous plastic surgeon in the world and especially renowned for his reconstructive work on the work on the war wounded and burns victims, to explain his problem. Gillies ran a hospital at Basingstoke which was to become well-known as a centre of excellence for plastic surgery. He replied to Michael's letter suggesting an interview, at which he examined him from all angles. At last, he said: 'I will put you down as an acute hypospadias.'

Gillies' biographer, Reginald Pound, said that Sir Harold was always sympathetic to 'nature's mistakes', as he termed them, and during his career as a plastic surgeon was to carry out several sex-change operations, many of them the first of their kind. Gillies probably realized that Michael was anatomically and chromosomally female, but the diagnosis of hypospadias gave him a valid reason for carrying out the operation, should awkward questions be asked.

Hypospadias is a rare condition, allied to cleft palate, in which the subject is actually male but possesses incompletely formed external genitalia. In the past, this had often led to boys being classified as girls. Another manifestation of hypospadias is that female-type breasts form at puberty.

In his chapter on sex reassignment and hermaphroditism in the book *Transsexualism and Sex Reassignment* John Money describes hypospadias as

> a condition in which the foetal differentiation of the penis remains incomplete. The skin of the penis does not wrap around the shaft of the organ and fuse on the under side as it should do to form the urethral tube. Instead of a tube, there is an open gutter. In somewhat similar fashion, the skin of the two sides of the scrotum does not properly fuse in the midline. There is an orifice where the base of the penis and the scrotum should join. This orifice houses the urinary opening and in some cases the opening of a vaginal pouch also. Prior to surgical repair, urination is accomplished from the sitting position only.
>
> There are varying degrees of hypospadias, so that the urinary opening may be located anywhere from the penoscrotal junction to near the tip of the penis. All can repaired surgically, the ultimate success being dependent on the size of the deformed penis to begin with. The penis may be little bigger than a normal clitoris. Then the outlook in terms of adult sexual life, for a child reared as a male, is very poor indeed.

Nowadays, an easy test can determine whether a hypospadiac infant should be brought up as a boy or girl. If the penis responds positively to a testosterone-ointment test, then the individual will be able to ejaculate and have erections. In the past, such infants were sometimes designated male, sometimes female. But such people are not transsexuals. All the studies carried out on hypospadiac patients have revealed that they prefer to remain in the sex in which they were reared and have no psychological longing to be other than this. Those reared as boys establish a masculine psychosexual identity, regardless of the size or function of the penis, and those brought up as girls prefer to remain that way, even though they may not be able to bear children. In no instance, John Money observes, has a hypospadiac individual demonstrated an overriding urge to have his or her sex reassigned. Quite the reverse: in all cases that have come to his attention, patients have been desperate for surgery that would enable them to live more fully within the sex in which they have been reared. Michael Dillon fell firmly into the transsexual rather than the hypospadiac category, as Sir Harold Gillies well knew.

Sir Harold Gillies is not much remembered today, but he introduced many pioneering surgical techniques and was always ready to try new experiments. He had never carried out the fashioning of a penis on a biological female before, but that was not to stop him from trying. Roberta Cowell, who got to know Michael Dillon well in later life, remarked: 'Gillies was making it up as he went along.'

Harold Gillies had, however, done several reconstructions of the penis on genuine hypospadiacs and developed the tube pedicle technique, by which a tube of flesh is raised on the thigh or abdomen to be transferred elsewhere. For the rest of his life, Michael was to remember Sir Harold Gillies with extreme gratitude. He was the person who eventually who made it possible for Dillon to look like a perfectly normal man, though he was never able to have a proper erection or to ejaculate – and he retained female organs inside him.

Harold Gillies told Michael that he could not fit him in for some time owing to the number of war wounded to whom he needed to attend (the landings in France had just begun). But Michael didn't mind. 'To wait with hope in one's heart is easy,' he said. 'And I had waited long enough without any. So back I went to study science and to park cars.'

If he was indeed to go to a university to study medicine, the authorities would want to see evidence of his Oxford M.A., which was made out in the name of Laura Maud. Michael wrote to his old tutor, Jimmy McKie, who was now a major in Army intelligence, explaining his predicament. He persuaded the Oxford University registrar to issue a new certificate with only initials, rather than the full name, so that no awkward questions would be asked. Michael felt that he had to keep the fact of his transsexuality a complete secret, telling only those who absolutely had to know. It was this perceived need for secrecy that made Michael's story all the more astounding when it eventually became public knowledge.

Michael did not find it easy to get accepted at a university. He failed the preliminary examinations at both Edinburgh and London. Then he tried Trinity College, Dublin – where his brother had read law – and, after an interview, was accepted.

The final task Michael completed before he went over to Dublin for the six-year medical course was his first book, which he had started writing in 1939 in the evenings after the garage was closed. He sent it to Heinemann, where it was accepted. The book was eventually published under the Heinemann Medical imprint in 1946. Although full of special pleading, it contains many passages that shed valuable light on Dillon's state of mind and attitudes.

The 'darkest days' of the garage years, as Michael was to see them later, had actually seen him accomplish a great deal: re-registration, acceptance as a man, having all his certificates changed, gaining a place at medical school and writing a publishable book. He had also made a lifelong friend of Gilbert Barrow and made his peace with the aunts. He could not persuade Bobby to accept him, but that was really Bobby's problem and was not to bother Michael much as he had so little in common with his brother; the rift between them had in any case been widening since early childhood.

He had also found Sir Harold Gillies and, miraculously, received an assurance that he could eventually be transformed, through plastic reconstructive surgery, into a cosmetically complete man. In 1945 Michael, aged 30, felt that his life was just beginning. He had never felt that he could live any kind of life while condemned to exist as a female. The male role – however that may be defined, and Michael never did define it – was the only one that felt natural to him.

5

Medical Student

ALTHOUGH Michael now felt far happier about taking his place in the man's world, he still asked himself ceaselessly whether he could have done anything other than what he did. By changing sex, he had accomplished what nobody else had ever previously achieved and few had probably ever contemplated. Although transsexuality appears to be as old as time, Michael Dillon was the first person – so far as records and medical textbooks show – to make so complete a change from female to male, taking advantage of the recently-isolated sex hormones and of advances in plastic surgery.

He came to the conclusion that he had had no choice but to take the path he had chosen, whatever the consequences, and whatever anybody else thought. His philosophy of life at the time is contained in the book he wrote while he was working in the garage and which was published when he was a first-year medical student.

The book, *Self: A Study in Endocrinology and Ethics*, examines the links between mind and body. Dillon argues passionately for greater openness about sexual matters, and for tolerance for those who do not appear to fit neatly into either the male or the female gender. The book is a distillation of his reflections of the previous few years and shows how far ahead of his time his opinions were. Writing about the phenomenon of sex change, he asks that far more sympathy and compassion should be extended to those who undergo it. They should be regarded as thinking, feeling human beings, not categorized as circus freaks.

In attempting to determine what makes some people believe they are of a gender other than that which they seem to be anatomically and biologically, he anticipates later researchers by coming to the conclusion that it is something which starts before birth and is most probably caused by 'some accident of foetal life'.

When, at Oxford, Dillon had come across the word 'homo-sexual' for the first time, he had at first thought that that was what he must be. Since those days, however, he had researched the phenomenon and had become convinced that, instead of just male and female, there were many graduations of sexuality.

He writes:

> It is fast becoming evident that there are not only two sexes but several grades . . . Both the mannish and the masculine woman and the effeminate and feminine man enjoy the habits and occupations of the other sex far more than they do of their own . . . Because they are not quite natural in their role, which is one of imitation, much ridicule attaches to them, unjustly, however, because they cannot of themselves alter the primary desire. Yet there is always an incongruity between their appearance and their habits.

Society and convention, says Dillon, often force these 'masculine' women and 'effeminate' men into roles which are unnatural for them. All too infrequently are they allowed to be themselves. Life, he states, can be sheer agony for those men and women who simply cannot fit into the roles that society has preordained for them; and he knew, as all other transsexuals have known, that psychiatric treatment can never bring about acceptance of the original gen-der. 'The psychologists' only suggestion is to make the mind fit the body, to which of course the patient will never accede,' he writes.

Self is well written, scholarly, intelligent and decades ahead of its time. Dillon understood that it is only by physical 'mutilation' that transsexuals can hope to lead a tolerably happy life, and not lose their sanity. These people are perfectly aware, he says, that they will always be incomplete specimens and never able to reproduce in either sex. But that doesn't really matter. All that is asked is that the body should be altered, as far as possible, to fit the mind.

Michael Dillon was the first to say this, and it has taken psy-chologists many years to accept the truth of his statement. He is generally scathing about psychologists, who, he says, have no experience themselves of the transsexual phenomenon. So how can they hope to be of much help?

71

Michael Dillon was also, at this stage of his life, feminist in outlook. He says in the book that centuries of conditioning have made women apparently weak and fearful, and it is hardly surprising that they have achieved hardly anything in the outside world, as they have been given so little chance to do so. Women have been conditioned, he says, into taking a secondary and passive role in life, and have adopted a slave mentality, a conviction that they are bound to please their masters – men. Women, says Dillon, have had to anticipate men's needs and moods, just to survive. There has never been any corresponding need on the part of men to think much about what would please the women in their lives. Such inequality, he claims, creates discord between the sexes. He considers it impossible for men and women to be able to live happily together, least of all as equals.

Dillon felt that the stultifying effects of conditioning meant that women could not truly benefit from teaching, even from higher education. They still regarded everything as glorified housewifery, he believed. Higher education, he says, cannot give women a man's mind – such as Dillon believed he himself possessed.

Dillon ends his book with a plea that those who do not fit neatly into stereotyped sex roles should not be regarded as freaks. They are as yet, he says, condemned to live in a twilight world, where they must either try to find others of their kind or attempt to conform with pre-existing rules. He suggests that since the war was now over, it was a good time for a new beginning, a new tolerance, a new understanding. He considers that the hardest thing of all is to reject society's 'freak' label and to find a means of reconciling its unthinking condemnation of anything outside the norm with a tolerable way of life.

It is tempting to speculate how such a book would be received today. The tone is measured, even intellectual, and is a truly remarkable achievement considering the circumstances under which it was written. In Dillon's day it seems to have been read mainly by those who identified with the conditions he describes – homosexuals, lesbians and potential transsexuals. At the time, it would have been hard to assess such a book without knowing something about the author – and Michael did not give away any secrets about himself. The book simply states his name as author, without the addition of biographical details. It is a matter for speculation whether Heinemann, the publishers, ever wondered or thought to ask what qualifications the author had for the highly original and unconventional (for the time) solutions that he was advocating to the transsexual problem. When the book was published the word 'transsexual' had not been coined; indeed, there was no term in existence to describe people like Michael.

Self not only enabled Michael to clarify his ideas but served to launch him on a career as a writer – something he was to pursue with incredible dedication a decade or so later.

For the moment, however, he was obliged to apply himself to his work as a medical student at Trinity College, Dublin. His brother, Sir Robert, was not at all pleased that Michael had won a place there. He himself lived only 26 miles away, and worried that Michael might call at his house, reveal that he was Robert's brother or otherwise cause him embarrassment. Michael had however promised never to do anything which would link Robert's name with his. He kept his word, even to the extent of continuing to be known as 'Laura Maud' in *Debrett*'s and *Burke*'s peerages. It was Robert who filled in the forms for the peerage entries, and nothing would ever induce him to change his sister into a brother, even on paper.

Michael Dillon entered medical school in the autumn of 1945 to find that most of the students were about twelve years younger than he was. His year was unusual for the time in that almost half the medical students were female. Michael was to be extremely rude about these female students for wanting 'equality' with the men at the same time as demanding what he saw as the privileges of their sex. By this time, his disidentification with the female sex was complete: Dillon never saw himself as a former woman. In his view he had always been a man, and it was just unfortunate that nature had provided him with the wrong equipment. The huge age gap between Michael and most of the other students meant that it was difficult for him to form any close relationships with the people in his year, who mainly remember him as having been 'aloof'. Very few knew his secret, although there were rumours that Michael Dillon may not be all that he seemed.

One firm friendship was forged, however, with one of the brightest female students in his year, Patricia Leeson, to whom he confided his past. She was begged to keep the secret to herself and managed to do so successfully.

Dr Leeson remembers:

Michael was always a keen rower and was very proud of that. He was also diabetic, and was on insulin when I knew him. [Several of Michael's contemporaries describe him, erroneously, as being diabetic, and mention that he often used to pass out.] He often passed out after rowing, as I recall. I remember the hassle of people trying to get him to eat something.

He was a very nice person, although always rather remote. We younger students put it down to him being so much older. He did seem to have a bit of a chip on his shoulder and certainly was not universally popular. There were those people who got on with him, and many others who didn't.

Dr Leeson considers that Michael was 'not sexy at all' – at this time he had had no sexual experience whatever, with either males or females. He had never taken the Oxford friend's advice to find a girlfriend, and of course there was never any question of his establishing any kind of emotional relationship with a man.

'He didn't make friends easily,' recalls Dr Leeson, 'but I became quite friendly with him for a time, and would go back with him to his flat. He did like a female to go out with on Saturday evenings for a meal or to the pictures. He acquired something of a reputation as a misogynist, and this was how he regarded himself, but it wasn't entirely accurate.'

Maybe by letting himself be thought of as a misogynist and 'confirmed bachelor' (the phrase had a more innocent connotation in the 1940s than it does today) Dillon was simply protecting himself: he knew he must never get closely involved with a woman as he could never became her sexual partner, as either lover or husband.

Dr Leeson remembers Michael as completely ordinary – and not with any outward characteristics that would lead anyone to suspect he was really female underneath. 'He was quite hard-working,' she says, 'although never a brilliant student.' In fact, Michael was to find it difficult to pass his medical examinations and despite his hard work did little more than scrape through them. 'He was always very borderline,' says Patricia Leeson.

> He told me quite a lot about himself. He said that he had been brought up by aunts and went to a girls' school in Folkestone. He told me that he had been brought up as a woman but always felt himself to be male and was completely lost among women.
>
> I didn't realize he was biologically female but thought he was a grossly underdeveloped male and that a mistake had been made at birth. He was obviously a little different from the rest of us and never quite fitted in.

Dr Leeson, who got to know Michael well in his first year, also remembers reading the proofs of his book, which she found very moving: 'It was the first time I had read anything about sex transformation, and the loneliness such people feel when they are living a life that seems completely alien to them.'

Michael also confided to Dr Leeson that he and his brother were not on good terms: 'I knew all about the title and remember him as being very anti the aristocracy. But that may have been because he was anti his brother. My impression was that Michael was brought up alone by the maiden aunts and that his brother had a different kind of upbringing.'

Dr James Morrow, another contemporary, recalls:

I had heard that he was once a woman but, to tell you the truth, I didn't believe it. We knew he was supposed to be an M.A. at Oxford and of course he was far older than most of the students.

As far as I can remember, he behaved like a perfectly normal male, and looked like one, too. He asked intelligent questions and seemed to be very well read. Yet he never did all that well in exams. The odd thing about Dillon was that every vacation he went off somewhere and came back very pale and shaken and ill. We used to wonder whatever was the matter, and why he always came back from the holidays looking so dreadful.

Michael's holidays were of course spent at Sir Harold Gillies' hospital at Basingstoke, where he underwent a vast number of protracted and extremely painful operations. It was because of these that he had to confide in somebody, as he needed the dressings changing for a while after resuming his medical studies. The man he trusted to do this job was at the time a house surgeon at the Royal City of Dublin Hospital. Somewhat embarrassingly, this doctor was a friend of Robert's. He was intrigued to discover what had happened to the sister Robert used to have but he never told Robert that he knew.

Few of the medical students in Dillon's year had any inkling of his background. One, Alec Meldrum, comments: 'I had no idea at all and was absolutely amazed when I found out. I'm sure nobody knew.' Another contemporary, Hillas Smith, admits that he was also 'staggered' to learn that Dillon had once been female: 'It doesn't say much for our powers of observation that we never guessed. He did seem rather chauvinistic and anti-women and was not himself all that aggressive or obviously masculine. But nothing untoward occurred to us at the time.'

In fact, most people who met Michael Dillon after 1945 would never have guessed his female past. For his part, he was delighted that when he walked down the street nobody ever gave him a second glance. Michael had in common with more recent transsexuals the feeling that if one can move about in public without exciting any attention at all the desired objective has been achieved. Michael looked like a perfectly ordinary young man. He dressed mainly in sports jackets and flannels, and in 1949, after a few years of medical school, he grew a beard, which was quite unusual for those days. He also continued to smoke his pipe, so perhaps he did rather look stereotypically masculine – though not in any way to make anybody stare. The massive doses of male hormone he had been taking since 1939 and was to take until he entered a monastery had the effect of deepening his voice so that it sounded absolutely male, as all those who remember Dillon have affirmed.

As soon as Michael became a medical student he found the temptation to row again overwhelming. One of the first things he did was to join the Boat Club. Thanks to the testosterone, he had now put on weight and was 11 stone 4 pounds, more or less the ideal male weight for his height of 5 feet 9 inches. His only problem was undressing in a man's changing room, as there were still telltale mastectomy scars on his chest. He decided to explain everything away, including the need for operations during the holidays, as war wounds, and seems to have got away with this story.

Eventually Michael won another rowing blue at Trinity College. He is probably the only person in history to gain a blue as both a female and a male. Michael was probably prouder of this achievement than of any other in his life – and his achievements were many. Naturally, he did not divulge to anyone that he had gained his Oxford blue while rowing for a women's eight; he told people instead that he had rowed for Brasenose, knowing that his fellow medical students were hardly likely to check.

The numerous operations that Dillon had – every vacation for the first four years of his medical course was spent entirely in hospital – made rowing rather difficult, but he was determined to continue. On the evening of the last day of each term he would rush off to London, taking the train to Basingstoke and arriving at the hospital at midnight. His operations were often scheduled for the following morning. During those four years he had a great many skin grafts but claimed that these did not interfere unduly with muscle function.

All of Michael's operations were performed by Sir Harold Gillies, whom Dillon was to regard almost as a god. Sir Harold specialized in skin grafts, and Dillon could not have chosen a better person to carry out these difficult operations. 'All of my former troubles were resolved,' he wrote on one occasion, 'by the good offices of one enlightened man with the courage of his convictions and the skill to carry them out.'

Sir Harold Gillies, born in New Zealand in 1882, is most famous for his 'tube pedicle' technique, which was first used in Russia in 1916. In 1936 Professor N.A. Bogoras, also working in Russia, used it to restore the major part of a penis lost in an accident. By the 1940s Gillies had perfected this technique as a means of reconstructing the penis. He did this by raising two abdominal tubes, one of which he inserted into the other, to produce a penile shaft and urethra. Into this he implanted a cartilage, to produce a semi-erectile condition. One of Gillies' contemporaries said of his work, 'The human machine had never known such confident engineering.' Gillies discovered that pedicles of living flesh could be raised almost anywhere on the body and transported to other areas. During the war the townsfolk of Basingstoke had become quite used to seeing young men from the hospital, Rooksdown House, with terrible burns or other war wounds walking around with their elbows attached to their foreheads (for example) by pedicles of flesh.

Sir Harold did much of his sex-change work in secret, but according to his biographer, Reginald Pound, he dealt with a 'welter of variants' on the sex theme. Some of the cases were people whose sex organs had never properly developed. In 1922 he transformed an apparent female into a 'grateful young man'.

'A simple operation,' recalled Gillies, 'and "she" was no longer of that gender.' That 1922 case was probably a typical hypospadias.

He also carried out breast reduction and augmentation operations, much nose remodelling and other operations which would now be considered routine cosmetic surgery. He knew that defects which might seem trivial to the onlooker can be terrible disfigurements in the eyes of the sufferer.

He became one of London's busiest surgeons and his income during the 1930s reached £30,000 a year – a massive amount for the time. He was never very interested in money, however, nor was he a good businessman, so he never became rich. He would often undertake operations at cut price if the patient could not afford to pay the full fee. He became known as a 'miracle surgeon', and this is certainly how Dillon came to regard him. Gillies often remarked that if an operation was going to make a great deal of difference to a patient's happiness, then that operation was justified. 'If it gives real happiness, that is the most that any surgeon or medicine can give,' he was fond of saying.

He declared that all people who are deformed, or who imagine they are deformed, suffer from extreme self-consciousness, which blights their personality.

Those whose defect is born with them, he used to say, present the greatest psychic disturbance, while people who suffer accidental injury are more inclined to regard their misfortune philosophically.

He used to say of his pedicles that he had raised so many that if they were laid end to end they would reach from Buckingham Palace, down the Mall and halfway up Nelson's Column. 'It is my ambition,' he told friends, 'that before my last pedicle is made we will reach to the top with at least one pedicle to go into the Admiral's palate.' Sir Harold had a sense of humour about his work, which was probably one reason why he was so popular and so greatly sought after. Another advantage was his excellent bedside manner. Nor was medicine his only interest in life. In his spare time Gillies was quite an accomplished landscape painter and held many exhibitions.

Although even he, their creator, laughed at the tube pedicles, they were really no laughing matter. They were an ingenious means of transporting living flesh from one part of the body to the other. However, each transportation required a serious operation. When a pedicle was raised (for example, on the abdomen) it would be slowly swung up or down until it reached the damaged area. A lengthy healing period was necessary between each movement before the pedicle could be moved again. This was the main reason why Dillon had to have to many operations: it took a long time for the pedicles to reach their final positions. Even then the job was not complete, for grafting an artificial penis was by no means the same as covering damaged skin: the part had to work, at least to the extent that the patient would be able to urinate out of it. Making working parts – fingers, hands, toes and so on – is the most difficult task undertaken by plastic surgeons. Grafting a penis and scrotum on to a female-to-male transsexual is so delicate an operation, even today, and in many cases so unsatisfactory, that many such people prefer to let well alone and go through life half-male, half-female. As Michael Dillon was the first biological female ever to have this operation, it is possible that no one knew just how difficult it would be.

Even with so skilful and compassionate a surgeon as Sir Harold Gillies, Dillon's operations did not always go smoothly. There was a continual risk of haematoma (blood clots occurring beneath the skin), and once one of these broke down serious infection could set in.

This happened on one occasion, which meant Michael had to spend three months in hospital for further skin grafts. He returned to college with no surface skin on the upper legs, and yet more haematomas: he looked as if his legs had been spread with strawberry jam. Weak and ill, he had to walk with a stick. Moreover he was obliged to urinate out of a catheter until the operations were completed.

Partly because of his medical ordeals Michael failed his anatomy examination at the first attempt; he only managed to scrape through, with 50 per cent, at the second attempt. He had to try to do a lot of studying in hospital, which he found very difficult, even though Rooksdown House was not, according to Michael, at all typical of a hospital. Sir Harold's waspish wit and friendly manner encouraged a jolly atmosphere – despite the fact that some patients were so badly burned that they were having to endure as many as 60 operations. Like Michael, they had to have the work done in stages, which meant coming back time and again. As so many of his patients were long-stay, Sir Harold tried to make the hospital as normal and as much like the outside world as possible. Otherwise, he reasoned, those who were mutilated or badly injured might not be able to face the outside world again.

The hospital had certain strict rules, however. One was that no-body, whatever his condition, was allowed to indulge in self-pity. Another was that nobody who could do something for himself, albeit slowly and with great difficulty, should have it done for him.

Some patients had no recognizable faces at all; gradually, replacement features were made, with skin taken from other areas of the body, very often the abdomen.

Michael Dillon had a fellow sufferer – a man whose private parts had been caught and torn off by naval machinery. 'The nature of his operations,' writes Dillon, with some delicacy, in his journal, 'was similar to mine.' However, this young engineer's story had a sad ending: when the operations were complete, he told his fiancée's father what had happened and was turned out of the house forthwith, for the man would have none but a 'proper' man for his daughter.

On the whole Michael enjoyed his time at Rooksdown, partly because Sir Harold took trouble to generate a cheerful ambiance and partly because he was among people who could understand his problems, their own injuries having necessitated equally major surgery. And Rooksdown put an end to Michael's lonely, friendless Christmases. On two occasions he was master of ceremonies at

Christmas functions, conducting events from a wheelchair. He was delighted to do this, feeling that it marked his re-entry into a social scene from which he had so long considered himself debarred, even if the Christmas parties were only 'practice runs' for the real world. On these occasions Sir Harold was expected to carve the turkey, which everybody imagined he would do with consummate skill, so used was he to cutting into human flesh. But Dillon recalls that he was so inept that a nurse quickly had to rescue him and do it herself.

The other reason why Michael found his stays at Rooksdown House relatively pleasant, despite the pain and suffering, was that they meant he was slowly being transformed into a 'complete' man. It was the place where he finally rid himself of all outward female characteristics.

In the same way, but on a social rather than a physical level, medical school was the place where he consolidated his 'Michael' identity. He also managed to make a few friends, some of whom he was to keep throughout his life. One was an African student, Tom Asuni, now a consultant surgeon in Nigeria, with whom Michael went on holiday in 1949, the first year he did not have to spend his vacations in Basingstoke. The holiday, lasting three weeks, was spent cycling in France and was yet another indication of Michael's social emancipation. It also signified the start of his wanderlust, which was to last until he died.

The holiday had another beneficial effect: Michael began to grow a beard and discovered it made an invaluable diguise, for he could now go anywhere without anyone guessing who he was – or had been.

Otherwise, his social life was still generally rather restricted and difficult. Several of Michael's contemporaries noticed that he was at all times rather remote. This was mainly because he did not want anybody to know, or to guess, his cover, and therefore felt that he had to keep his distance. In particular, he could not risk any of the female students falling in love with him, or he with them, because that would all too soon destroy his cover. He made a point of treating girls in a 'rough, brotherly fashion', as he himself describes it, and came to realize that he had earned himself a reputation as a woman-hater. An evening's flirting at a dance was all very well, he told a friend, but matters could never be taken further. He regarded it as a simple fact that he could never marry, or have a proper girlfriend, and that he was bound to walk alone, always. (More recent female-to-male transsexuals have, by contrast, formed very close, lasting partnerships, rather refuting his assumptions about human relationships.) Even though Michael was so much happier now than he had been as Laura, it was still a source of occasional resentment that he could never be a husband or father.

Actually, there is little indication that Michael ever wanted children. He never felt at home with them and was unlikely to have made a very good father. More probably he was attracted by the *idea* of having children and being married, as this would have set the final seal on his recently acquired manhood.

By 1949 he had finished at Rooksdown, complete with a new, operational artificial penis and scrotum. Once his operations were finally over and the tubes taken out, doctors gathered round and asked Dillon to urinate out of the new organs. Of course, he was unable to – as one never can when specifically asked to do so. Eventually a tap was turned on and he managed a trickle, much to the delight of the hospital staff. The operation was a success. Michael was never to mention, in later life, any problems with the constructed organs, so presumably they continued to function satisfactorily.

Theoretically, some sort of sexual intercourse might have been possible for him, although there could be no ejaculation. If ever Michael *had* attempted a full sexual relationship he would undoubted-ly have had to offer a frank explanation of what had happened to him, as it is unlikely that he would have been able to pass his constructed organ off as a 'war wound'. As it turned out, however, he never allowed himself to get into such a situation.

Michael wanted to keep the fact of his re-registration as a male an absolute secret and was astonished when, a few years later, transsexuals started publishing their autobiographies and proclaiming to the world who they were. Even nowadays many feel they should not divulge this secret, except to those who absolutely have to know. There is after all still a great deal of prejudice, ignorance and misunderstanding, for all that the subject is now so much more out in the open.

Michael feared that if people knew he had been born a woman they would not understand, but while he could pass himself off as a normal man and disappear into the crowd he could be relatively happy. In-deed, owing to his fear of being recognized, he had revisited his childhood town of Folkestone only once in the last few years, when Daisy and Toto wanted to return to their house after the war. Michael's job was to get the garden into some sort of order and to clean and air the rooms. He found the house in a dreadful state and was appalled at what had happened to Folkestone itself. It was absolutely desolate, even though it had suffered little actual damage. Many people had been evacuated, for fear of aid raids, and the town had acquired a lost, uninhabited air as a result.

Daisy and Toto had agreed with their 'nephew' that he should not return to Folkestone again, as they too felt it was vital that he should not be recognized. The last thing they – and Michael – wanted was publicity. However, once his beard had grown to a reasonable length Michael did start to go to Folkestone again. Nobody recognized him at all, which pleased him because it meant he could keep an eye on Daisy and Toto, now in their eighties, without risking discovery.

The problem of how to pay for the six-year medical course and the many operations at Rooksdown had not been easy to solve. Michael had decided to use the money which his father had left him to finance these two ventures. It would mean he had nothing left of the bequest when he finished, but then his earning capacity as a doctor would be high, so he should not have to worry. Michael spent some of his capital on buying a house and then assured himself of an income by letting off part of it. He also bought a Renault car, which he called 'Rennie', with £500 left him by Daphne, who had died in an internment camp during the war. Not long after this his Aunt Maudie died and left him a third of her estate of about £20,000. This useful sum of money, almost £7000, relieved Michael of his immediate financial worries and gave him some security for when he had qualified. The other two main beneficiaries named in the will were his brother Robert and Joan, the daughter of his Aunt Evie (Maudie's twin sister). Michael was to keep up a lasting relationship with Joan, who was fond of Michael and was to stay with him on occasion in his house in Dublin. (Evie wrote to say that this was most improper now that Laura was a man.)

Having bought a house, Michael could now have the kind of home he had always wanted. He soon created for himself a comfortable bachelor environment. His sitting room contained leather chairs and sofa, shelves he had made himself and which were soon covered with books, and rowing photographs on the walls. He also had the cups he had won on display, and on an occasional table gin, Irish whiskey and sherry. Although aunts never drank, and although his father had been an alcoholic, Michael was not an abstainer. He had started drinking occasionally while at Oxford, but he vowed that never would he become drunk and incapable like his father, whose example was forever in his consciousness.

Those Christmases which Michael had not spent at Basingstoke in a wheelchair had been passed with a fellow medical student whose parents were both doctors. This family made a practice of inviting to their home those who would otherwise be alone on Christmas Day. They already had a connection with the Dillons: the student's grandfather had been Robert's trustee in Ireland, while his grandmother had spoken out about 'that woman', Mrs Hearne. When the family asked whether Michael was related in any way to Robert, he at first denied it emphatically, as he had been asked to do by his brother; but two years later, when he felt he could trust them enough to let them in on the secret, he admitted the relationship.

Dillon admits that he made no other close friends at all during his medical student years, partly because of the age factor and partly because he still found it very difficult to be natural in a social context. He was unsure of his place in the world and of how to act for the best. He felt himself to be shy, and recalled all too well how he had been laughed at and shunned in the past. He also had continual nightmares about waking up and finding himself back in the garage, still a woman longing to be a man. Despite occasional loneliness, Dillon felt most of the time that he was very fortunate; indeed, he could hardly believe his luck. Everything he had dreamed about had happened: he was no longer a woman, he was officially a man, and almost all his female attributes had long since disappeared.

Michael bought himself a white tie and tails and forced himself to go to dances. For the first time he felt proud of his appearance, and absolutely right in the garments. Before, he had not felt comfortable in any kind of evening dress, so he had avoided going to any dance or evening function where dressing up would be required, quite apart from the fact that if, as Laura, he had gone to a dance and a man had put his arm round him, he would have found the experience horrifying.

By 1950 Michael's life seemed pretty settled. He had managed to scrape through five years of medical school, both the written examinations and the many hours of practical work in hospitals that were required by the Irish medical authorities; he had a house of his own; he had acquired a circle of friends; he had his rowing, and enough money to keep him going until he qualified. He had made his peace with Daisy and Toto and, now that he had grown a beard, was even able to go to Folkestone to visit them. He particularly wanted to keep an eye on Daisy, who even at eighty was still totally under

Toto's thumb. The one cloud on the horizon was that his brother had firmly adhered to his avowed intention of never acknowledging their relationship, and privately Michael thought it was 'rather horrid to be estranged from one's relations'. This, however, was a minor drawback.

Overall Michael was probably happier than he had been for many years. Although he never shone as a medical student (he found anatomy and physiology hard, and would moan about having to reproduce the textbook) he was assured of a well-paid, prestigious job if he managed to qualify. Having done so, he could take his place in the world as a doctor with confidence. There was no longer any need for him to hide himself away and take menial jobs. In addition, the four years of his surgical ordeal were now over.

Life, it seemed, could only get better from now on.

6

In Love

A T some time during 1950 Michael Dillon fell violently in love. The object of his affections was Roberta Cowell, who four years later was herself to cause a worldwide sensation by publishing her autobiography.

Roberta had begun life as Robert Cowell, elder son of Major General Sir Ernest Cowell, Winston Churchill's surgeon. Robert was born in Croydon, read engineering at University College, London, and then became a well-known racing driver. Highly skilled and talented in both mechanics and mathematics, he also qualified as a pilot. When Robert was in his twenties, however, startling changes began to happen to his body. Extensive medical tests showed that underneath the masculine exterior he was biologically female. Reports suggested – somewhat amazingly – that female characteristics had begun asserting themselves in his twenties, rather than at puberty, owing to Robert's overwhelming need to be super-masculine in everything he did.

By 1950, however, the physical changes that had begun to manifest themselves were far advanced, and Robert was halfway to becoming a woman. He chanced on Michael's book *Self*, and, intrigued, decided to write to the author, saying he would like to meet him.

Michael Dillon's initial reply was guarded, for by now he had received a number of letters from readers who identified with the problems outlined in the book.

Dear Mr Cowell [he wrote from the Royal City of Dublin Hospital],

Thank you for your letter which was forwarded to me here as I am in residence for six weeks. I think before you fork out the huge sum required for getting over here we had better find out if it would be profitable or not. I have had various letters from readers and only one did I meet because I happened to be in London at the time. He turned out to be a homosexual who wanted names of people of like turn of mind living in London and I was quite unable to help him in anything; he was neither a case for the psychologist nor for the surgeon. So if you care to write and let me know what it is you want to talk about I will consider if it would be worth a meeting. Anything you say will of course be completely confidential but I don't guarantee being able to help beyond either what is said in the book or referring you to plastic surgeons if you are interested in any form of physical conversion.

Yours sincerely,

Michael Dillon.

Roberta (then still officially Robert) felt that a meeting would be useful. This eventually took place, in London, and was subsequently described in her autobiography, *Roberta Cowell's Story*:

He was a good deal younger than I had expected, and wore a full beard. His hair was beginning to thin and had receded at the temples. Not bad-looking, he was a very masculine type. He was apparently a misogynist, and appeared to have a low opinion of women.

After lunch we sat talking over coffee, and he lit his pipe. We were discussing the connection between sex and intelligence, I of course maintaining that, given equal opportunities, women can be the mental equal of men. He disagreed violently.

Then came the surprise, a surprise so shattering that the scene will be crystal-clear in my memory for the rest of my life. He sat there, sucking at his pipe and toying with his coffee cup. He was silent for a minute or two, and I was idly wondering how long that beard of his had taken to grow.

Suddenly, 'I don't really see why I shouldn't tell you,' he said, 'but five years ago I was a woman.'

Such a possibility had never entered my head for one moment. As I looked at him now, it seemed absolutely and utterly fantastic, quite unbelievable, but I was not then fully aware of all that modern medical science could do.

He had been born as a perfectly normal girl, physically at least. Mentally he felt like an interloper in his own body. He hated anything feminine and was a gawky, desperately unhappy child. By no means bad-looking, he became a brilliant scholar and was also an outstanding athlete. He wore men's clothes whenever possible and was frequently assumed to be a man.

One day a doctor friend suggested that he might be helped by hormone treatment, and gave him a supply. The results were more than satisfactory and, years later, after intensive therapy and some thirteen operations, he was certified legally a man . . . For some time he had lived on an income of £5 a week, out of which he spent £2 .10*s* [£2.50] on hormones.

Although the final result was so satisfactory, he had endured immense hardships, and had to have constant medical supervision. He suffered intermittently from hypoglycaemia, which is caused by a deficiency of sugar in the blood.

Immensely strong, even for a man, I found it impossible to imagine him as a girl. He was as genuine a man as any I have met.

This favourable first impression led to many more meetings with Dillon. Letters were exchanged, too. Michael was always a highly prolific letter-writer, although Roberta was not. Robert Cowell was able to re-register, as a female, in 1951. In those days, because re-registration was easier than it is today and both were allowed to re-register, Roberta and Michael could legally have married. The problem was that the love-affair was almost completely one-sided. Although Roberta admired much about Michael, she considered that the two of them did not have anything at all in common. Unfortunately, Michael thought otherwise.

'He was convinced that it was destiny which had brought us together,' Roberta recalls. 'He thought that we were absolutely similar and should get married and set up house together. But as far as I was concerned, it would have been two females getting married, and I was certainly not interested in him in that kind of way.'

Since leaving Oxford, Michael had had to spend much time with people who were not of his own social class, in the garage and in digs, and, although he did not want to be considered a snob, was far more comfortable with people of his own kind of background. Roberta fitted the bill here. Her father was one of the leading surgeons of his day, her background was upper-middle-class, and she spoke with the correct vowel sounds, which was always vitally important to Dillon. But in character they could not have been more different. Whereas Michael was always rather serious, wanting to discuss deep philosophical themes and ponder the meaning of life, Roberta was witty, humorous and light-hearted.

With an almost wilful disregard of the warning signs, Michael plunged ahead into a fully-fledged one-sided love affair and started to write passionate letters to Roberta, whom he called 'Bobbie'. Her replies to Michael have, unfortunately, not survived, but many of his letters to her remain, and they show a side of his character that had not emerged until now. The letters reveal him by turns to be chauvinistic and importunate; he rode roughshod over Roberta's feelings, never stopping to ask himself whether his regard for her was reciprocated. He plunged ahead, trying to force Roberta into acquiescence by sheer force of will and persistence. These were qualities which had often got him his own way with the aunts; they had worked at Oxford and had played a part in enabling him to change his sex. 'When I determine to do a thing,' Michael wrote in an early letter, 'I do it.' But the same tactics were not to work with Roberta, who was a strong, tough character herself.

Although he was now 35 years of age, Michael had had no sexual experience of any kind. Neither had he ever been properly in love. There had been one or two girls at Oxford for whom he had felt a special affinity, but he had never wanted to have a lesbian relationship. Since leaving Oxford and undergoing the many operations, he had felt afraid to approach a girl in that way. He felt, however, that Roberta, who had been through a similar ordeal herself in reverse, would understand. There was nothing that he need hide from her. He said to her soon after they first met: 'You are the only person to have learned my past history within an hour and a half of meeting.'

Michael had the confidence to show Roberta his body, 'in a completely dispassionate and objective way,' she recalls, while their relationship was still in its infancy.

He showed me the triangular mastectomy scars and then whipped out the penis, which he was very proud of. It wasn't any kind of seduction scene, and he just wanted me to see what medical science had achieved.

I had never seen anything like it. It was huge, and in a constant state of semi-erection. I said to him then, I don't know about destiny shaping our ends, rough-hew them how we will, as this object was certainly rough-hewn. It looked as if it had been cut out of wood with an axe, as it was so deeply scored.

But I'm not sure whether he got the joke. Dillon did not exactly have the most perfectly-developed sense of humour. But anyway, it was absolutely ridiculous for him to pretend that we had anything in common. We were poles apart. His idea of a holiday was cycling round Ireland and camping.

He used to want me to accompany him – but nothing could have appealed to me less.

Michael would not be put off, and persisted in writing letter after letter to Roberta, sometimes more than one a day. 'I am not a wolf,' he wrote on one occasion, and: 'The chief feeling you arouse in me, Bobbie, is a desire to protect you and to treat you gently and to steer you along.' It is hard to imagine anybody less in need of protection than Roberta, who, as a wartime pilot, had been involved in many dangerous and difficult assignments, and who was now running a very successful dress business as well as occasionally still motor-racing at weekends.

But still Michael persisted. He wrote poems to 'Bobbie' – unfortunately (or perhaps fortunately) not preserved, and many of his letters included proposals of marriage. 'I am trying to assemble something together for a decent home so that I will have something to offer you other than a rather bare bachelor establishment,' he wrote. 'Because, whether you accept it or not, it will still be offered. All that's mine is yours.'

On another occasion (many of his letters are undated, and dashed off on hospital notepaper, or whatever scrap of paper came to hand), he wrote: 'I need to have two whiskies in me before I could start off "my beloved Bobbie", as I have never called anyone that before and you know what my inhibitions are like. Anyway, no inhibitions are going to stop me saying, "I love you." I love you with the whole of me. *Te amo, ergo habebo te, Q.E.D.*'

Roberta said: 'Dillon thought of me as monstrously uneducated and was always wanting to take me to see plays in Greek and so on. He also tried to teach me Latin – which I had refused to learn at school. He couldn't really see that I wasn't interested.' He bought Roberta a Latin dictionary and asked in a letter: 'How is Bobbie getting on with her Latin dictionary?' In one letter Michael was to write: 'Your lack of education affects me.' He told her: 'Your spelling makes me shudder at times, especially of words with well-known derivatives.' In this love affair, Michael tried desperately to take the conventional male part; he was often patronizing, and saw himself as the one who would take control and command in the relationship. He was three years older than Roberta.

He carried on writing letters, buying presents and purchasing tea services and other household items for the day when he and

'Bobbie' (a character he had in fact invented, and about whom he then fantasized) would be able to set up home together. One day he saw a brooch in a Dublin jewellers which he thought would make an ideal present for 'Bobbie', and wrote:

> I shall get it for you and give it to you on some special occasion, e.g. the day you say 'yes' or something like that, because you're going to, don't forget, whenever you have become acclimatized to things. I am not rushing anything, I just know it, as I have said before. The whole thing is too incredible otherwise.

Still trying to play the part of the great lover, Michael wrote that he would like to take Bobbie away to a hotel for a weekend, 'with a "gold" ring from Woolworth's to appease the manager'. There are hints of sexual frustration in several of his letters. 'If you let me know you merely want to be fraternal,' he wrote when planning some kind of weekend meeting, 'I won't bother you, and if you feel able to cope I will – er – go further.' In another letter, he confided that he was feeling 'in an indelicate mood'. 'Oh Bobbie, Oh Bobb-bee, come to me soon, I am wanting you all the time,' he pleaded. And: 'Personally, I cannot conceive of there being any indelicacy between you and me simply because we are what we are and because I love you very much.

'You have probably had experience in "zones of eroticism",' he wrote, 'and I have had none. Still, you could teach me.' He went on to explain the reason for his lack of any kind of sexual experience: 'I never felt I ought to try anything beyond kissing with a girl, and that has been limited to two or three times. I must say I sorely wanted to take you to bed that night.'

As time went on, Michael acquired photographs of Roberta, which he displayed prominently in his flat, and relayed to her the comments he received from other people. One girl who visited Michael's flat said, 'She's lovely, isn't she?' and added that whereas Michael had seemed lonely before, he now appeared happy and content. A Mrs Colquhoun, who 'did' for him, thought he had 'chosen a good looker, anyway'. 'So do I,' he added in parenthesis.

Occasionally, Michael must have realized that the affair was almost completely one-sided as in other letters he chides 'Bobbie' for the lack of amorousness in her letters to him, her lack of kisses at the bottom, and the scrawled 'B' for a signature. He chose to interpret this as shyness and 'feminine delicacy' but must have known underneath that his feelings were not returned with anything like the same intensity.

Laura Dillon on the beach at Folkestone, aged about 16.

Above right:
Laura Dillon aged 22 in the garden of her aunts' home in Bouverie Street West, Folkestone. The young man on the left is Laura's brother, Sir Robert Dillon, then aged 23.

Already androgynous: Foreign Office picture of Laura aged 23.

CERTIFIED COPY OF AN ENTRY OF BIRTH

REGISTRATION DISTRICT _Kensington_

1915. **BIRTH in the Sub-district of** _Kensington Central_

Form A502   Dd 8924061   45M   1/87   Mcr(733638)

Columns:—	1	2	3	4	5	6
No.	When and where born	Name, if any	Sex	Name, and surname of father	Name, surname, and maiden surname of mother	Occupa of fath
54	First May 1915 20 Ladbroke Gardens	Laura Maud	Girl	Robert Arthur Dillon	Laura maud Dillon Late macliver Formerly Reese	of independ mean

CERTIFIED to be a true copy of an entry in the certified copy of a Register of Births in the Dis

Given at the GENERAL REGISTER OFFICE, LONDON, under the Seal of the said Office the, _7th_

BCA 195209

This certificate is issued in pursuance of the Births and Deaths Registration Act 1953.

Section 34 provides that any certified copy of an entry purporting to be sealed or stamped with the seal or death to which it relates without any further or other proof of the entry, and no certified copy purpo unless it is sealed or stamped as aforesaid.

CAUTION:—It is an offence to falsify a certificate or to make or knowingly use a false certificate or a prejudice of any person, or to possess a certificate knowing it to be false without lawful authority.

Sir Harold Gillies, the plastic surgeon who carried out most of Michael's sex-change operations.

EN AT THE GENERAL REGISTER OFFICE, LONDON.

Application Number _693330_

the _County of London._

7	8	9	10*	
Signature, description and residence of informant	When registered	Signature of registrar	Name entered after registration	In entry no's Col 2 for Laura maud read Laurence michael and Col 3 for "Girl" read "Boy" Corrected on 14th April 1944 by C.E. West Supt Reg S on production of Statutory declaration
Jessie Emily Third Present t the birth 0 Ladbroke Gardens	Third June 1915	A.S. Pearson Deputy Registrar		

ve mentioned. Made by John Burdon Cooper and Maude Eileen Beauchamp _See note overleaf._

day of _January_ 19_88_.

al Register Office shall be received as evidence of the birth been given in the said Office shall be of any force or effect

lse certificate intending it to be accepted as genuine to the

_MB7188_

Laura Dillon's birth certificate, showing the correction by marginal note in 1944.

Laura as Michael: a portrait taken soon after the alteration of the birth certificate in 1944.

Graduation at Trinity College,
Dublin, in June 1951. Dr
Michael Dillon is standing
second from left, next to the
Nigerian, Tom Asuni, who was
a great friend of Michael's in
his medical student days.

In 1950 Michael fell deeply in love with
Roberta, formerly Robert, Cowell, whose
own story caused a worldwide sensation
in 1954. This portrait of her was taken in
the early 1950s.

Once he had grown a beard, Michael
could safely visit Folkestone without fear
of recognition. He is pictured here with
Aunt Daisy, aged 80, in 1950.

Michael as a ship's doctor, 1955.

Portrait of Dr Michael Dillon,
taken in about 1955.

DILLON.

Sir Robert William Charlier Dillon, 8th Bt., of Lismullen, co. Meath, a Baron of the Holy Roman Empire, B.A. Trin. Coll. Dublin, called to the Irish Bar 1936, *b.* 17 Jan. 1914 ; *s.* his kinsman 1925 ; *m.* 18 Feb. 1947, ●Synolda, dau. of late Cholmondeley Butler Clarke, of The Hermitage, Holycross, co. Tipperary.

Lineage—Sir John Dillon, 1st Bt., M.P., of Lismullen, co. Meath, M.P. for Wicklow 1771–6 and for Blesington 1776–83 (only son of Arthur Dillon, descended from a common ancestor with the Lords Roscommon and Dillon, by Elizabeth, dau. of Dr. Ralph Lambert, Bishop of Meath), was created a Baronet 31 July, 1801. He *m.* 23 June, 1767, Millicent, dau. of George Drake of Fernhill, Berkshire, by whom he had issue,

1. CHARLES DRAKE (Sir), 2nd Bt.
2. ARTHUR RICHARD (Sir), 3rd Bt.
3. WILLIAM (Sir), 4th Bt.
4. Ralph (Rev.), Rector of Ballymacward, co. Galway, *b.* 18 Dec. 1779 ; *m.* Jane, sister of Thomas Charles Steuart Corry, and *d.* April, 1834, leaving issue,
    1. JOHN (Sir), 6th Bt.
    2. Charles James, *m.* Charlotte, dau. of Rev. John Swiny, and *d.s.p.* 1872.
    1. Anne Rebecca, *d. unm.* 7 May, 1883, aged 75.
    2. Jane Elizabeth, *m.* Rev. Richard Mills, and *d.* 1883.
5. Robert, Major 32nd Regt., *b.* in 1787 ; *m.* 4 March, 1814, Eliza, dau. of John Swiny, K.C., and *d.* 27 Jan. 1864, having had issue, one son,
    Robert, Lt.-Col. late 30th Regt., *b.* 6 Oct. 1818 ; *m.* 17 June, 1862, Minerva Margaretta (who *d.* 10 Feb. 1924), 2nd dau. of Hon. Samuel Mills, U.E., of Stafford House and Westlawn, Hamilton, Ontario, Senator of the Dominion of Canada, and *d.* 20 Jan. 1916, leaving issue,
    (1) Robert Arthur, late Lieut. R.N., *b.* 3 July, 1865 ; *m.* 21 May, 1913, Laura Maud, widow of J. Lachlin McCliver, of New Zealand, and *d.* 6 Oct. 1925, having by her (who *d.* 11 May, 1915) had issue, ROBERT WILLIAM CHARLIER (Sir), 8th and present Bt.
    ●Laura Maude, *b.* 1 May, 1915.
    (1) Grace Minnie, *m.* 19 April, 1893, Charles Edward Bonner, of the Manor House, Spalding, co. Lincoln, eldest son of Charles Foster Bonner, of Ayscoughfee Hall, Spalding, and *d.* 11 Feb. 1939, leaving issue. He *d.* 30 April, 1907.
    (2) Katharine Welden, *m.* 1886, Richard J. Crookes, of Raithby House, Spilsby, and *d.* 13 Jan. 1938, leaving issue. He *d.* 25 Aug. 1899.
    (3) ●Melita Edith Almeria (97, *Bouverie Road West, Folkestone*).
    (4) ●Minna Marguerite (97, *Bouverie Road West, Folkestone*).
    (5) Evelyn Drake, *m.* 3 Nov. 1916, Capt. Lancelot Joseph Hicks, I.A.R.O., 3rd son of Arthur Hicks, and *d.* Oct. 1951.
    (6) Alice Maude, twin with her sister, *d. unm.* July, 1949.
1. Elizabeth, *m.* 5 June, 1794, William Mills, Barrister-at-Law and had issue.
2. Anne Grace, *m.* Thomas C. S. Corry, M.P.
3. Millicent Sarah, *m.* 2 Oct. 1820, Thomas Corneck, and *d.* leaving issue.

Sir John Dillon had
Empire conferred up
II, with reversion
authorized by Roya

The entries in *Debrett's* and *Burke's Peerages* for 1956. The discrepancies led to Michael's exposure in 1958.

DILLON, Creation (U.K.) 1801, of Lismullen, Meath.

Sir ROBERT WILLIAM CHARLIER DILLON, 8th, *Baronet*, and a Baron of the Holy Roman Empire, son of the late Robert Arthur Dillon (who *d.* Oct. 1925), great-great-grandson of 1st baronet ; *b.* Jan. 17th, 1914 ; *s.* his kinsman, *Sir* JOHN FOX, Nov. 1925 : *m.* 1947, Synolda, da. of the late Cholmondeley Clarke.

Arms—Argent, a lion rampant between three crescents gules, issuant from each crescent a star with six points of the field, over all a fesse azure. **Crest**—On a chapeau gules turned up ermine, a falcon rising argent, beaked, legged and belled or. **Second Motto**—"Auxilium ab alto" (*Help from on high*).

Seat—Lismullen, Navan, co. Meath.

Whilst I breathe I hope.

Brother living—LAURENCE MICHAEL, *b.* May 1st, 1915 ; M.A. Oxford; M.B. and B.Ch. Trin. Coll., Dublin 1951.

Aunts living—Melita Edith Almeria. *Residence*, 97, Bouverie Road West, Folkestone.——Minna Marguerite. *Residence*, 97, Bouverie Road West, Folkestone.

Daughter living of 7th Baronet—Millicent, *b.* 1895. *Residence*, Hendregadred, Pentrefelin, Criccieth, N. Wales.

This family is descended from a common ancestor with the Earls Roscommon and Barons Dillon and Clonbrock. The 1st baronet, Sir John, M.P., was created a Baron of the Holy Roman Empire, 1782, with reversion to male and female descendants, and was authorized by Roy. licence to bear the title in this country.

Left and below:
Aboard ship, mid-1950s.

Rizong Monastery in Ladakh, where Michael spent three
months as a novice monk. (Photo: Christopher Portway).

Michael Dillon, now Lobzang Jivaka, pictured with his fellow monks at Rizong in 1960. He was already in an advanced state of emaciation.

This portrait of Michael Dillon was taken shortly before his death at Dalhousie, India, in May 1962.

He sometimes wondered if it was his own letters which were causing the coolness. 'I can't write the pretty things women like to hear,' he complained to her, as if this would have made any difference to Roberta's attitude towards him.

Be that as it may, by March 1951 Michael considered himself engaged to Roberta and wrote to the aunts, enclosing a photograph of his intended. Daisy wrote back: 'I hope you will be very happy, dear, and I think you will. I think she will be a lovable companion.' Michael also told Roberta that Toto had been very taken with Roberta, whom she pronounced 'very nice'. On one occasion Michael had taken her to meet the aunts. He also wrote to 'Mrs Mac' (the wife of his Oxford tutor Jimmy McKie) telling her he was engaged. 'She was delighted,' Michael reported back to Roberta. Another item of information he passed on to her was that several of his friends had expressed surprise that a woman had at last 'captured that misogynist and confirmed bachelor Dillon'. Joan, the cousin who had been to stay with him in Dublin, commented that Roberta was 'delicious, and had very kind eyes'.

Michael in due course gave Roberta an engagement ring. She has described how this came about:

One day this package arrived, wrapped up in an old Players' cigarette packet. The letter which accompanied it told me to put it away in a drawer and not open it until he had passed his finals. Of course, I put it away and never thought any more about it until I got another letter saying that he was now a doctor, and had I opened the package. When eventually I found it, it was a huge diamond ring, some kind of family heirloom. That was Dillon's way of saying that we were now formally engaged.

Undeterred by the total coolness on his 'fiancée's' part, Michael pressed ahead with plans for the wedding. 'Today,' he wrote in an undated letter, 'I bought a complement to our dinner service. So I think you should now be able to entertain at dinner quite well.' He added that they would not be using the dinner service, however, except on very special occasions. He also told Roberta that she would look 'well in white – especially on our wedding day'.

Michael saw Roberta as a future housewife and mother, and as somebody who would be more than happy to look after him, wash his shirts and so on. He even went so far as to suggest the possibility of having children – adopted, of course: 'You will have to design a soundproof room for ours when they want to howl,' he wrote in a letter dated 9 February 1951. 'How are your maternal instincts, by the way?' He wondered how her leisure interests – that is, motor-racing, flying, engineering – would fit in with her 'chosen mode of life', by which he meant cooking, sewing and housework. However, as Michael had been brought up in a house with servants he did not assume that 'Bobbie' would be carrying out all the drudgery herself. He wrote: 'I have the greatest respect for the way you handle people – I can see Bobbie running the domestic staff on similar lines.'

'A church wedding', he wrote solemnly to 'my own dearest Bobbie', 'is going to have some difficulties. I can't see your father giving us [sic] away, nor can I see your mother being allowed to give a little reception. Other alternatives are to be married at sea, and then have it ratified in church later – so there's plenty of food for thought.

'One thing certain is that at our wedding I want the hymn "Father, hear the prayer we offer! Not for ease that prayer shall be, but for strength that we may ever live our lives courageously."'

'I wish,' he wrote in another letter, 'that we were on the eve of getting married.'

To Roberta Michael poured out all his thoughts, his deepest longings, his fantasies. He gave her pictures of himself as a female and as a male, told her all about the aunts and his brother, the many operations, the fears he had about not passing his finals in the summer and therefore not qualifying as a doctor, and the problems he had encountered before and after the change from female to male, in being accepted by family and friends.

'People I thought were friends,' he wrote, 'found they couldn't afford to be laughed at by associating with an oddity.'

He also offered his general thoughts on women, female emancipation and the correct place of women in the modern world – an inferior one, of course. 'Most females,' he said, 'get enjoyment out of leading men on so far and then dropping them.'

On another occasion he wrote: 'Man is no longer able to assert himself as rightful lord and master. Woman is now trying to be equal and getting uppish. After all, it is even contrary to Holy Writ.'

Michael truly felt that he and Roberta were meant for each other, that they were fated to meet and spend the rest of their lives together, and that she was the one person with whom he could honestly and openly share his feelings. 'There are very few people,' he told her, 'that I can trust until I have known them a long time, which makes it all the more remarkable that Bob learned my past history within one and a half hours of just meeting me. I have often thought how peculiarly I felt at home with you right from the start.'

'Dillon always thought we were totally similar,' Roberta comments. 'In fact, we could hardly have been more different.'

In many ways, the letters indicate that Michael was trying over-hard to be the conventional husband and provider, and was attempting to force Roberta into the unnatural role of dutiful housewife. He must have known at the bottom of his heart that it could never work out, and certainly it would have been disastrous if Roberta had in the slightest degree returned his affections. The letters show a side of Michael's character that must have got on other people's nerves: the wilful persistence, the inability to take no for an answer, the complete blindness to hints and signs from others. For instance, Michael was always booking phone calls to London, where Roberta shared a flat with a girlfriend, and then writing that he had not much hope of finding her in. In fact, she would deliberately make arrangements to be out when he phoned, or simply not answer the phone.

'He used to plead to meet me alone, and kept coming over to London for weekends,' Roberta recalls. 'I used to take my flatmate with me so that we wouldn't be alone. In fact, I was so often away at the weekends, motor-racing or on business, that he went out with my flatmate more often than with me. She remembers going to Greek plays with him – I don't know how much she understood.'

At this time Michael's hormone tablets were costing him £2 17s (£2.85) for a bottle which lasted three weeks. Apart from these he was not having any further treatment, and so his change-over could be considered complete. But as he still had ovaries they would have been trying to put out female hormone, which would have to have been counteracted by huge quantities of testosterone. 'It beats me,' Roberta said, 'why Dillon never had a hysterectomy. It would have seemed the obvious thing to do.'

Maybe there was simply no one to perform the operation, which would have had to have been carried out by a gynaecologist. Also, at the time when Dillon was having his operations, a hysterectomy does not seem to have been suggested. But Michael apparently mentioned to Roberta another case of a woman who wanted to become a man, remarking that in her case only a mastectomy and the use of testosterone were recommended. Hysterectomies were undoubtedly not a routine procedure in those days, as they have since become.

In spite of being in love, and sending daily, sometimes twice-daily, letters to Roberta across the Irish Channel, Michael had somehow to get through his medical course. He wrote to her, 'I have very little hope of passing in the summer,' enclosing his latest examination grades, which were all barely above the pass mark.

The final examinations in medicine and surgery were held at the end of term. Failure would mean the student would have to retake the whole year – not, in Dillon's case, a very inviting prospect. Course examinations took place at the end of each academic year, and Michael considered that he had passed the previous year's important examination in obstetrics and gynaecology only by luck. Finals encompassed written, practical and oral examinations. The practical was taken on real patients at real hospitals and nobody knew until the very morning of the examination to which hospital he or she would be sent, which prevented students checking out cases before the examination.

In the surgery examination, Michael had a huge stroke of good fortune. One of the examiners was an Oxford man; having noted that Michael was wearing a university tie, which he always did for examinations, he simply asked questions about the university. The Trinity examiner arrived late and hurriedly asked questions about post-operative treatment of appendectomies, an operation Michael had undergone a few years previously himself and therefore felt fairly confident about answering.

He did not feel too many qualms about the medical part, as his many years as a hospital patient, together with the large amount of residential hospital work require by the course, had enabled him to develop a good bedside manner. His extra maturity also helped here. 'As I had been so much a patient myself,' Michael wrote in a journal, 'I always managed to get on well with the sick.' The patient he had been assigned for the practical examination was terminally ill, so Michael asked him his medical history, to which he replied in a whisper.

'The history is all important,' Michael stated later, 'and many students fail because they rub the patient up the wrong way. But this man was an advanced heart case and all went well. The examiners did not want to pull him about either.'

The other part of the practical examination – which consisted of a major and a minor diagnosis – did not go so well. 'This patient is contrary to all the medical textbooks,' he said miserably to the examiner, unable to offer a diagnosis. The patient concerned had mysteriously become paralysed in both legs after falling down unconscious while cooking breakfast in her home one morning. Her knee and plantar reflexes were working, yet the ankle reflexes had gone. There seemed no possible explanation as to why this should have happened.

Dillon said: 'The plantar and knee reflexes are present and the ankle ones have gone. It's impossible.'

'And the abdominal?' asked the examiner.

'They're about to, sir, but then she's not yet fifty.' (The problem they were discussing is in fact one which disappears with age.)

The examiner said: 'Let's see.'

Michael waited in an agony of despair lest the examiner's diagnosis were different from his own.

In the end he said, 'Yes, you're right. What do you suppose it is?'

'Some sort of cerebral haemorrhage, I suppose,' Michael answered. The second examiner now joined them and confirmed the findings of them both.

Despite this, Michael was certain he had failed, because what they had observed would appear to have been impossible.

But he passed – much to his own surprise and that of many of the other medical students. He also passed all the other final examinations and so, in July 1951, formally became Dr Laurence Michael Dillon.

He records that all the former students celebrated in the traditional way with whisky, beer, gin and any other alcoholic liquid they could find, but Michael stopped before inebriation set in. Always he had before him the example of his drunken father; he felt that if he were not careful the same fate might befall him.

'Next morning,' he wrote, 'I had to tell myself that I was at last a doctor, and for many mornings after, as it seemed so unlikely. My life had been so strange and at one time so impossible that now as a respectable member of the community and accepted at my face value, it was too good, far too good to be true. Within me I felt an intense gratitude and devotion to that, whatever it was, an Absolute, a Father-God or what you will, who had brought me out of the slough of despond on to level ground from which the far-off hills could be seen to be green. I went into a church and gave thanks.'

There remained the question of Roberta Cowell to resolve. Michael had told her that he had 'very little hope' of passing in the summer, and yet he had passed. Moreover, he had given her a valuable ring, wrapped up in silver paper and shoved into a cigarette packet.

'When I realized he was really serious,' said Roberta, 'I had to tell him that, although I liked and respected him very much as a person, there was no possible way I could ever think of marrying him.'

Michael, deeply disappointed, probably realized that this was his last chance of finding anybody with whom he could form a truly close relationship. He had tried to bulldoze Roberta into accepting him, a tactic which was almost certain to have the opposite effect from the one intended. She was not Daisy or Toto, who could be dragooned into submission. But Roberta does not think Michael was ever really in love. 'He thought it was all fate, and that we had to be together. But it was absolutely ridiculous of him to suppose that we were similar in any way.'

In the event, Michael managed to get over this blow without too much pain and upset. After he had recovered from what was after all mainly hurt pride, he set about having a long holiday and then found himself a job as a medical officer in a nearby hospital. Never again did he venture into the realms of romance.

After writing all those letters and pouring out all that passion on paper, Michael still had no sexual experience of any kind: his frustrations were left intact. Most transsexuals have an extremely low sex drive, however, and in Michael Dillon's case it is probable that his frustrations were more apparent than real. After all, he could not have proper erections, or produce sperm, and the artificial penis could never have responded to touch as a natural one would. So Dillon could not possibly have experienced the kind of sexual frustrations that biological males often endure. He probably thought that it was time that he felt in love and had some sexual experience, and it just so happened that a suitable person presented herself at the right time. He realized, as many people have done since, that Roberta was (and is) an extremely strong, charismatic and attractive character, and he was momentarily bowled over. But as for being genuinely in love – perhaps he was deceiving himself. His letters show how he did everything by the book, in imitation of a genuine lover, wanting to feel a passion that possibly, underneath, he did not feel.

Most likely, what Michael was experiencing was not so much sexual desire but a deep urge and need to feel loved and wanted. He had been rejected by his father when only ten days old, had never had a mother, and was brought up by people who had never wanted to bring up children. His brother, too, had eventually rejected him, and although the aunts had been won over they were so old and doddery by now that they could not offer Michael any true support or affection. If anything, it was now his place to support and look after them.

Gilbert Barrow, Michael's friend from the garage days, was now married and embarking on family life, so the friendship between the two could no longer be what it had once been. The former medical students, all now doctors, were about to scatter; once again, Michael would be on his own, having to face life without any close companion. Although he gave thanks in church for his deliverance from hated femaleness, and for his new status as a doctor, he was still desperately lonely at heart. Roberta had understood him, that was certain, and he had trusted her and confided in her. But for the time being there was no one else who was at all close to him.

He was never again to fall in love or find anybody who was genuinely interested in him or concerned for his welfare. One of the reasons for this was not that he was so unlovable, but because he could not bear anybody to know the truth about himself. Roberta was different in this respect as she had been through traumas of a similar kind to his. If Michael could have brought himself to confide in more people he could have made more friends, for he was essentially a kindly, honest, intelligent and tolerant person. But the perceived need for distance, the fear of being hurt and rejected, made him more lonely than he need have been.

Many present-day transsexuals speak of the deep relief when their secrets are out and they no longer have to hide the truth about themselves. Most have found that people do not automatically shun them but behave in a normal and friendly towards them.

However, although Michael Dillon was never able to make close friends after the change-over, he determined that he would do some good in the world and help people wherever he could. Above all, he would not lead the kind of selfish and narrow life that the aunts had led, hoarding their money and never going out or having anybody in the house. He would be, to the best of his ability, warm, open-hearted and generous.

7

Dr Dillon

ALTHOUGH Michael Dillon had now qualified as a doctor, he had no clear idea of what he would do in the future. When his one-sided affair with Roberta Cowell was at its height he had begun to write some plays, which he hoped might be performed on the London stage. One of these, called *The Prime Minister*, he described as 'Aristophanic' in construction, and he sent it to Roberta in the hope that she might be able to put him in touch with agents who would take it further.

But he never got anywhere as a playwright. His plays simply do not come alive. He had no gift for dialogue or for depicting character, possibly because he was too self-absorbed. Like many transsexuals, Michael was more given to introspection and finding out the truth about himself than to communicating with others. However, he kept alive the idea that one day he might be able to make a living as a writer. He had, after all, one published book to his credit, and while a medical student had had a paper on the hypothalamus published in the *Irish Medical Journal*. He had also won first prize in the All-Ireland students' essay competition, speaking out about the newly introduced National Health Service. All his life Michael was against nationalized medicine.

As yet, however, there was little indication that he would ever be able to earn a living as a writer. His first book, *Self*, had sold out of its first edition but was not reprinted – rather to Michael's disappointment, as he had considered it an original and provocative work. So it was, and if the world had known of its author's background it would undoubtedly have caused an enormous stir. But

Michael could not bring himself to let the public know about this, and for this reason the book remained simply an interesting curiosity. Indeed, it is probable that few people could understand exactly what it was about, or what its purpose was. The publishers, Heinemann, never asked Michael for any more works, although they were to publish, in 1954, Roberta Cowell's autobiography, which caused a huge sensation lasting for several years. Another sex-change case which excited global interest was that of the American Christine Jorgensen, born George, and later a G.I., who was the first biological man to undergo sex-transformation surgery. Christine's autobiography was not to appear until 1967, five years after Michael Dillon's death. The first 'respectable' sex-change story (unaccompanied by media sensationalism and untainted by any freakshow aura) was that of Jan (formerly James) Morris, in the early 1970s.

Given that Dillon had no wish to go down in history as the first surgically transformed female-to-male transsexual by writing a potential bestseller about his experiences and becoming a celebrity, he had to pursue another course of action. In the short term he had to complete his medical studies by working as a house physician for a year. He had expected to be offered an appointment at the City of Dublin hospital where he had already worked, especially as he was the only student of his year to have had papers published in an outside journal before qualifying. But those chosen for these plum posts were the four with the highest marks in the final examinations.

As Michael had regarded this appointment almost as a foregone conclusion he had not made any other plans. He had no idea where to go or what to do. In the end, he accepted a post at a small hospital in the north of Dublin which had only 50 beds and required just one resident medical officer. This sounded quite a pleasant job, as it would offer the opportunity to do a wide variety of work, but the pay was only £1 a week – less than he had earned at the garage and nowhere near enough to live on. This was the main reason why the job had been hard to fill: – even in 1951 it was nothing like a living wage. Michael could accept it because he still had the £7000 left to him by his Aunt Maudie. (Such a sum would equate to about £100,000 in the late 1980s.)

After a lone holiday in Naples, Dillon went to take up his first post as a doctor. He later recalled that he felt as new and strange there as a boy at his first boarding school. Now aged 36, and therefore about thirteen years older than most housemen, he was, it seemed, almost back at the beginning again. This sensation of always being back at the beginning, always a new boy, was one which Michael was to experience repeatedly all his life.

He soon found that some of the ideas he had picked up from Rooksdown House, where he had undergone his sex-change operations, came in useful. There, as so many of them were long-stay, all the patients had to learn some form of occupational therapy. Michael had during his time at Rooksdown learned many handicrafts, which he felt would be a good idea for tubercular and other long-stay patients who were lying in their beds all day with nothing whatever to do. Michael obtained some money from hospital funds and bought leather and tools, embroidery silks, knitting wool and parchment for lampshades. He designed a cowboy belt with thiefproof pockets and a sheath and cartridge loops. These, he said, proved very popular when the items were offered for sale on visiting days. Michael records that the response 'surpassed all belief' and produced useful profits for the hospital funds. By Christmas there was enough money to take all the patients who were mobile to a pantomime, and provide a big tea for those confined to bed.

The thought then occurred to Michael that it would be sensible to fit all the beds with headphones so that the patients could listen to the radio when they liked. This was also paid for out of the money raised from the sale of handicrafts. In addition, Michael used to take several of the tubercular patients into town in his car, and to the cinema with him. Gradually, he was making these hospital patients his 'family': by now he had no other. Robert, although only 26 miles away, showed no sign of relenting over his decision never to own Michael or speak to him ever again. His great friend Gilbert Barrow was no longer available for holidays and excursions as he was married with a young family, and most of the students in his year had now dispersed to other parts of Ireland, or to England.

Michael still lived in his house at 9 Oaklands Park, Ballsbridge, and sometimes he would take patients back to the house with him, lend them books and try to 'educate' them, as he had tried to educate Roberta. He found that some of the younger patients responded to this, so his next self-appointed task at the hospital was to make a bookcase with glass doors to house an educational library for those patients who wanted to learn something while they were lying on their backs. Whenever there was any money to spare Michael would go to the secondhand bookshops in Dublin to buy volumes for the hospital library.

The books he chose were not exactly light reading: they included French, Italian, German and other dictionaries, books on classical and other literature and on grammar, astronomy, science and music. Whenever a particular patient expressed interest in a specific subject Michael would try to find a suitable book to add to the library.

Soon the surgeon in charge remarked that the hospital wards were more like factories than hospitals. Tables were covered in leather and cloth and all the 'up' patients would be working away and helping those confined to bed.

As the weather grew warmer, Michael would take some of the long-term patients out for days in his car.

'Those who lie in bed day after day and see only the same limited landscape feel a happiness out of all proportion to the little trouble involved, when they are suddenly taken from the prison of their room and allowed to see once again trees, flowers, people and the shops, or the sea,' he wrote years later when in hospital himself in India. He ensured that his own patients had the opportunity of keeping in contact with the outside world by taking them out for picnics and to the theatre, and teaching them how to use the telephone and send telegrams. Very many patients, he said, had never seen a play or used the phone. Most came from what he called 'the peasantry' and had been used to a very simple life before Michael Dillon entered their lives. Some could hardly read and write, and Michael naturally took it upon himself to teach them.

There is no indication that he communicated at all with Roberta once he finally realized that nothing would come of his determination to win her. Instead, he plunged himself into his hospital work, and the patients became his social as well as his professional life. He was probably still rather lonely at heart because he found it hard to meet people of his own kind – if indeed any existed.

Michael took particular trouble over one tubercular patient, an 18-year-old lad who had received no education whatever. Michael became a Professor Higgins to him, showing him how to dress, how to use a knife and fork, introducing him to civilized people and, finally, through Gilbert Barrow, finding him a job in a wine-bottling factory. He and Gilbert, records Dillon, got on well, as their origins were similar.

Michael then had the idea that when he was earning good money he would give one-tenth of his yearly earnings to help struggling students complete university courses. A scheme had been devised to provide grants, for students whose families could not afford to pay for their courses, by Canon Arthur Millbourn of Bristol Cathedral, whom Michael had got to know while still Laura and who had become a great friend despite the fact that he was some 30 years older than Dillon. Canon Millbourn always lent a listening ear to Michael and in later years acted as intermediary for him between literary agents and publishers. Michael gave all his donations to the student aid scheme anonymously but was kept informed as to who benefited. His first beneficiary was a girl who had won a scholarship to Oxford but whose family could not afford to pay for books, club subscriptions and all the other necessities of college life. Michael was gratified to learn in time that this girl had gained a first-class degree and then won another scholarship to a French university. Another student whom he helped had been born in a London slum; he had later joined the navy and tried to educate himself by joining the Seafarers' Education Society. Then he had won a place at a theological college, intending to take holy orders, but after a year could no longer pay the fees. He heard of Canon Millbourn and applied to him directly for assistance. He was given £20 immediately and then helped to finish the course.

Michael's desire to help these struggling people no doubt stemmed from his continuing gratitude to those who had helped him live what he considered a normal life when there seemed no way out of his dilemma. 'Those who thirst for knowledge and can find none through poverty or circumstances, these were the ones I wanted to help most,' he wrote. Michael was now beginning to be able to shed some of the self-pity which had dogged him all his life. He began to read the works of Gurdjieff and his pupil Ouspensky, and found them a revelation. He learned that most people glory in their self-pity, feeding and watering it to allow it to grow, and failing to realize that they can, if they like, choose not to feel any kind of self-pity at all.

Michael began to work on his personality, attempting to shed everything that was negative in it. His great desire to become positive, loving and useful was eventually to lead him to Buddhism.

Ever since childhood Michael had had a restless, questing streak, a trait which had prevented him from putting down roots and living what others might have considered to be an ordinary kind of life. He was never to stay anywhere for long, never to put down roots of any kind, and in so far as he considered he had a home, it was Oxford. He had not, it is true, always been happy there, but he was to look back on it as a golden time, compared with his subsequent existence. This feeling persisted, even though he had been Laura at Oxford and therefore cut off from most social and leisure activities apart from sport.

When his house year finished Michael was 37. Emptiness stretched in front of him. There were no open arms to welcome him anywhere, and he once again felt the desolation of loneliness as his year drew to a close. But whenever he felt a little sorry for himself he reminded himself how much more intolerable everything would have been if he were still Laura. Life would have been completely impossible, not just unsatisfactory on occasion.

Since re-registering Michael had travelled as much as his free time and his pocket allowed. He now decided to see if he could join a ship as a naval doctor and travel the world at somebody else's expense. He had a vague intention of doing some kind of research job after that, perhaps concerned with human brains again, so that he could further investigate the links between mind and body which had interested him since adolescence and which provided the subject matter of his first book.

But first he wanted to try to get some kind of job on board ship. After all, he had no ties at all and nobody much cared what he did. He had come from a moneyed and leisured family and very few of his relations, male or female, had had any kind of job. His father was described on Dillon's birth certificate as being 'of independent means', and his brother Robert, after qualifying as a barrister and being called to the Irish bar, did not practise, preferring to run his farm and family estates in County Meath. There was therefore no family tradition, nor financial necessity (he still had a healthy capital sum to draw on if required), for Dillon to pursue any specific career with dedication: the world was his oyster and he could please himself what he did with his life.

Michael wrote off to several shipping companies and was accepted over by the P.&O./B.&I. (Pacific and Orient/British and Irish) combine after interview and medical examination. Michael Dillon always had cause to dread medicals, which made it necessary for him to explain the mastectomy scars and his extremely odd-looking male organs. He had by this time got his story worked out: he had lost most of his private parts in a wartime accident, and the surgeon had done the most effective reconstruction job possible. The scars on his chest he explained away by saying they were caused by wounds received during the Blitz. The fact that he had lived in Bristol, an area of heavy raids, during the war, lent credence to this story. No one at the time would have been likely to guess, in any case, that the person standing before him was a woman who had undergone the world's first-ever sex-reassignment surgery. So unlikely was it that such an idea should have entered the examining doctor's head that Michael could be reasonably certain of being passed fit. And he was.

Michael's first job was on a P.&O. cargo vessel just back from Hong Kong, where the regular surgeon had had to be given leave. Michael was measured for his 'blues' by a naval tailor and was also given all the other items of uniform – mess kit, tropical wear and so on – that he would need for the trip.

Before setting off for his new life at sea, which was to occupy six years of his life in all, he decided to pay a trip to Folkestone to see his aunts. The beard ensured that he need not fear being recognized or asked awkward questions by people who knew the family, although some of them no doubt gossiped about the apparent disappearance of that strange, mannish Laura Dillon. By this time Daisy and Toto were long past being surprised at anything Michael might do, though they were slightly shocked that he had joined the Merchant Navy; in their eyes, only the *Royal* Navy was suitable for gentlemen. Michael's father had been a lieutenant in the Royal Navy, as had many previous. Dillons, and Daisy and Toto considered the Merchant Navy far inferior. Their opinion was, however, not an informed one: they knew nothing about either navy and their reaction was one of blind prejudice.

After spending three days with Toto and Daisy, Michael went out and bought a Merchant Navy tie, with narrow red, white and green stripes on blue.

When he entered the King George V docks in London to enter yet another completely new kind of life, he felt the old familiar panic. Surprises lay in store. The first was being allotted his own personal servant, who laid out his uniform on the bed and generally looked after him.

Most of the ship's crew members were Indian and spoke only Hindustani, of which Michael had been advised to learn a little before coming on board. He had bought two Hindustani phrase books but soon discovered that they were of little value to a physician. Although they could readily provide the Hindustani for 'How far is the railway station?' and 'How much does this cost?' (two phrases infrequently used on board ship), they did not offer much that would be of use to a doctor attending patients, such as 'Have you vomited?' or 'Have your bowels opened today?'

As Michael dressed himself for dinner in the new uniform he felt both proud and yet painfully self-conscious. Can this really be me? he asked himself as he surveyed the image in the mirror. If so, what a long way this smart, self-assured-looking fellow had come from being a grease monkey in a garage – that strange creature who hid himself away while all who came into contact with him wondered to which sex he belonged. Now there could be no possible doubt: he was a man. Not only did he have a beard, but his hair had now started to thin, owing to the huge doses of male hormone he was still taking.

A photograph taken of him in uniform at this time shows Dillon in exactly the same stance as that adopted by Laura in a much earlier snapshot, standing on the beach in a swimming costume. His arms hang by his side, hands lightly resting on his thighs, his legs are fairly wide apart, the head is at an identical angle, and the expression is similar – rather stern and forbidding. Michael used to say to friends that many things he had thought would change did not, when he changed sex – and his stance is one feature that remained unaltered.

Dillon left his cabin to go to dinner. He found the other officers perfectly friendly and complete gentlemen, thus proving Daisy and Toto wrong, as they had been about so many things. Dillon's first ship would be away only three weeks, to load and unload cargo from the Far East. It was a kind of 'practice run' for Dillon, to break him in before he joined the B.I. ship, which had two hundred passengers on board. This one had only crew.

Soon Michael was sure that being at sea was the life for him. Ever since he was a small child he had been attracted to the sea, and he had often watched the ships come and go from the 'gentry's' side of The Leas at Folkestone.

He felt intensely grateful to those who had made his new situation possible, by rescuing him from the terrible half-life he had felt condemned to lead while still Laura. Even if he had not so fervently felt he was male, despite his female anatomy, he would hardly have been able to achieve, as a woman, what he had done so far.

It would probably have been more difficult, although not impossible, for him to qualify as a doctor; he could not have embarked upon lone camping holidays on the Continent, or travelled round Ireland with just one other friend, and it would have been out of the question for him to have become a ship's doctor. He realized that men have much greater freedom than women; even so, Dillon never took the woman's part, believing that women were ordained by both nature and holy writ to be inferior and secondary to men. In view of this belief, it was somewhat odd that he had fallen in love with Roberta Cowell, who, although biologically female, was far more intrinsically masculine than Dillon could ever hope to be, in addition to possessing a temperamental affinity with all things mathematical and mechanical. Roberta was in many ways a stronger, and certainly more self-confident, character than Michael, too: the fact that he was at all times somewhat shy and reserved might also be interpreted as a less than manly trait.

Revelling in his new freedom, Michael so much enjoyed his first three weeks at sea that he was sad to leave his first ship, which was going on to Japan. But there was no question of his staying with it, as he had merely been on loan to P.&O. and had now to join his proper ship. He then realized that he must make up his mind once and for all never to try to cling to the past but always to be ready to face new ventures. Although Michael felt that he had a tendency to cleave to what he had known before, he had in fact already charted unknown and perilous territories by taking on a new sex in adulthood. But Michael dismissed this as an act of courage, having always felt himself to be male. His problem, he considered, was that he hated to leave behind anything he had come to know and love. Thus, he had not wanted to move up to the senior school at the age of eleven; he had been sad when Bobby went to school and left Laura in the nursery; he would have liked to do his year in hospital at a place he had already come to know. But the years at sea were to kill any vestiges of Michael's temptation to hang on to the past. After leaving his first ship, he never looked back to any ship with regrets when it was necessary to leave it for another one.

One of the reasons why Michael tended to cling to the past may have been because he was shy about making new friends, and unsure of his ability to do so. On board the passenger ship, bound for Beira, Portugal, he had to force himself to make conversation with the passengers. He found this quite difficult and painful, for small talk did not come naturally to him; he preferred serious discussions about major philosophical issues. He quickly became aware that he was not much of a conversationalist, and sometimes felt rather awkward when he had to play host to the passengers, for he found it hard to think of things to say to them. Possibly people found him something of a bore – anxious to please and be helpful, but with no notion at all of when he was becoming tedious to his listeners. He certainly showed strong signs of this trait in his letters to Roberta – and to other, later correspondents.

Once again, Michael came up with ideas which were to benefit both himself and his charges – in this case, the passengers – and so to some extent alleviate the need to make polite conversation with them. He soon noticed that the daily five-course lunches, seven-course dinners and no exercise were having an adverse effect on both the passengers and himself. So he decided to hold gymnastics sessions every day after tea. In response to a notice he put up, about twenty passengers met for the first of these, attired in swimming costumes, and Michael organized ball games and other exercise routines. 'This,' said Michael, 'brought me into closer contact with the passengers than anything else could have done.' The games also provided amusement for the less active passengers, who came out to watch. Another benevolent activity for which Michael volunteered was looking after the children in the swimming pool during the afternoons; this gave their parents a rest and himself a valid excuse for getting out of uniform. He also taught the children to swim. In this way Michael became a known and popular figure and built up far more useful contact with the passengers than he would have done simply by drinking with them in the bar. Indeed, he had been warned of the dangers of drinking with passengers in the bar, for having to stand his round of expensive drinks time and time again would soon have taken its toll on his pay packet. Quite apart from that, he could not risk having too much to drink when he could be called upon at any time to attend a sick passenger – and perhaps to operate on one. On every voyage he made, Michael found he had to contend with the cliché of the 'gin-drinking ship's doc'. ('Doc' was an abbreviation which, like 'prof', 'cap' and 'Mike' – as he was frequently called at sea – Dillon hated.)

The ship went to Port Said, the Suez Canal, Port Sudan and Mombasa, where most of the passengers disembarked. Michael flew on to Nairobi for a weekend in a small aeroplane, his only companion a man who came from the same road in Folkestone, Bouverie Street West, where Michael had spent his teenage years as Laura. Fortunately, the two had not known each other at all at that time.

He was initially disappointed with Africa as the parts where he spent time – Dar-es-Salaam and Mombasa – were nothing like the thick jungle he had imagined from his days of reading *Tarzan* books. As he had little to do when the ship docked in Mombasa, he decided to take classes for his lifeboat qualification; he took the appropriate examination when he arrived back in London.

Michael undertook one more voyage in the same ship, which was then scrapped. As he had a long time to wait for his next ship, he resolved to take what he expected to be the very last step in altering his documents from Laura Maud to Laurence Michael. Since he had re-registered in 1944, he had managed to get all his records changed, including his birth certificate, and he had had the certificate for his Oxford M.A. issued with only initials. But as late as 1953 his entries in both *Debrett*'s and *Burke*'s peerages said 'Laura Maud' (or 'Maude'). So he called on the editor of *Debrett*'s with his birth certificate and requested that the name should now be changed. The editor, Michael recalled, was extremely kind and helpful and acknowledged Michael's claim to the baronetcy in the event of his surviving his brother. On 18 February 1947 Sir Robert had married Synolda, daughter of Cholmondeley Butler Clarke of County Tipperary, but no children had been born to them. The fact that Sir Robert was childless meant that Michael was now heir to the title. The *Debrett* editor assured Michael that any changes made there would automatically be followed in *Burke*'s, and so it seemed that the last vestige of Laura would now be swept away. It says much for the sexism of the two peerages that as soon as Laura Maud was elevated to man's estate her name appeared in capital letters: LAURENCE MICHAEL. As it turned out, *Burke*'s did not follow *Debrett*'s practice, and it was the resulting discrepancy, unnoticed for several years, which eventually led to Michael's exposure.

When Robert heard that Michael had set the *Debrett* changes in motion he was very angry. He was certain this would lead to unwanted publicity, and in this, of course, he was eventually proved right.

Meanwhile Michael had been offered the *Dunera*, a troop ship which was to sail for Japan, to fetch troops who had been serving in Korea and who were now waiting in Kobe. It was in Japan that Michael saw his first Buddhist temple, but he comments that he was not much impressed by the sight.

He found that when the ship reached Kobe, many of the troops were strangely reluctant to go home. The reason for this was that when they were first taken to Kobe, near Osaka, they had been given all their back pay and told to have a good time. This they did in the time-honoured way, with Japanese prostitutes. The result was that the soldiers had soon lost all their money and a large number became infected with VD, which was almost universal among the Japanese prostitutes. Many of the servicemen, says Michael, did not know how they were going to face their families. Michael also had to deal with several cases of beatings among the soldiers, for informing on their companions when in prison camps. Before long, a number of battered soldiers had been admitted to the ship's hospital. One soldier was discovered in the lavatory with his throat cut; he lived for only 20 minutes after being found. The body was put in the refrigerator for the journey home, where a verdict of suicide was returned. 'It suited the politicians to have these men treated as heroes,' Michael commented. As the soldiers began to see themselves described in newspapers as national heroes, their behaviour got worse and they became ever more insolent to the officers. They even demanded to be treated as civilians, now that their term of service had long since expired, and they did not see why they should still be subject to military discipline.

The commanding officer agreed, but said that if they were to be regarded as civilians their army pay would have to stop from that day. That, according to Michael, shut them up.

He was extremely glad this time to dock in Southampton. Leaving the ship with relief, he reflected that being on board a troop vessel was not really in his line. Having enjoyed his previous trips on passenger ships, he set about looking for a job on one of these. Eventually he signed a contract with the China Navigation Company and flew from Heathrow to Hong Kong. In those days, flights to Hong Kong took five days.

On signing this contract, Michael committed himself for four years. The chief job of the company was to take Muslim pilgrims from Singapore and Penang to Jeddah so that they could go on to Mecca, the trip to the holy city which every Muslim is supposed to make at least once in his lifetime. Michael Dillon's life was becoming ever stranger.

Before Michael went out to Hong Kong he had bought every single book he could find about Gurdjieff and Ouspensky, the Russian mystics whose ideas were popular in some circles in the 1930s and 1940s, so that he would have plenty to read on arriving in Hong Kong. Unfortunately he did not have these books when he needed them most, as he was kept in Hong Kong for five weeks while most of his luggage went ahead by sea.

On many occasions in his life Michael had found himself utterly alone, in strange places without friends or other contacts. This pattern was to reassert itself now in Hong Kong, where he knew nobody, and he became ever more depressed and discontented, especially as Christmas approached. Having spent many Christmases entirely alone when working at the garage in Bristol, he always dreaded the approach to Christmas, for it reminded him all too vividly of the solitary path he had chosen for himself. He retained clear memories of magical Christmases spent in Folkestone with Daisy, Toto, Maudie and Granny when he and Bobby had been small children, and when letters had been sent up the chimney to Father Christmas. Now he had no one. Even the padre from the Mission to Seamen was ill. Michael faced the prospect of spending the festive season in Hong Kong all by himself. While wandering round the cathedral grounds one morning, despondently contemplating a Christmas devoid of festivity, he met a young clergyman in a hurry. Feeling rather desperate, Michael told the young man about his appalling loneliness and was soon asked to supper with his family. Immediately a rapport was established between them. Michael discovered the clergyman's wife had been to Oxford, while the clergyman himself was a Cambridge graduate. Michael was invited to spend Christmas with the couple and their two small children, and so it was that he managed to have a good Christmas after all.

It was during this time that Michael started to think in earnest about the way his life was proceeding, and to wonder whether there was anything he could do to overcome the lengthy bouts of self-pity which had marred his happiness and which had also, in his opinion, curtailed his activities, since childhood. The books he had brought with him from England, Nicoll's *Psychological Commentaries* on the works of Gurdjieff, said that self-pity was one of the worst emotions in which anybody could indulge, because it made all other negative emotions so much worse. Michael was avid for information and advice on how to tackle negative mental states, as he felt he had been plagued with them all his life and that they had always come between him and any chance of real happiness. He learned then that negative emotions do not arise from outside circumstances, but from one's own attitude to these circumstances. Although most people, if asked, would say they prized happiness above everything, in fact what most of us do all the time is to indulge self-pity and wallow in it whenever the opportunity arises. Most of us, according to Gurdjieff, do not realize that we have the power within ourselves to overcome self-pity permanently. We suffer from it mainly because it has become an ingrained habit. But it is not innate, and with sustained effort it *can* be removed from the personality.

As soon as Michael read these words he knew that they were true. He decided that from now on he would make every effort to overcome the self-pity which had dogged him from early childhood, and to become the happy, contented and positive individual he wished to be. Like many people who undergo cosmetic surgery, Michael had expected a new personality to evolve along with the new body, but had in due course found that his character remained untouched by the surgeon's knife and the hormone tablets. 'Many things I thought would change did not,' he wrote to a correspondent who had asked him for advice on changing sex.

He now felt he had to work hard on his mind to become the kind of person he wanted to be. He was learning that 'running away to sea' was not the answer: he had not been able to run away from all the deficiencies in his character. It was his avid reading of Gurdjieff during those weeks of isolation in Hong Kong which was eventually to lead to Dillon becoming ordained as a Buddhist monk.

8

A Quest for the Self

FOR the next three years Michael Dillon was to satisfy to the full his urge to see exotic places. In the ship carrying pilgrims to Mecca he sailed first to Indonesia and then to Japan, and after that to Singapore, which was to be the headquarters for the Haj, the once-in-a-lifetime pilgrimage to Mecca. The ship could take up to 1200 pilgrims, many of whom, having long since run out of money, would be starving and ill on the return journey. As there were often a great many sick passengers two surgeons were required for each journey. On the first journey Michael's assistant was a doctor far senior to him in years and experience, but who had suffered a stroke and could no longer practise ashore. It was doubtful whether he should have been allowed to do *any* medical work on board ship, as his brain had been affected by the stroke so badly that he could not follow a conversation for more than a minute or two. He was, Dillon said, quite incapable of taking a case history by this time and his standard treatment for all patients was to give them a purgative, without troubling to find out what was wrong. For this reason, the Malayan medical assistant made sure that any really ill people attended only Dr Dillon's surgery.

Although the passengers were supposed to be passed fit before the voyage, one was found, after he told Michael he had not passed water for six days, to have advanced cancer of the prostate. A tube was inserted through his abdominal wall under local anaesthetic to enable his bladder to be relieved, but he died of a heart attack six days later. Nobody mourned for this passenger, however, because, according to Islam, as he was en route for Mecca he would go straight to Allah.

Although Michael had suffered several hypoglycaemic attacks during his years at medical school – his frequent passing out while at Trinity College was something most of his student colleagues remembered about him – the good food on board ship had enabled him to stave these off without too much trouble. As a precaution, he used to carry glucose with him everywhere in case he went for too long without food. On his return to Singapore on the pilgrim ship he took a day trip by plane to Sarawak, where he could find nothing to eat. By the time he landed he had been ten hours without food. He passed out on the wharf and later woke up in hospital with a huge bump on his head and a long scalp wound.

On the whole Michael did not enjoy his time shipping Muslim Malayans to Mecca. The completely different culture and religion felt alien, and he was not able to establish any kind of rapport with either the passengers or the crew. But all the time he continued to read Gurdjieff and try to put his precepts into practice. Michael felt he was being given golden Gurdjieffian opportunities to become a better person, and to get to know himself, as he did not really get on with the others and the only friend he had was the captain, with whom he was engaged in making a rug. In the evenings and when off-duty Michael and the captain would sit one each end and work on it. Michael does not record anywhere whether it was ever finished. After a year he felt he could no longer work for the company and applied for a discharge. He requested a berth to Australia instead of being repatriated to England.

The reason he was anxious to visit Australia was because his mother's only surviving relative, her sister Mary, lived in Australia. Michael was keen to contact her, having only ever met the Dillon side of his family before. She and Michael had exchanged letters for many years and he had told her of his sex change. She appears to have accepted it without comment.

On meeting for the first time, in Sydney, both felt extremely shy. Michael was all his life hampered by shyness and found it hard to get into easy conversation with people. He was due to spend five weeks in Australia, and spent most of the time trying to find his aunt somewhere decent to live. He was appalled at her lodgings – a single room in a decrepit house with wallpaper hanging off the walls in long strips. Aunt Mary had to do everything – sleep, eat, cook and entertain – in this one squalid room. Cooking was by no means a simple matter as all water had to be fetched up from the floor below.

After discovering that she owned a plot of land in Adelaide and wanted to build a house of it, Michael helped his aunt with the money and was later to return to see the finished home. His real aim was to try to find out a little more about his mother, but by this time Aunt Mary was 75 and did not appear to be able to remember much.

When the five weeks were up, Michael bought a berth back to England, having failed to find a job on any of the returning ships. He found members of every nationality on board and soon formed a 'university' where they could instruct each other in their various areas of knowledge and expertise. Michael himself gave classes in philosophy which, he recorded rather pompously, 'became more popular than one might have expected'.

During this voyage the ship called at an Egyptian port, which enabled him to see the pyramids and the Sphinx. Naples was another port of call. Although Michael was interested to see the various sights in the countries he visited, his journals reveal no particular insights or anything other than travellers' clichés. These voyages made him realize, however, how fundamentally lonely a person he was: much as he longed for company, friends and love, he never seemed able to find them. Nor did he have the happy knack, so useful on board ship, of being able to get on with everybody easily, and he found it hard to engage complete strangers in conversation.

By the time he returned to Southampton he had been away for a year and a half. The future was as uncertain as ever. Should he get another job on board ship or try for something else? He decided that first he would go to Oxford, his favourite city in all the world, to celebrate his birthday; then he would see whether Gilbert Barrow, his friend from the Bristol garage days, would be able to join him in a fortnight's holiday cycling round Italy.

Before that, however, Michael went to Folkestone to see how his now ancient aunts, Daisy and Toto, were getting on and whether they needed anything. He was horrified at what he saw. Always miserly, the aunts now lived like complete paupers, with holes in their slippers and patched and ragged clothes. When he went to their house – they were still living in the large house in Bouverie Street West – he found that they were both crouching over a tiny fire which had been banked up with bricks so that they would not need to put so much coal on. As the old ladies seemed so poor, the inhabitants of Folkestone repeatedly asked why the two children whom Daisy and Toto had brought up never did anything for their aged relatives.

Why, neighbours wondered, did they let them live in such poverty? Most of them sincerely believed that Daisy and Toto had no money of their own. In fact, both of them had large personal incomes which they were loath to touch. When Toto died in 1957, she left more than £24,000 – the equivalent of £500,000 today.

Nobody at all in Folkestone connected Michael with the girl Laura, and Daisy and Toto never revealed who the bearded stranger was.

He wanted to buy them new dressing-gowns, but they refused, saying, 'What's the good when there is nobody to see us?' None the less, he did buy them a pair of slippers each, which he thought they might wear. And every day he took Daisy to lunch in the town, as she was being kept half-starved by Toto – who would never go out to lunch with them herself.

Daisy and Toto carefully mixed all their butter with margarine, and hoarded it until it went bad. Going through their larder, Michael found two big chocolate Easter eggs he had bought them in Dublin when chocolate was rationed in England. Now, years later, they remained wrapped in paper, the chocolate having faded to an unappetizing white. The aunts' explanation was that they had looked too pretty to break into and eat – so they had just left them. They maintained that they could not afford a servant, and when Michael offered to pay for a lady to come and live in they brushed the idea aside. 'We prefer it like this,' Toto would say whenever Michael tried to help make their life better.

After Michael had done what he could for his aunts, who by now were well into their eighties, he paid a visit to Canon Millbourn and contributed more money to the Canon's educational fund. Michael enjoyed meeting Canon Millbourn, as he could talk to him about all the things that interested him, the major issues of life, rather than just making small talk.

Then Michael visited Gilbert Barrow, now living in a prefab and working in a post office. (Barrow later became a tax inspector.) After talking to Gilbert's 6-year-old son, Michael decided that the boy was wasting his time at the local elementary school and offered to pay for him to go to prep school. Young Barrow later justified Michael's faith in him by winning a scholarship to public school. Michael had very kindly told Gilbert that he would see his son through public school, but only if he won a scholarship: he felt some effort had to come from the boy himself.

This was the way in which Michael tried to repay Gilbert for his kindness and friendship during the dismal days at the garage, when the little lad from the orphanage had been the only one with the courage to accept Michael – the weird man/woman with the Oxford degree and the posh voice – as a friend.

Having re-established contact with family and friends, and after celebrating his fortieth birthday as planned in Oxford, Michael thought about doing the Merchant Navy Defence Training. A major rail and dock strike was then at its height, for which reason he would be unlikely to find another ship just yet, although he had applied to, and been accepted by, Ellerman Lines. They had told him they would not have a ship ready for at least three weeks after the dock strike as all their vessels were lying idle at Liverpool.

The idea for the training course came from Michael's extensive reading of Gurdjieff, who had advocated taking on new and unusual activities whenever possible, to open up different areas of the brain.

Michael went to stay at the Mission to Seamen in Victoria Dock Road, where he soon found himself serving in the canteen on Sundays and going country dancing on Saturday evenings. He enjoyed these occasions far more than the formal balls on board ship. On finishing the defence training, Michael became eligible to have another stamp put in his Discharge Book – and thus notched up for himself another first: the only ship's surgeon to have completed the defence training course.

He then set off with Gilbert Barrow on the planned cycling holiday in Italy. The two spent a night in Folkestone with Daisy and Toto before crossing the Channel. The very day after Michael returned to Folkestone a telegram arrived at the aunts' house, which Michael usually gave as his permanent address; it was from Ellerman Lines, asking if he could fly to New York straight away to join the *City of Johannesburg,* her regular surgeon having fallen ill. The ship was to complete a round-the-world voyage, and Michael accepted instantly.

His was the usual Englishman's impression of New York at the time – 'all size and money and shouting about both', he wrote in his journal, adding that it was 'only what might have been expected'. In the 1950s most English people were very snobbish about Americans and their country, thinking themselves infinitely superior. (In one of Enid Blyton's *Famous Five* stories written at about this time, an American boy is actually taught to speak 'proper' English by the eponymous children and say 'wonderful' instead of 'wunnerful'.) This attitude has so completely disappeared that it is hard to realize just how strong it was when Michael Dillon was a ship's surgeon.

Ever wanting to please and be helpful, Michael became a 'deck hand' on the first part of the voyage, as there were no passengers and he had hardly anything to do. This experience came in useful later, when he wrote the book *Imji Getsul* and told a white lie, to protect his true identity, about signing on as a deck hand in order to go round the world.

Before long Michael he became an enthusiastic chipper and painter, and found something very satisfying about using a paint-chipping hammer. He always enjoyed hard physical labour. In lieu of exercise, this work was the next best thing, although the captain did not consider it an entirely suitable occupation for a highly qualified ship's doctor.

On reaching China, the ship continued up the Yangtse River to Shanghai, which did not impress Michael much. He knew a little about its past, but although he felt it had not quite lost its prosperous look, he thought the goods in the shops were shoddy and the roads and houses were in a bad state of repair. At the Seamen's Club, Michael bought four lengths of brocade which he sent to the matron and nurses at his Dublin hospital. To these women, he thought, brocade dress lengths would be a luxury beyond belief. Michael's identification with the male sex was so complete that he regarded women very much as the 'other', or opposite, sex. There is no hint in any of his writings that he had any true rapport with women. He never thought of himself as a refugee from hated womanhood but as somebody who had always been male, despite biological evidence to the contrary. It was only the external female manifestations of himself that he had hated. Once these were removed, he felt able to move quite naturally in a man's world.

After the Roberta incident there was no hint of his forming any romantic attachment of any kind. Michael never seemed to think of women in that way again, and there is no indication that he missed having a constant female companion. Perhaps he realized that he was basically a loner and an adventurer, who could never settle to the kind of life most other people would consider normal.

He had been out for five and a half months when he came back to London again, and was immediately offered a job on *The City of Bath*. But before that voyage started, he went down to Folkestone again to see the aunts, having received a letter from Daisy informing him that Toto had broken her leg in a fall and was in hospital. Daisy had provided a vivid description of how she had found Toto lying on the kitchen floor one morning and could not lift her up. Robert had come over from Ireland to see to the aunts and had written to Michael (the aunts were the only matter on which the pair now corresponded) to tell him that when he arrived at the hospital all the staff thought she was a pauper; he had had to go straight out and buy her some decent nightdresses as all her own were in rags. By the time Michael's ship docked, however, Toto had left hospital, and she and Daisy had decided to abandon their house and go to live in a guest house in Earls Avenue.

Here Michael found Daisy looking much better, as she was being properly fed, while Toto was up and about, walking with a stick. She was now 87 and Daisy was 83. Michael said that he would go and clear the furniture from the house, as they were never going to return, and if their belongings remained there they would have to go on paying rates. He began in the attic, where despair quickly set in, for he found that nothing whatever had been thrown away since 1929, when the aunts had first moved there. Aware that all the furniture had been willed to him, Michael decided to sell most of it.

In Toto's room he opened an ottoman and found the moccasins he had bought a year previously to replace her worn-out slippers; they were still wrapped in their tissue paper, presumably put away as they were 'too good to use'. Beneath that he found boxes and boxes of writing paper bearing their family crest – again, never used as it was 'too good'. Toto always wrote letters on cheap lined paper from Woolworth's. Further down he came across a child's fancy dress, a red flannel petticoat and two pairs of striped flannel drawers with open crotch, as were worn in Victorian days. Underneath these ancient clothes he found a strip of cloth on which were pinned his 22 Girl Guide badges, and a doll's tea-set dating from Toto's own childhood. Michael took his grandfather's sword and the paintings and books that had belonged to his ancestors but put all the furniture up for sale. Old-fashioned and out of date, though presumably not of antique value, it fetched only £25.

At first Michael loved being on *The City of Bath*. It sailed for New York early in December with its cargo of passengers and then went on to India. Michael went ashore in Bombay and cycled round that bewildering city, learning something of the Ba'hai faith while having a cup of tea in a café. He was by now becoming seriously interested in religion, and was questioning the bland Christianity of his upbringing. More than ever, since he had started his career as a ship's surgeon, he wanted to find the meaning of life or, more precisely, the meaning of *his* life.

In Calcutta the temperature was 125 degrees Fahrenheit and one of the crew, the third engineer, died on board. Michael himself went down with amoebic dysentery and had to be put ashore and taken to hospital. He remained in the hospital for two weeks, after which he was given an air ticket for London. Although glad to get out of the heat of Calcutta he was still ill on the plane home. He vomited all the time and was so weak on landing at Northolt that he was taken by ambulance straight to the Greenwich Seamen's Hospital. He was there for another two and a half weeks before he was allowed to leave and then, still weak, he went to Belfast to recuperate.

All the time he had been at sea Michael had been writing poems. In Belfast he completed these poems and attempted to get them published. They were the first poems he had written for many years, although he had tried his hand at several forms of verse when a teenager. This had been discouraged by Toto, who asked Laura one day what she wanted to be, and she had replied, 'a poet'. Toto laughed and said, 'Don't be silly, you haven't got it in you.'

Although Toto had probably never read any of Michael's poems, she was right when she said he had not got the makings of a poet. Some of Michael's 'Poems of Truth' have been preserved, although the volume itself, which was eventually privately printed, seems to have disappeared without trace. The poems are derivative, sombre, hymn-like in sentiment and archaic in language, with nothing really original in them. Michael's originality lay in his life, which must surely be one of the most unusual ever lived. One might have expected his unique experiences and outlook to have given him a poet's vision, but they did not. Michael could never get away from himself, his own preoccupations or his corroding self-pity, nor could he empathize with other people. He might be able to refer, like Alexander Pope, to 'this long disease, my life', but he had not the gift, or genius, to turn his thoughts into any kind of memorable verse. Maybe this was because all his life he had struggled to be something he was not.

The poems never come alive, nor are they interesting even as curiosities, in the way that his conventionally published books are. Yet Michael decided that what he had to say as a poet was so

119

important that he should pay for publication of a thousand copies of a collected edition. He considered these poems were 'strongly Gurdjieffian' in sentiment, but this was not enough to make people flock to buy them. The following is an example of one of them, entitled 'Understanding and Compassion', which he regarded as his best:

Deep black the night save when the lightning flashed,
Which showed the foaming crests and spray flung high;
Sheer wall of water rearing to the sky
As waves on waves against each other crashed.
No rest, the struggle raging
As when a war is waging,
The sea against itself – against its will;
When suddenly a gentle Voice was heard,
Fraught with Compassion came the needful word:
'Peace!' Then the storm was stayed and all was still.

Tossed this way and that, a soul in torment,
Thoughts recurring o'er and o'er again,
Long wakeful nights and days of mental strain,
Love strove with hate and jealousy till spent.
No rest, the struggle raging
As when a war is waging,
A man against himself – against his will.
He took his life for lack of friendly hand,
For want of one to say 'I understand'.
This time no peace was there, though all was still.

After the 'publication' of *Poems of Truth*, by Linden Press in 1957, Michael managed to get one shop to stock his poems. Soon after that he departed to sea again, never to return.

He was still trying to reach a condition of calmness and positivity within himself. Although perhaps no longer positively unhappy as he had been when Laura, Michael was still by no means settled in his life, or in his mind. Now over 40, the best years of his life were slipping away, and to what effect? He had maintained a strong desire not to lead a life as useless as he considered those of Daisy and Toto to be; but what *was* a useful kind of life?

To try to find out, Michael joined an Ouspensky discussion group in London. But he was soon disappointed, for although the members of the group enthusiastically adopted Ouspensky's ideas none of them, in Michael's opinion, succeeded in living up to them. After the discussions the members of the group would go to a nearby pub, where they would joke and talk just like anyone else. They seemed so very unexceptional, so basically untouched by Ouspensky's ideas, that Michael could not help wondering what they had gained from the group. In this, he felt much as many people do when they first go to a religious or spiritual meeting, expecting the other people attending to be above the common herd, unconcerned with petty jealousies or small talk. Newcomers usually discover that the members are just as lacking in the 'higher' qualities, just as ordinary, just as tedious, as anybody else. Such visitors often go away disappointed, wondering what if anything the meetings have given the members. What they may not realize, and what Michael probably did not recognize, is that the reason why people attend them is because they feel there is something desperately lacking in themselves; unhappy and ill at ease with themselves and their surroundings, they hope to fill the perceived emptiness in their lives.

When Michael was pronounced fit again, he was assigned to a different ship, *The City of Oxford*. He felt it was his fate to accept the assignment, as anything with the word 'Oxford' in its name felt instinctively right for him. This ship, currently loading in Hull, was to go first to South Africa, then Australia. This run would in itself be a new experience for Michael.

A few days after the ship started its run Michael had a cable from his brother Robert to say that Toto had died of a femoral hernia, and so Robert was taking Daisy over to live with him in Ireland. At last she would be free of her sister's miserliness and constant nagging, and would spend her remaining few years eating well and being treated well. Although the rift between Michael and Robert had never been healed, and Robert still refused to acknowledge his former sister as a brother, Michael was never bitter about him. He always felt he understood how Robert felt. Few people, surely, would have found it easy to cope with having their younger sister turn into a man, thus becoming a serious contender for the family title. As the years went by and it became ever more unlikely that Robert would produce any heirs, it seemed increasingly certain that if he outlived Robert Michael would inherit the baronetcy.

Meanwhile, Michael was putting his painting and chipping skills into practice, painting the whole of the fo'c'sle himself. By now he had become quite expert and enjoyed the work under a pleasantly warm sun. Perhaps one reason why Michael was so enthusiastic about this kind of work was that it gave him a valid excuse to be away from everybody else and therefore removed the need to make conversation.

On landing in South Africa, Michael observed, with dismay, the day-to-day operation of the colour bar, but was gratified to learn that it did not extend to the Mission to Seamen in Durban. There, he said, blacks, Chinese and Europeans all sat together: no distinction was made between seamen. He made quite a close friend of the fourth engineer, who wanted Michael to teach him Latin. This he was glad to do, as it offered human contact without the need for general conversation (Michael never managed to lose his paralysing shyness). He also introduced the engineer, named Dennis, to the works of Gurdjieff and Ouspensky. One night Michael gave the engineer a copy of Ouspensky's lectures on how to avoid negative emotions.

The engineer burst into Michael's cabin soon after saying, 'This is it, Mike! It's what I've been looking for all my life. Who is this man and what else has he written?' Dennis had confided to Michael that he was bored and frustrated with his present life; he wanted to leave the sea and become a doctor himself.

At last Michael had a willing pupil. He had for so long tried to bend the ear of those who were not in the slightest bit interested in his philosophical ideas, and now here was somebody who actually *wanted* to learn. This friendship grew: when Michael landed at Adelaide and went to stay with his Aunt Mary, Dennis came with him – and was a great help in digging the garden and putting in plants.

The ideas which had so excited the fourth engineer were the ones by which Michael was now desperately, and with only partial successs, trying to live. The most important of these was the notion that each human being is not one but many different people. The most urgent task for the individual is to integrate all these disparate entities to make one whole self. It was this idea which was eventually to lead to Michael's wholehearted adoption of Buddhism.

Another important idea was that no one is a victim of circumstances; on the contrary, people actually attract circumstances to themselves by being what they are. Many people imagine that if things had been different, if they had had better parents, a more loving and stable background, or a better education, they might have been more successful, richer and more lovable. But according to Gurdjieff the circumstances into which you are born are exactly the right ones for you to make the best of. One can see why this doctrine would have appealed so much to Michael Dillon: he had spent years and years railing against the adverse circumstances that had caused him to be born a girl and brought up by aunts who did not try, and did not want, to understand him.

An idea which particularly appealed to Michael was that nothing can hurt you if you do not allow it to do so. We cannot change the course of events, or affect them in any way, but what we can do is to determine our own attitude to these events. He was to find, however, like the people he met in the London Ouspensky group, that there was a wide discrepancy between the theory and the practice of Gurdjieffism.

Through reading Gurdjieff, Michael felt he had discovered the answer to his childhood question about the purpose of life: it was, he felt, to evolve spiritually and to become an integrated person. Like many people, he had always been very ready to try to reform and educate other people, without realizing that it is not in anybody's power to change another person. All one can hope to do is change oneself for the better. The contemplation of these ideas over the years helped drive Michael towards Buddhism.

The most important task, Michael discovered, was to get to know yourself, and the best way of doing this is to listen to the criticisms that other people may have of you. Whenever people abuse you, or are hostile, you should ask yourself whether there is any truth in what they are saying rather than simply rejecting their behaviour out of hand.

It was 1956 when Michael was mulling over Gurdjieffian ideas. After leaving Australia, his ship went home via the Suez Canal, where it dropped anchor in the gulf to await orders. The Suez crisis, over the administration of the right of passage through the canal, was then at its height and the officers were worried in case Britain declared war against Egypt, as the crew were mainly Muslims. Just about all of the officers, including Michael, were on the British Prime Minister Anthony Eden's side and gave him moral support, although there was little they could do in practical terms.

After a day and a half at anchor, they were ordered to sail via the Cape of Good Hope, and eventually they arrived home. Michael, having now been a ship's surgeon for four years, instinctively felt that this life would not continue much longer. He spent the return journey chipping and painting as a deckhand as usual, much preferring this to reading all morning, propping up the bar before luncheon, eating a vast meal and then sleeping or playing tennis until the bar re-opened.

He wrote in his unpublished memoirs:

This voyage I had a growing feeling that this life would soon end, that chipping and painting and manual work had served its purpose and soon would come a change. When I first went to sea I knew there would come a time when I should have to leave it again, when its use would be exhausted, and then the next door would be opened for me, since all else was subservient to this Search for Truth. I was still being pushed along by I knew not what and my medical career seemed primarily for the purpose of my seeing the world. It was never an end in itself.

Although Michael's life had never been orthodox, he had always wanted to fit in, to be like other people, to feel right. He discovered that he did not feel much more right as a male than he had as a female, and that there was still not really a place for him in normal society. Always he was a loner, cut off from other people by his shyness, which people often mistook for rudeness, and also by his experiences, which prevented him from relating easily to others. On the whole, the people with whom he became friendly were themselves outsiders, in one way or another. He had singled out Gilbert Barrow, who had been brought up in an orphanage and had therefore never had what one might call a 'proper' upbringing; he had become friendly at Trinity College with Tom Asuni, the only black medical student in his year and also, therefore, an outsider. As a houseman he had befriended those who had never had a real chance in life, and as a benefactor he had given money anonymously to students who wanted to learn but who could not pay for their own education – people who wanted to elevate themselves above their backgrounds. Michael liked to help people who were worse off than himself – for example, his Aunt Mary in Australia – and he had rallied round Daisy and Toto when they became too old to look after themselves. But he was never able to find a permanent niche for himself, he never put down roots, and he never had what might be described as a circle of friends.

People who remember Michael say that his most noticeable quality was his remoteness: it seemed that he could never get close to another person. It is hard to know whether the phenomenon of his sex-change experience had caused this or whether his aloneness was simply a character trait entrenched deep within him.

9

Exposure

HAVING no particular job planned, Michael decided that he would look around for a few months and find out more about some of the topics that had begun to fascinate him. Over the past few years he had become increasingly interested in alternative medicine, Eastern religions, mysticism and reincarnation. So while on extended shore leave he decided to research further into arcane areas which were, in the late 1950s, generally regarded with deep suspicion and mistrust. As ever, Michael was to be a pioneer – forming his own conclusions, and not taking too much notice of the prejudices and ignorance of others.

As he no longer had any contacts in Folkestone he decided to call on Sir Harold Gillies, now in his late seventies and working at the London Clinic. Michael felt he could never repay his debt to Sir Harold, who had enabled him to live as a cosmetically acceptable member of the male sex. 'His one aim,' Michael wrote, 'had always been to make life tolerable for those whom either nature or man had ill-treated, without regard to conventional views. To many he must have given renewed hope and a new start.'

Michael had decided to take a temporary job as casualty officer at a Docklands hospital in London until he could set sail again. It was now 1957, and this was his first experience of what he called nationalized medicine – he had never previously worked within the NHS. He soon realized that he hated it. He had always been against it in theory, and now he was shocked at what he found. The first shock was that he was expected to give penicillin and anti-tetanus injections routinely for every scratch and then daily for five days. The idea was that one would thereby create permanent immunity. According to Michael

Dillon, however, the injections were quite unnecessary, and were one reason why NHS costs were rocketing – even in those days. Moreover he believed that the constant injections of penicillin and anti-tetanus could be dangerous in themselves. However, he was told he must give injections, otherwise the patient might bring a claim of negligence. You could kill patients by over-medication and nobody would say a word – but if you failed to prescribe something you could be accused of dereliction of duty.

He discovered that there was far too much unnecessary treatment and far too much unnecessary medication in general. Every person who had suffered a fall had to be X-rayed, in case there was a fracture. All patients had to stay for a long time in hospital, too, even after they were perfectly able to go home. After three months Michael could stand no more, and left.

But the lure of the East – alternative medicine, new ways of expanding consciousness and new ways of healing – was becoming ever stronger. Michael met Lobzang Rampa, author of *The Third Eye*, a book full of occult wisdom about reincarnation which caused widespread interest when published, and was fascinated by this man. The book describes its author's previous incarnation as a Tibetan monk. At the time Michael knew nothing whatever of Tibetan Buddhism, but he liked Rampa, a Devonshire farmer's son, and believed him to be completely genuine.

He also attended Ouspensky meetings again while in London, for he was anxious to try to understand his own personality. A ship's captain had once informed Michael, during his days at sea, that he was an extremely selfish person; Michael had been amazed at this, considering himself to be somebody who would always put himself out for others. But the captain had explained that, in arguments, for example, Michael was always overbearingly dogmatic: he considered his opinion to be the only correct one, and that everybody else was wrong. As soon as the captain had drawn attention to this characteristic Michael realized he was right; now he resolved to do something about his dogmatism. He discovered, by going to the meetings, that the trait one most often criticizes in other people is the one that is uppermost in oneself – although it is rare for individuals to spot this.

Michael now tried to be less dogmatic, and to allow other people their opinions and the opportunity to express them. He found the meetings useful but concluded that most people who attended them were far more interested in the intellectual idea of Gurdjieffism than in working on themselves and trying to improve their own personalities. Perhaps the idea of self-improvement was too painful for most to face. It was different for Michael because he had always been an outsider, never readily fitting into any niche in society. Now that he considered he had overcome the problems connected with living in his original body, he turned his attention to altering his mind as well, so that he could be happy mentally as well as physically.

After resigning from the NHS hospital, Michael went to Oxford, always his favourite city. For a couple of years now he had been interested in radionics, a diagnostic and healing method based on the belief that the universe is composed of interlocking fields of energy that pervade everything, both animate and inanimate. Now came his chance to find out more about this branch of alternative medicine. He applied for, and got, a job working in the De La Warr Laboratories in Oxford and found himself some digs behind Pembroke College. He felt thrilled to be in Oxford once more, and this time not just for a short visit but for several months.

Michael felt that going back to Oxford was a sign that his old life was coming to an end and a new one was about to start. Oxford always seemed to act as the catalyst for change, but now he felt that Oxford itself had changed. His former tutor, Jimmy McKie, told him that most students were now from grammar schools, on scholarships, and wanted to be told things they could regurgitate rather than seeking to work things out for themselves. Wherever Michael went in Oxford he heard provincial accents, which grated on him. He still possessed traces of the snobbery and class-consciousness he had unsuccessfully tried to eradicate over the years.

Michael found that apart from his former tutor there was now nobody he knew in Oxford, but he set about making new acquaintances. Unable to resist the lure of the river, he became a rowing coach for one of the town clubs, and was only too glad to take an oar whenever a member of the crew failed to turn up.

The De La Warr Laboratories were situated three miles outside Oxford, on the Botley Road. There were three main laboratories and patients were received in a little country cottage with roses round the door. The whole set-up was designed, Michael noted, to impart confidence to the patient, who may well have been trying out something very new and strange.

The theory behind radionics certainly sounds strange enough. It was invented by a Dr Albert Abrams, an American neurologist, who discovered by chance that the human abdomen could be used as an accurate diagnostic tool. If he connected samples of diseased tissue in a container to a healthy subject by means of a wire, certain electrical signals could be detected. This phenomenon occurred only when the subject turned due west, however. Dr Abrams never found the scientific reason for this, but it seemed to work.

Later practitioners of radionics invented special boxes which could diagnose illnesses by translating disease wavelengths into ohms. As time went on more and more complicated machinery was invented, including cameras which could take photographs of human organs at long distances. The De La Warr instrument used what came to be known as a 'stick pad'. A thin sheet of rubber was stretched over a metal plate under which was an oblong cavity. The practitioner stroked the rubber lightly with his fingers while setting the dials to different diseases and illnesses. When the resistance matched the radiation emitted by the condition, the rubber stuck to the fingers and the diagnosis was confirmed. It was soon discovered that patients could be treated at great distances and did not have to have personal consultations. The rubber pad worked by means of the practitioner concentrating his or her mind on the illness. It is when concentration coincides with fact that the rubber starts to respond, according to the theory.

As might be expected, the early practitioners of radionics were soon accused of charlatanism and trickery, and court cases were brought against them. (One, in 1965, was brought against American radionics pioneer Dr Ruth Drown, who had invented some long-range cameras. She was accused of fraud and the verdict went against her on the grounds that her instruments were not scientifically valid. Dr Drown was sent to prison. She died the following year, aged 72, her life in ruins, after a couple of strokes brought on by the stress of the court case and of being discredited.)

George de la Warr was a civil engineer who had been asked, during the war, when imports from America were banned, to make some radionics 'black boxes' for a group of interested people living in Oxford. The boxes consisted mainly of a set of dials, and de la Warr was to design many such ingenious instruments. Indeed, he became so interested in radionics that he decided to devote all his life to this field. He carried out many experiments, built long-range cameras, and attracted many patients to his Oxford laboratories. In 1960, in the celebrated 'Black Box' case, George de la Warr was charged with fraud by a Miss Phillips, who claimed that she had been reduced to a nervous wreck by trying to operate one of the diagnostic instruments. The judge, Mr Justice Davies, dismissed allegations of fraud but could not accept the viability of the diagnostic camera. He claimed that it was impossible to take pictures of human organs at long range, and expert witnesses were called in to corroborate this. The upshot was that de la Warr won his case but was faced with crippling costs (Miss Phillips was receiving legal aid and therefore did not have to pay anything herself).

When Dr Abrams first developed radionics, he taught the technique only to already qualified doctors. By Michael Dillon's time, however, others were being taught it.

Radionics is based on the belief that all illnesses are caused by imbalances in the etheric body, or the 'aura' that surrounds us all. The theory is that energy patterns are emitted by all forms of matter, and that these patterns are distorted whenever there is negative emotion, stress or tension. The radionics instruments can supposedly pick up these tensions and diagnose them. Radionics is part of what we would now call 'holistic' medicine, as it takes the whole person into account, not just the symptoms. Health, according to radionics practitioners, is maintained when energy is flowing freely round the body. This energy is blocked whenever the patient is troubled by anxieties.

Radionics is not considered a form of faith healing. Practitioners stress that the success of radionics does not depend on whether the patient believes in the treatment. The only important requirement is that the patient should genuinely want to get well. Strange as it may seem, not all ill people *do* want to recover: some would prefer to be ill, for by being ill they can evade responsibilities and escape decisions. Moreover, when ill they get looked after, which may not be the case when they are well.

Radionics works by means of hair analysis. All that is needed for an accurate diagnosis is for the patient to send a sample of hair. The box, in the hands of a skilled operator, will do the rest. The whole thing sounds so peculiar that all through the 'fifties journalists and other investigators from the media sent samples of cats' hair and birds' blood, along with phoney symptoms, to see what practitioners made of these. Nowadays radionics has taken its place in the pantheon of alternative therapies, but in Michael Dillon's time it was considered very strange and cranky indeed. That did not stop him from being interested, however, for he was beginning to realize himself that physical illness tended to occur mainly when the mind and emotions were disturbed. It is easy to see why Michael was attracted to this form of therapy, as it very much ties in with Gurdjieff's theories, and also the Eastern ideas he was now embracing.

As soon as Michael arrived at the laboratories, he was given a 'black box' from which to try to diagnose patients' illnesses. When de la Warr was taken to court in 1960, Canon Millbourn sent cuttings relating to the trial to Michael in India. He wrote back to the Canon to say that, had he been still in England, he would have gladly testified on behalf of de la Warr, for he knew from experience that the black box really did work and that it had the capacity to help many people.

Michael quickly discovered that the theory of the box is one which does not stand up to scientific investigation. In order to work the box a practitioner has to be sensitive and intuitive, and in this Marjorie de la Warr, George's wife, was supreme. She worked the box easily and had startling successes, simply by concentrating on the name of the patient. She did not even need to use a sample of blood or hair in order to make an accurate diagnosis.

Only sensitive individuals could use the box. Some practitioners have compared using the box to playing a violin. Although anybody can buy such an instrument, and most can learn to play it up to a point, only a few people will ever become concert virtuosi. It was the same with the box – by no means everybody got good results. De la Warr himself said that people who were too materialistic in outlook could never learn to use it properly. When Michael Dillon was working at the laboratories, a few students from the university asked if they could have a go. Some were able to get results from it, but most could get no sense out of the stick pad.

Michael soon came to realize that the box was invaluable for diagnosing those illnesses which have a strong psychosomatic basis, such as ulcers, dermatitis, high blood pressure, cancer, arthritis, asthma and eczema. 'The box can determine such psychological causes much more easily than the psychiatrist, and with less ill effects on the patient,' he observed.

Just for fun, Michael thought he would try the box out on some of his friends. He started with his old tutor, Jimmy McKie, and was alarmed to find that coronary thrombosis was strongly indicated, through a very high level of friction on the rubber pad. He tried it again, just to make sure, and the diagnosis was the same. So he rang Mrs McKie and told her, but she informed Michael that her husband was perfectly well. That was in 1957. Two years later he had his first coronary and a year later he died of a second. This could, Michael reflected, have been coincidence, of course, but the evidence of the box had been so very strong that he doubted it.

Although the black box was not accepted in orthodox medical circles – and, for that matter, still isn't – the laboratories received a steady stream of patients whose own doctors could do nothing more for them. Michael was very impressed by the results, which he felt were amazingly accurate, although many people who came to the laboratories were at too advanced a stage in their illness to be cured.

He was not so impressed with the long-range camera which was supposed to be able to take photographs of human organs from vast distances. A peculiar factor about these cameras was that they could be worked only by one person, the individual for whom they had been designed in the first place. They were not like ordinary cameras, which can be operated by anybody who knows which buttons to press. It was these strange cameras, above all, which made people think that radionics was so much rubbish – a form of quack medicine to be taken seriously only by the naive and gullible.

Nor was Michael at all impressed with the photographs that the De La Warr camera supposedly took. He did not entirely dismiss the idea of 'thought photography', whereby a photographic image could be produced by concentrating on that object, and he felt that the De La Warr process undoubtedly had a scientific basis of some kind. But he could find no rational or logical explanation for why and how it might work.

As was so often the case with Michael Dillon, initial enthusiasm and happiness soon gave way to discontent and dissatisfaction. He was happy working at the laboratories for a few months and was impressed by the talent and ingenuity of the de la Warrs. But he was abruptly dismissed from the establishment, ostensibly for two reasons: first, because its finances were highly precarious, despite appearances to the contrary; second, because he refused to write up an experiment which he felt had not been conducted under proper scientific conditions. He felt that de la Warr's enthusiasm sometimes led him to hasty conclusions and slipshod methods. Michael, always scrupulously honest, indeed occasionally over-honest, and undiplomatic told him at the time that there was a major difference between scientific honesty and spectacular, unsubstantiated claims. This did not endear him to de la Warr and the two fell out.

By this time, however, Michael had had enough of radionics, much as he had enjoyed his interlude in Oxford, and was eager for the next phase of his life to begin. Meanwhile he arranged to go on another cycling holiday through France with Gilbert Barrow.

Michael had now lost all remnants of his belief in orthodox Christianity, which he felt could not possibly be the one true religion. He was yearning for something in which he *could* believe, but knew he had not found it yet. Radionics had been useful, but it was not something to which he wanted to dedicate his life.

He had now set himself the discipline of not allowing small disappointments and setbacks to upset him, and was determined that he would stay cheerful and positive throughout the continental holiday with Gilbert Barrow. When something did go wrong – for example, while travelling to their destination by train they slept past their station and had to go back almost to the beginning of their journey – Michael managed to stay calm, much to Gilbert's surprise. Michael told Gilbert about Gurdjieff, about radionics and about Lobzang Rampa, the author whom he revered so greatly. Much of this was above the younger man's head. Gilbert Barrow has said: 'I counted him as one of my best friends, but I never understood his various [intellectual] ventures.'

On his return from the trip, Michael went over to Ireland to spend a week or two with Lobzang Rampa, who at the time lived in a flat overlooking Dublin Bay. Although Lobzang Rampa was largely discredited later, Michael felt at the time that this strange man held the key to the next stage of his life.

The question as to whether he really was a reincarnated Tibetan lama did not unduly bother Michael because by any standards Rampa was a highly unusual man. Later, Michael was to become extremely sceptical of Rampa's claims to be a reincarnated wise man, but was glad that he had not questioned this too energetically at the time. If he had, he might have missed two weeks which were to be of immense value to the next stage of his life.

Michael took great pleasure in spending this time in Rampa's company, for the two of them talked endlessly on subjects which were beginning to hold more than a passing fascination for Michael. He learned later that many of Rampa's statements were false: much of what he said about Tibetan monasteries, for example, was simply

not true. Michael realized this when he came to live in one himself –
which, of course, Rampa had never done, unless he did so during the
claimed previous incarnation. But, be that as it may, Michael became
convinced that the man had indisputable psychic powers and had also
possessed the ability to influence his – Michael's – dreams. While with
Rampa, Michael also had experiences of 'astral travelling', of which he
had never previously heard.

On Michael's last day Rampa took him for a long car drive in
the evening, then offered him some advice: 'Do one more sea voyage
and then go to India and look for a monastery where you can learn
meditation, Michael.'

This was something Michael had never for one moment considered.
The monastic life had never appealed to him in the slightest; he could
never think of becoming a Christian monk because he was not an
orthodox believer, and he had no idea how one might set about
entering the sort of monastery Rampa had in mind – one dedicated
to Tibetan Buddhism. Rampa assured him, however, that there were
some Tibetan monasteries which took Europeans; in the meantime he
advised Michael to practise meditation.

By now money was running short, and as Michael was still committed to paying the school fees of Gilbert Barrow's son, as well as
contributing to Canon Millbourn's trust fund, he had to look for
another job. His previous employer, Ellerman's, still had only the *City
of Bath* available, still on the same run and needing a new crew, but
not before the end of November, which was over three months away.
That was too long to wait, he decided. He made a concerted effort to
find something else, but no vacancies were available. Then Ellerman's
wrote to tell him it had a vacancy for a relief surgeon on the *City of
Port Elizabeth*, but it was only for three weeks. Michael took it
rather than hanging around any longer.

This ship was only coasting round the Continent to unload, and
there would be hardly anything for Michael to do, but it was a legal
requirement for large ships to have a qualified doctor on board. It was
an uneventful trip, and when Michael came back he accepted the job
on the *City of Bath*, at that moment berthed at Baltimore, Maryland.
Michael and the crew crossed the Atlantic on the French ship *Liberté*.
When he joined the *Bath*, things immediately began to go wrong.
First of all the second mate left, as he had a feeling there was going
to be trouble on the ship, although he had no idea what. The ship's
carpenter had gone ashore one evening and been knocked down by a

taxi, whereupon a new carpenter had had to be flown out. The new captain had a bad reputation among the crew and nobody liked him. At first Michael could not understand why, for on the voyage out on the *Liberté* he had seemed very kindly and charming. The final straw was that the purser was out to save money, and made most of his savings on the crew's food. Usually food on board ship is extremely good, as Michael knew, and when it was not complaints and abuse would follow in abundance. All in all, the atmosphere was charged with tension even before the ship set off.

They sailed from New York to India and once again Michael travelled round India on his trusty bicycle. This time he was not just a tourist but was looking for a suitable meditation centre, although he found nothing that was just right. Back on board, Michael found he had nothing to do, and so he started to write some short stories which he hoped to be able to publish in one volume when he returned to England.

In Calcutta he was given permission to be away from the ship for a weekend and bought a first-class ticket to Bodh Gaya in the state of Bihar, not far from Benares. He wanted to visit Bodh Gaya's famous Buddhist temple. There he also saw his first Tibetan lama, very old and wrinkled and wearing a dirty red robe. Entering a bookshop which had the words Maha Bodhi Society over the door, Michael asked in English whether there was anywhere he could stay to learn Buddhist meditation. The Indian bookseller, who happened to speak excellent English, took Michael over the road and introduced him to the abbot of the local Tibetan monastery. Michael's first thought was that the abbot was dressed exactly like a woman.

The abbot took Michael into the head lama's room, where tea and biscuits were served. The head lama, Dhardoh Rimpoche, invited Michael to spend the night in the guest room. Later, salty buttered Tibetan tea was served. They also had *tsampa,* a sort of porridge made with barley which formed the staple diet of Tibetan monks. Michael found the supper quite inedible and in fact was never to get used to the food eaten in these establishments.

Thus Michael received his first taste of Tibetan monastery life. He watched processions, meditations and the monks at their labours, doing needlework and even taking part in a kind of sports-day programme. He found it all very strange, if not incomprehensible.

After a couple of days Michael had to leave to join his ship 300 miles away. There he found the atmosphere on board if anything even worse. The personality of the captain appeared to have changed: instead of being jovial and paternalistic, he seemed hostile and aggressive. Michael learned later he had a manic nature, alternating between high spirits and depression, which made life extremely difficult.

By the time Michael reached America once more, he thought that the *City of Bath* was the unhappiest ship he had ever been on. The standard of the meals had deteriorated even further on the journey back as there were then no passengers to please, and the crew had no fresh fruit on the entire journey. Also, because the crew had little to do, they started drinking heavily, which made quarrels and complaints increasingly frequent.

Michael made one more trip ashore, in Baltimore, which took the form of a bus trip arranged by the Mission to Seamen. He saw the house in which George Washington planned his last political strategy and ate his last meal. Michael and the four other crew members who joined the trip enjoyed themselves and returned late at night.

The following morning, while the ship lay in Baltimore harbour being loaded for India, Michael went down to the surgery as usual before breakfast to see if any members of the crew had any medical problems. A steward put his head round the door and handed Michael a cable. At first he thought it must be from Lobzang Rampa, who had by this time been exposed in British newspapers as a fake. Nobody else, he fancied, would be likely to send him a cable when he was out at sea.

The cable read: 'Do you intend to claim the title since your change-over? Kindly cable *Daily Express*.'

At that moment, he recalls in his memoirs, his heart stood still. The secret which had been closely kept for fifteen years had leaked out. But how had the paper found out? Michael's first thought, as far as he was capable of logical thought, was that Bobby – Sir Robert – had died, triggering a search for his heir. His hand trembled violently as he screwed the cable up and threw it away. But its contents were already etched on his heart. They were to change the course of his existence forever – and may even have hastened its end. He in fact felt that his life was effectively over, and he even contemplated suicide, as he had done so many times before when in the depths of despair as Laura. It was now a very long time since anyone had given him so much as a second glance in the street. For nearly fifteen years, he had taken his place in the world of men without challenge or question. Yet Laura had come back to haunt him.

While he was considering what to do next the company agent came to tell him two reporters from the *Baltimore Sun* were waiting on the wharf demanding to see him. Michael decided there was nothing for it but to light his pipe and face the music as best he could. There was, he felt, nothing that could stave off the inevitable.

To meet the reporters, Michael assumed once more the poker-face expression which he had worn more or less permanently as Laura. Here was the ultimate Gurdjieffian test – could he pass it without negative emotions, without self-pity, with equanimity? He could not.

The reporters, having sniffed out an excellent story, would not budge until Michael admitted that he had indeed changed sex. After the interview, they wanted a photograph; he sat puffing away at his pipe and let them take it.

He then went to the captain's cabin and told him about the reporters and why they were there; he explained that the press had somehow discovered that he was both heir to a title and had changed his sex, a secret which had been kept for fifteen years.

The captain became kindly and sympathetic at once, his hostility and aggression immediately evaporating. He promised to do all he could to help, and said he would try to keep the reporters away from Michael.

Neither of them was naive enough to suppose that this one interview would be the end of the matter. As they were sailing to New York in a day or two, the ship's captain cabled the shipping agents in New York asking them to have a police guard on the gangway ready for Dr Dillon.

Michael did not 'kindly cable' the *Daily Express* but braced himself for the reaction to the story when it appeared in the *Baltimore Sun*. He reckoned he had about eight hours' grace before everybody on the ship knew his secret. Then he went into breakfast trying to keep calm and to remind himself of Gurdjieffian doctrine: 'Nothing can hurt you if only you learn not to react,' he kept repeating to himself. He also tried to keep himself occupied by playing *Scrabble*. He reckoned that his adherence to Gurdjieff's teachings reduced his reaction by about half, but he could by no means obliterate the shock to his system.

The next morning the story was printed in the local (Baltimore) papers. His secret was common knowledge. Dr Dillon was a woman! Who would have guessed? Michael sat in his cabin and nobody came near him, possibly out of embarrassment. After all, what could you say to him? The first sign of life was when the third mate looked in to say there was a photographer on the gangway: what should he do with him? Michael signalled the third mate to tell him to go to hell.

The original story had appeared in the *Sunday Express* (London) on 11 May 1958, four days before Michael's 43rd birthday. Situated in the Ephraim Hardcastle gossip column under the headline 'From Laura to Laurence – and now a baronet's heir', it carried no direct quotes from Michael:

> A strange discrepancy exists between the two main reference books of the aristocracy. It concerns the family of Sir Robert Dillon, the eighth baronet of Lismullen, in the south of Ireland.
>
> *Burke's Peerage* lists a sister to Sir Robert – Laura Maud – born May 1, 1915.
>
> *Debrett* says Sir Robert has a brother called Laurence Michael with the same date of birth.
>
> The explanation – a few years ago Laura Maud Dillon registered a change of sex, and became Laurence Michael Dillon. He qualified as a doctor in 1951.
>
> Says Sir Robert: 'Dr Dillon became my brother some years ago. This is a matter of great delicacy and I don't wish to say too much about it.'
>
> Says Mr C.F. Hankinson, editor of *Debrett*: 'I cannot get out of saying that Dr Dillon must be the heir to the baronetcy. If a person is registered as a male, and recognized by the Registrar-General as such, then, as far as I am concerned, that person must be recognized as the heir.'
>
> Sir Robert, 44, is married, but has no children. He is reluctant to discuss the matter of inheritance. 'Who should inherit the title is purely a family matter and not for general discussion.'
>
> Dr Dillon is at the moment practising somewhere in England. Says Sir Robert: 'I do not know where he is living.'

It was after receiving a tip-off about the discrepancy between *Burke's* and *Debrett's* – nobody knows to this day who discovered it – that the *Sunday Express* made its enquiries and traced Sir Robert Dillon to Lismullen, there to 'doorstep' him until he answered at least some of their questions. But he would not tell them where Michael was. The very day the *Express* story appeared it went round the world courtesy of Reuter's news agency, and this was how the American papers had picked it up.

Michael soon found out how it had all happened. His friend Gilbert Barrow sent him a copy of the *Sunday Express*, where he read the original story for himself and realized it was accurate. He also learned that reporters had camped outside Robert's home after the story appeared and had grilled him continually until he broke down and gave them the name of Michael's ship. From there, it was a simple matter for the journalists to consult Lloyd's Register of Shipping to find out where she was. A further story in the *Daily Sketch* elaborated on the strange case of Dr Dillon, whom it described as a bearded, pipe-smoking British doctor: 'Dr Laurence Michael Dillon's delicate features showed surprise when he was told the secret was out,' commented the *Sketch*. Michael told his friends that most of the *Sketch* story was inaccurate, but did not mention that he had himself compounded the inaccuracies by making out that he was really a biological male who had been wrongly designated female, and that it was not too late for him to have a son, who would then inherit the title. This was, of course, patently impossible after what he had been through at the hands of Sir Harold Gillies.

The quotes that Michael gave to the *Daily Sketch* – which it in all probability lifted from the American papers – were as follows:

> It wasn't until I was in my early teens that I first sensed I was the victim of a sex mix-up.
> My voice began to crack. It became deeper than a female's, but higher than a male's.
> I began to grow hair on my face – but I didn't have to shave regularly. It wasn't a sudden thing. It developed slowly.

The story ended by saying that in 1945 he underwent the first of a series of operations that were completed four years later when he registered his change of sex. The *Daily Sketch* also carried a picture of Michael, bearded and smoking a pipe.

For the next ten days Michael was confined not just to the ship but to the starboard deck, furthest away from the wharf. On the first morning that he had peered out he saw a milling throng of spectators, all intent on glimpsing the male doctor who was really a woman. Most of these people were holding cameras, in the hope of getting a picture, too. The novelty value of Michael's story was, after all, immense, for in those days few people had even heard of changing sex.

Finding himself an object of curiosity, to a far greater degree than he had experienced even in the later stages of being Laura,

Michael paced up and down wondering what to do. Letters started arriving from his friends – Sir Harold Gillies, the lady warden from the Mission to Seamen in London, and Lobzang Rampa, himself a recent victim of press investigations. All offered sympathy and encouragement, but none could have imagined how Michael felt. Since the change-over he had striven to be as normal and ordinary a man as possible, taking care not to attract any undue attention to himself. Now everybody knew. The clock could never be turned back, and the general awareness of his past must make a huge difference to the way he would be regarded in future. He felt that his career at sea was over. Who now would want to take him on as a ship's surgeon?

In the meantime Michael composed a letter to Ellerman Lines, apologizing for involving the company in such unwelcome and unsought publicity. He had two letters back, one from the medical superintendant saying that he hoped Michael would feel he could still stay with the company. But Michael knew this would be impossible, however understanding Ellerman's executives may have been. From now on, wherever he went, he would be the butt of stares, comments and whispers. As Laura, Michael had known all too well what it was like to be considered an oddity: he could not endure the thought of being in that situation again.

He then wrote to his London club offering his resignation, assuming that it would no longer want to have him as a member.

Perhaps Michael over-reacted to his exposure: there is a possibility that in some perverse way he welcomed the publicity because it gave him a valid excuse to finish with a way of life that was becoming increasingly meaningless.

Michael's club (its identity is unknown) wrote back to say that the committee had considered his letter and decided to refuse his resignation as no blame attached to him. He was not a criminal and had done nothing wrong. The club requested, however, that its name should be withheld from the press. Michael promptly sent the club a cheque for two years' subscription, thanked the officials for their kindness and assured them that he would never leak the club's name to the papers; he also informed them that he would be at sea for the next two years.

Michael did not in fact intend to stay at sea for this length of time, but to 'disappear' to India in the hope that he might be able to find a monastery, learn meditation and lie low until the world forgot about him. Then, perhaps, when nobody remembered the great scandal of Dr Laurence Michael Dillon who was really Laura Maud, he could return and take up a different sort of life.

Michael wrote two more letters, one to the medical officer of the shipping company asking to be released in Calcutta, and the other to John Gordon, editor of the *Sunday Express*, asking whether he had stopped to think before publishing what might be the effect on a doctor's career of such publicity – a doctor who had, he argued, committed no crime and sought no publicity. For the rest of his short life – only four years – Michael could neither forgive nor forget. He was full of indignation and very angry. The whole situation brought unpleasant memories of his only previous brush with the press, which had also been highly embarrassing, when in 1937 the *Daily Mirror* printed a picture of Laura Dillon rowing, and asked 'Man or Woman?'

John Gordon wrote back to say he had been deeply moved by Dr Dillon's letter but would not publish it, as it would only mean further publicity. He added that he had a 'duty to the public' to reveal such matters.

Michael felt gratified to learn, some weeks later, that Gordon had been arraigned before the Press Council for having pursued the family of a murderer around the world. Again, Michael noted, he had pleaded a duty to the public.

Meanwhile Michael had to go with the ship to Calcutta. On board ship, he found a different atmosphere. Other members of the crew now looked at him oddly, and he overheard some saying that they had always thought there was something strange about Dr Dillon. Although no longer suicidal, Michael felt that his whole world was shattered; all his careful efforts to avoid publicity, and to have all his documentation changed so that nobody would ever know his background, had been wiped out in an instant.

Four years later, on his deathbed, Michael was to write:

By what sense of values did a newspaper editor and reporter think that five minutes' light reading by the public justified such an assault on a doctor's career? Or did they stop to think at all? When they realized that the secret was an old one, might they not have considered that publicity was unsought and, having found I was a doctor, although they did not know at first where practising, might they not have gauged the destructive impact on his job such an unnecessary dénouement would be? And finally, when they had discovered I was in the Merchant Navy, surely some feeling of what life on a ship would be like under such circumstances might have been expected from them – by virtue of their calling themselves human?

My career at sea would have been ended anyhow by this thoughtless act. The fact that circumstances quite apart from these were leading me on to a new life in any case, of which they knew nothing, makes no difference to the inhumanity of the deed.

Michael comforted himself by telling himself that the publicity only hastened his 'search for truth' and brought forward what he was intending to do for a while in any case – enter a Buddhist monastery.

In so doing, he was never to return to the West again.

10

India

NOW began the most curious phase of all in Michael Dillon's life. Having received permission from his ship's captain to be put ashore at Calcutta, for the rest of the sea journey Michael tried to prepare himself for the way ahead. His intention at the outset was to find a monastery where he could learn about meditation, and where he could stay for a couple of years until the world had forgotten about the strange case of Dr Dillon. He may well have been over-estimating the degree of public interest in him: to assume, after all, that the world would forever after be interested in all his doings, and that the press would follow him everywhere if it knew where to find him, was probably the sign of an inflated ego at work.

He began to practise sitting in the correct cross-legged position for meditation. Like most Westerners, particularly middle-aged ones, he found this extremely difficult, indeed impossible at first. His knees would not go down on the floor, but stayed high in the air. Michael practised the position in his cabin only to find that after ten minutes it was sheer agony. In fact he was never able to sit cross-legged comfortably. He started playing *Scrabble* against himself while sitting in this position to distract himself from the pain, and by the time he was due to go ashore he could manage three-quarters of an hour without too much trouble. He also practised kneeling, in case he might have to endure long stretches in this position as well.

At the time Michael knew nothing about Buddhism or meditation, and he had no thought of embracing the life of a Buddhist monk permanently. He just wanted to find out more about himself, and thought that Buddhism might hold the key to many unanswered

questions. Moreover, learning about a new religion would give him
something worthwhile and interesting to do during the period he
spent away from ordinary life. He had at this stage no clear idea of
what he would do when the two years were up, but had no thoughts
of going back to sea. That phase was now, he considered, at an end,
whatever might happen in the future.

He also prepared his friends for his 'disappearance'. Michael
wrote to everybody he thought ought to know something about
his whereabouts, telling them that he intended to stay in India for a
couple of years, and that they were not on any account to try to find
out where he was. Once he was settled, he would tell them where he
was; he added that he intended to return to England at some time in
1961. In his letter to Gilbert Barrow Michael enclosed a cheque for
another year of school fees for Barrow junior, and assured Gilbert
that they would never be forgotten.

On his last night on board ship he had a warm bath, wondering as he did so how long it would be before he could have the
next one. He knew that the life ahead would be physically tough, and
in order to prepare himself for it he had spent several nights sleeping
out on the deck with only a blanket beneath him, to try to get used to
the idea of sleeping on a hard bed, or perhaps the floor. The food on
the ship had not been good, but Michael had decided not to complain,
realizing that he would probably look back on these meals as the
height of gastronomic luxury compared with the food he would be
eating in the near future. In this prediction he was entirely accurate.

Reflecting on his life at sea over the past six years, he decided
that on the whole he had enjoyed them, as they had enabled him
to see the world several times over at other people's expense. Not only
that, but the life of a ship's surgeon was hardly arduous. On many
voyages he was there simply to comply with shipping regulations.
Michael had few regrets about leaving the *City of Bath*, however, as
the ship had not been a happy one, over all, and he could not forget
the nightmare of his exposure by the press. Once the cable had arrived
and everybody knew his secret, Michael had become a changed person,
withdrawn, silent, morose – in fact, very much as he had been during
the war while working at the garage. He had tried so hard to be a
normal, proper man. Then, suddenly, all the crew knew that he was
not, that he was a fake male after all. In an instant he had lost all the
credibility he had tried so hard to build up over the past fifteen years.
Now the only true friends he had left were those who had known him

as Laura: Canon Millbourn, Gilbert Barrow, Sir Harold Gillies, and his former Oxford tutor Jimmy McKie. There was nobody else he felt he could trust.

The remainder of the voyage, from when the crowds had milled round the ship at Baltimore to when he docked at Calcutta, was a far greater agony than trying to sit cross-legged. Despite his study of Gurdjieff, Michael could not come to terms with what had happened to him. The fact that he could not deny the press statements at all made it worse. He felt a sham, a total failure. Perhaps his intention to live a life of the utmost hardship for the next couple of years was, in a sense, a kind of self-punishment. He had been found out, and now he would have to atone for his 'sin'.

On arrival in Calcutta he withdrew his pay, amounting to about £200, and decided to try to live on that during the time he was in India. In a monastery, he reasoned, he would not have very much need of money. It is a mystery what he did about the male hormone tablets, which he had been taking regularly since 1939. Normally, when transsexuals change over, they must continue taking the appropriate sex hormones for the rest of their lives, as the body will always try to revert to its original state, however long ago the conversion has been effected. Michael Dillon never refers to this problem, although it is hardly likely that testosterone would have been available to him in India – and certainly not in a Buddhist monastery. It must also be remembered that he still possessed ovaries, although these would have atrophied considerably by now owing to the continual onslaught of male hormone over the years.

The lack of male hormone seems, however, to have been the least of Michael's worries; nowhere does he refer to it as a problem. When he landed in Calcutta, Michael had no idea at all to which monastery he might be allowed admission, or which form of meditation he might practise, and he still knew hardly anything about the Buddhist religion.

As usual for Michael Dillon, nothing was simple. First he was told in Calcutta that to comply with regulations he would have to take a plane to Chittagong and back again because he had entered India as a seaman and it was necessary for him to re-enter as a tourist. There was no way in which he could get round this.

Michael's intention was to go once more to the monastery where he had previously met the Tibetan lama and ask permission to stay there for a while, as a guest, to learn how to meditate and receive instruction in the Buddhist religion. He felt that he should use this opportunity to change himself, become a better person. If he could change himself, then his life would change for the better, he felt.

The next four years were to be more physically, mentally and emotionally exhausting than anything else Michael had ever known. Even changing sex was not as alien an experience as going to India and trying to enter a Buddhist monastery. He had no letters of introduction, he knew nobody and he was entirely alone. As a middle-aged Westerner who had neither read about nor otherwise come into contact with Buddhist ideas, and with health that was never good at the best of times, nobody could have been less prepared for the life that lay ahead.

Once he had re-entered India in accordance with the regulations, he took a plane to Siliguri, the nearest airfield to Kalimpong, where the monastery he had previously visited was situated. He carried the card of the head lama, Dhardoh Rimpoche, in his pocket. From Siliguri airport he had to take a bus to the monastery, where he expected to be welcomed with the equivalent of open arms.

But in the year or so that had elapsed since Michael's last visit a peculiar incident had occurred which was to make the monastery very wary of middle-aged Westerners announcing that they wanted to become Buddhists, or monks, and live the Eastern contemplative life. A French former Catholic nun had persuaded the Rimpoche to make her a Buddhist nun, or *getsulma*. The result was sheer havoc, for no sooner had the woman been accepted than she began to bring charges of rape and sexual assault against various monks and laymen in the area. It transpired that she was also a communist agent and was endeavouring to obtain sensitive information from the area. In the end the Prime Minister, Jawaharlal Nehru, got to hear of it, and finished the affair by declaring that the woman must be mentally ill. The story caused a huge scandal in India in 1958 and ended with the former nun returning to France to write a book about Buddhism.

As this incident was so fresh in their memories, the monks were not exactly enthusiastic about welcoming another odd Westerner who had suddenly arrived on their doorstep without any warning. Michael arrived at the Rimpoche's house tired and hungry, anticipating a rapturous welcome. But the Rimpoche would not see him. He sent his attendant down with a brief message that he was ill –

together with some tea and biscuits for Michael. Having been refused admittance, Michael sat down by the door with his bag, wondering what to do next.

Hours later the attendant came out again and said he had been ordered to take Michael to another monastery in Kalimpong, one which was run by an Englishman who had become a monk there. Michael was deeply disappointed; at the time he knew nothing of the reason for his being refused admittance.

Before entering this monastery, he made one last break with his former life, by throwing his pipe, reliable comforter since Oxford days, over a cliff. It was something he knew he would have to renounce if he were to live the life of a monk.

Once at the English monastery, Michael confided his whole story to the English monk, the *bhikshu*, mistakenly believing that in a holy place his confidences would be respected. He was to stay in this monastery for four months, paying five rupees a day for his keep and making himself useful by typing out manuscripts for his host and working in the garden. Michael had always enjoyed gardening, from the time when he bought his house in Ballsbridge, Dublin.

The monastery was set, Michael records, in a beautiful spot, on top of a mountain two miles from Kalimpong. Darjeeling could be glimpsed from the verandah and, below, the river Teesta. Michael's accommodation consisted of a room eight feet by six, containing a hard wooden bed. As he lay down on this bed at night, he blessed his foresight in sleeping out on deck while still on the *City of Bath*.

Although Michael was not yet a Buddhist and still knew very little about the religion, he took part in all the services, which started at six o'clock in the morning with *puja*, or temple service. This service would be followed by meditation lasting up to an hour. Soon, Michael forgot his despondency and disappointment at not being able to stay at the 'real' monastery. He went down to visit the Rimpoche, who on this occasion accepted the pictures which Michael had bought as a present.

As his own monastery was run by an Englishman, Westerners often came to visit. Michael requested that on no account should his true identity be revealed, and the *bhikshu* gave him the name of Jivaka ('doctor'). He was to adopt this name as his own, renouncing Michael Dillon completely. When, later, Michael came to write books about Buddhism and his experiences, he used only the name Lobzang ('ordained monk') Jivaka.

Michael took trouble to learn all he could about Buddhism at the English monastery, but the *bhikshu* refused to teach him anything formally, his excuse being that Michael 'learned too fast'; and rather than giving him the run of his library, as Michael had hoped, he picked out books himself for Michael to read.

One day a Tibetan lama came to the English monastery and offered to take Michael to the town of Sarnath, a place he had not previously heard of but was soon to get to know well. Michael would be able to stay for a time in the *Dharmsala*, or pilgrims' resting place, free, and only have to provide his own food. At the same time he could learn more about Buddhism as there was a huge library at Sarnath. He would also be able to attend the Sanskrit University at Varanasi, a few miles away from Sarnath.

Michael's serious interest in Buddhism now began. While at Sarnath he read everything he could about it and started to write prolifically, too. It now became his intention to earn a living solely by writing, and not to rely on his capital. Indeed, it was not long before he wrote to his lawyer, John Duff of Messrs Orpen and Co. in Dublin, asking him to dispose of his estate while he was still alive, so that he could cut off ties as completely as possible from his old life.

Michael soon realized that Gurdjieff, whom he had admired for so long, had taken very many of his precepts from Buddhism. From studying Gurdjieff it was a comparatively short step to becoming a Buddhist and embracing all the ideas wholeheartedly.

While at Sarnath Michael completed his first book on Buddhism, called *Practising*, which was published by an Indian publisher; this book was never to appear in the West.

As his interest in Buddhism deepened, Michael began to contemplate renouncing the world forever. After all, it had let him down badly in his view. Increasingly, the values of the world were to have little appeal for him, and before long he asked to become ordained. Michael was at first ordained a *sramenera*, or novice-monk, of the Theravadin Order of the Hinayana school, the form of Buddhism generally adopted in Burma, Ceylon, Thailand and Cambodia. Later he was to repudiate this order for another one, the Mahayana (found mainly in Tibet, China and Japan), although he kept the name Lobzang Jivaka. The Hinayana division of Buddhism, whose followers wear yellow robes, is directed towards self-salvation.

Michael adopted this one because it was the sect favoured by his English guru. Later, when he came into contact with Tibetan monks who favoured the Mahayana school, he felt this was more suitable for him. Mahayana Buddhists wear dark red robes rather than yellow ones.

Michael had been ordained a *sramenera* in Sarnath, and when he returned to Kalimpong he decided to give up the last of his worldly possessions – the remains of his navy pay-off, about £130, and his treasured signet ring bearing the family crest, which had been given to him by his cousin Daphne on his 21st birthday. He gave them to the English monk. It did not cause him much sorrow to part with the money, but it was a real wrench to let go of the signet ring. Over the years it had acquired an almost talismanic value. It had served to remind Michael of who he was when working in the garage, and of being laughed at by the other garage hands for being a boy-woman; it had accompanied him to Rooksdown House during the terrible years of the surgical operations; it had been with him all round the world. It had been with him when his brother Robert rejected him; and it was with him when he passed his finals and became a qualified doctor. Until now, it had never been taken off his finger. But Michael felt that the last links with his old life had to be broken. Also, he no longer wanted to be reminded that he came from the English aristocracy. He just wanted to be a humble Buddhist monk, living the same life as all other Buddhist monks, with no special privileges or favours granted him.

Michael soon realized that the gifts and the money from his navy pay-off were not put to good effect at all. The *bhikshu* used to provide board and lodging for a large number of Hindu youths who were glad to escape from their strict families while they went to school. The Hindu youths took every advantage of the *bhikshu*, and even told Michael they only liked him for what they could get out of him. For his part, the *bhikshu* regarded them as his extended family, as if they were his own sons.

When the *bhikshu* was out of funds he could not afford to have the youths to stay, but now he had a huge sum of money. Their fathers paid only one rupee a day for their upkeep, and for the rest they sponged off the *bhikshu*. The youths were loud and noisy, and interrupted Michael when he tried to work, write or meditate. When Michael complained about them, the *bhikshu* just told him to find himself another room. Before very long Michael was sadly disillusioned. He finally accepted that the English *bhikshu*, whom he had regarded as a guru and to whom he had donated all his worldly wealth, was not interested in him at all and did not want to teach him anything.

There were other problems. With so many youths now living in the monastery, the money ran out quickly and food became scarce. Without any preparation, Michael had suddenly had to change to a vegetarian diet, which he found hard to take. As is well known, any radical change of diet – even from an unhealthy to a healthy one – takes time to get used to, and at first the stomach may rebel. All his life Michael had been a hearty eater and a dedicated carnivore. Now he was presented with rice and curried vegetables at every meal. In the 1950s Indian restaurants were not very common in England, so this would have been almost Michael's first experience of Indian food of any kind. It did not seem to suit him at all. He simply could not eat enough of the rice to keep himself full, for he suffered from stomach bloating after eating only a little. He found that within half an hour of eating the rice he would be ravenously hungry again, and yet he could not eat enough to satisfy himself at mealtimes.

At first one egg a day had been provided at breakfast for the former meat-eaters, but soon the supply of eggs ran out and, not long after that, the butter – always quite a luxury in India at the best of times. So breakfast was reduced to two small slices of dry bread, there being no money for any more interesting food.

Michael wondered what the *bhikshu* could have done with all the money, as the sum given him was at the time a truly vast one in the context of an Indian monastery. He soon discovered that the *bhikshu* often 'lent' sums to the Hindu youths. Before long Michael was starving, and in desperation he went to an Englishwoman, married to a local landowner, who lived nearby, and begged her for breakfast.

It soon became clear to Michael that he could not stay at the monastery. The atmosphere was no longer conducive to work or meditation and, in addition, he was not getting anything like enough to eat. Michael records in his book *Imji Getsul* that within a year of arriving in India he lost two stone. But he makes no mention of his hypoglycaemia, and in spite of being constantly underfed he never seemed to pass out in India.

Something else was now troubling Michael deeply. From his avid reading about Buddhism he had discovered a reference to a 'third sex', referring to people who are not properly either male or female. He found that anybody belonging to this 'third sex' would be automatically denied Higher Ordination, which was the next step after the initial ordination procedure. He learned also that anybody who had suffered any form of bodily mutilation, such as the loss of a hand, foot or eye, or who suffered from certain diseases, would be banned from this Higher Ordination. By this time Michael had become anxious to receive Higher Ordination himself, and naturally wondered how the ban in the Buddhist canon would apply to his own case. He was obviously a member of the 'third sex', and in addition had undergone many surgical mutilations – removal of breasts, numerous skin grafts, the construction of a penis. He also suffered from low blood sugar and was prone to pass out. Would all this past history mean that he could never become a fully-fledged Buddhist monk?

In the Buddha's day there had been logical reasons for the ban on anybody who was mutilated or disabled. In the first place, many of those who had lost a hand, or an eye, may have suffered judicial mutilation for being criminals. Clearly, the Buddha would not want those among his followers. In those early days, moreover, monks often lived in the jungle and had to walk through it while begging. Naturally, they would have to have been able-bodied to be able to cope with this life. Michael learned later that in modern times, when many people are mutilated as a result of traffic or other accidents, or wounded in war, the ban has all but disappeared. Nevertheless, he was very worried about whether his past history would preclude him from the type of ordination he now sought. So he asked the *bhikshu,* to whom he had already confided everything, about it.

The *bhikshu,* who was an adherent of the Hinayana school of Buddhism, was extremely contemptuous when Michael anxiously asked him about the Higher Ordination. He replied that it might be a possibility eventually, but not for at least another three or four years.

Michael felt sick at heart at being so let down, especially as he had given his most precious possession, his signet ring, to this man. He also felt he understood the Englishman's reluctance to teach him, or to take any real notice of him. The reason was, he suspected, that the *bhikshu* had been so used to exerting his authority over the natives that he did not kindly welcome a rival – somebody who was upper-class, well-educated and well-connected. Michael decided that he could no longer stay at the monastery.

So sadly, after three months, he left. He was beginning to wonder already, however, whether he had chosen correctly in becoming ordained in the Hinayana school which, he said, adhered strongly to the letter, rather than the spirit, of the law.

Michael went back to Sarnath, where after a few months he was offered Higher Ordination by one of the *bhikshus* there. He decided to come clean and mention that he came under one of the absolute bans – and even told him which one, which must have been extremely difficult for him. Part of the reason why Michael had been so shattered when the press found out about him was that he never wanted to admit to himself, let alone anybody else, that he was really female. He had done everything he possibly could to repudiate any signs of femaleness in himself and present himself as a true male. Now, wherever he went, he was having to tell people who and what he really was. It is impossible to guess what the reaction of these Buddhist monks must have been. Few people in India even today have heard of sex change, and the idea must have been even more incongruous in the late 1950s. But at any rate the monks did not turn Michael out, or impose the ban on his Higher Ordination. Meanwhile, however, no one could decide exactly what to do; until such time as this happened Michael was to remain at the Maha Bodhi Society at Sarnath, near Varanasi.

He spent his time reading and writing. By now completely poverty-stricken, he thought he would attempt to earn some money quickly by writing. So he sent off articles, short stories and poems to Indian and Buddhist newspapers and magazines. Occasionally these were accepted. He managed to sell a short story about his faithful blue and white bicycle – which he had had to sell on arrival in Calcutta – to *The Sunday Statesman* for 90 rupees (about £6 at the time). But always there was a long wait between sending off the typescript and receiving payment, so he was constantly short. Letters he wrote at the time to English friends reveal that he often had to send several letters to different people in one envelope, as he simply did not have the money to send them separately. The recipient would be asked to post them on in England.

Before leaving the English monastery, he had started writing a popular version of a book entitled *The Life of Milarepa* (Milarepa was a famous eleventh-century Tibetan yogi), which was an adaptation of the original translation by W. Y. Evans-Wentz published in 1928. The existing version was, Michael felt, too academic and inaccessible for a general readership. He also wrote for it a general introduction about the Tibetan form of Buddhism.

He finished the book in the middle of 1959, about a year after he had 'disappeared'. No more stories had appeared about him in the newspapers and the world appeared to have forgotten about the unusual ship's doctor. His friends had kept their word and not revealed his identity to anybody. In search of a publisher, Michael wrote first to the Oxford University Press, which was not interested at all as it had published the original Evans-Wentz edition and did not want to issue another book on the same subject. Dr Evans-Wentz, an American scholar, was still alive, although very elderly. Michael then tried John Murray in London, which published books on Eastern religions as part of its list and was at that time engaged in a big series entitled *Wisdom of the East*, edited by Jack Cranmer-Byng. Murray seemed eminently suitable as a potential publisher, and so Michael Dillon wrote from Sarnath on 7 December 1959:

> Dear Sir,
>
> I am writing to enquire whether you would be interested in a popular edition version of Milarepa; the only edition in English being Evans-Wentz in Oxford University Press, which is not a publisher much frequented by the general public. Yet the story of Milarepa is full of human interest. I have rewritten it from Evans-Wentz' edition, omitting the archaic 'thees' and 'thous', paraphrasing where it is too dismissive or too technical for the lay reader and altering it somewhat. It is in a racy style (as the original Tibetan was) to make for easy reading. At the end there is about 5000 words to explain the main principle of Buddhism and questions that might arise out of the work. If you think you might be interested I will try and raise the postage to send it to you.
> The whole is 55,000 words.
>
> Yours faithfully,
>
> Jivaka (*sramenera* = novice monk) M.A., M.B., B.Ch.

On 17 December Simon Young, then a senior editor at John Murray, wrote back as follows:

> Dear Mr Jivaka,
>
> Thank you for your letter offering us a popular version of Milarepa. As it happens, we have just published a translation of some of his poems by Sir Humphrey Clarke in our *Wisdom of the East* series.

Perhaps you could get hold of a copy (they are distributed by the Allied Publishers Ltd, 15, Graham Road, Ballard Estate, Bombay) to see if this covers the same ground as your project would. It is not quite clear from your letter whether you intended to do a version of his life or of his poems. Incidentally, we would be interested to hear your opinion of Sir Humphrey Clarke's book.

Encouraged by this response, Michael wrote back to Simon Young on receipt of his letter, on 23 December:

Dear Sir,

In reply to your letter of Dec. 17, I have indeed seen and enjoyed Clarke's little volume of Milarepa's poems. Christmas Humphreys (a famous British lawyer and practising Buddhist) gave us £5 of books for the library here according to our selection from a catalogue, and it was the one I chose. No, my ms. does not cover the same ground at all. Rather, it is complementary. You must have read Evans-Wentz' 'Milarepa: Tibet's Great Yogi', Oxford U.P., a second edition was published a couple of years ago after about 20 years. OUP publications are usually too learned for the man in the street and E-W's version is no less so, with innumerable footnotes, abstruse Tibetan terms and long introductions; also the use of 'thees' and 'thous'. What I have done is to *use his translation* to make an abbreviated and simpler version in a reasonably up to date style (the original was colloquial and I have kept to that) leaving out parts that deal with Tibetan ritual or technicalities, and just giving the life in a readable way. The story is so full of human interest, even in E-W's edition, that updated thus, it could well become very popular. A knowledge of the life of Milarepa is really a necessary background to those poems you have published, to give them a meaningful background; and apart from E.W. there is no other translation or version. *I have given full acknowledgement to him at the start as I am not competent to retranslate at this stage.* If you think you might be interested I will try to raise the air mail postage for it. It is not my first book either under my present name or my Western one.

Yours faithfully,

Jivaka (*sramenera*) M.A. Oxon.

After this letter, Simon Young asked Michael to send the manuscript, adding that it would be necessary to clear the copyright question with Oxford University Press. He added that, as the book was an abridgement of the original Evans-Wentz one, the latter would be entitled to a share of the royalties, were it to be published. Young voiced the possibility that the royalties might be too high for it to be a commercial prospect for John Murray. However, he ended his letter by saying that if the copyright matter could be sorted out they might well be interested in publishing the book in their *Wisdom of the East* series.

On receipt of this letter, Michael got to work. He wrote to Oxford University Press and received a reply to the effect that it would not object to a popular version of *The Life of Milarepa* being published, as it did not imagine that this publication would damage the sale of the original. Having received this assurance, Michael wrote again to Simon Young saying that he would send the manuscript as soon as he could raise the postage. These references to raising the postage in each letter so far sent to John Murray underline how precarious Michael's financial situation was at this time. It is never easy to be in a foreign country without money, but in India it is almost impossible, for although the Indians have a tradition of begging they expect all foreigners – particularly English doctors – to be well off. Help is not therefore readily extended. In his third letter Michael asked Simon Young to send the manuscript to Mrs McKie, wife of his former tutor, in Oxford, rather than back to him in Sarnath.

On 3 February 1960 Michael posted the manuscript off to Simon Young, the covering note containing the final sentence 'Here's hoping!'

He did not hope in vain. John Murray accepted the manuscript on 29 March and set about getting it edited. They wanted the end section put at the beginning as an introduction to Buddhism, as this, according to Simon Young, would be more in keeping with the other books in the series. 'The moment we have arrived at a final version we shall send you an agreement,' Simon Young promised, and asked to know the titles and publishers of his previous works, as the 'Western name' did not seem to be forthcoming.

This posed yet another dilemma for Michael, as he had no intention of allowing his identity to be discovered, even by his publishers. So he had to explain as much as he could in his next letter, dated 4 May 1960:

Dear Mr Young,

That was indeed a welcome letter! By all means transpose the postface into a preface if you think it better . . . I am only too delighted that it is going to be got across to the Western public.

My previous [London] publications [are] two: one half-medical, half-philosophical (I am a doctor as well as a 'Greats' man of Oxford) and a book of Poems, but I do not wish my Western name known. I am heir to a title and have no desire for publicity. Only six people know where I am or what I am doing. My first Buddhist book was published by the Maha Bodhi society of Sarnath last year, but it was stillborn from atrocious printing. The number of mistakes was incredible. Unless it is redone it is no good, although it had a good review in 'World Buddhism' – a full page. The second, 'Growing Up into Buddhism', is for teenagers and young people, and is in press now.

Michael ended his letter with a plea for a 'wee advance' of £12, once the agreement had been drawn up, as he had run completely out of money and could not even buy food. Starvation was, he said in his letter, alleviated only by the arrival of the occasional food parcel from England, which would provide him with what he considered 'real' eatables. For the whole of his time in India Michael was to consider rice and curry his penance for being there.

Of course, Simon Young was much intrigued by Michael's latest letter. An Oxford 'Greats' man, a doctor, heir to a title – was it all true, and, if so, what could Jivaka be doing in India? Simon wrote to Canon Millbourn for more information. However, on the subject of Jivaka's identity he would not budge; he told Young that Jivaka's intentions were perfectly honourable, and that he had his own very good reasons for wanting to remain incognito.

Matters progressed rapidly with *The Life of Milarepa*, although, as it turned out, it was not to be published until April 1962, a month before Michael died. John Murray agreed to send him £4 to cover postage, and expressed interest in any further manuscripts that he might have on related subjects. Michael did not need telling twice: over the next year or so he was to deluge John Murray and later his literary agent John Johnson, whom John Murray found for him, with manuscripts, poems, synopses and outlines for further books. In the event, John Johnson succeeded in placing only one more, *Imji Getsul*, although he would undoubtedly have had much greater success if it had been known that 'Jivaka' was the same Dr Dillon whose story had so astonished the world only a couple of years previously.

The *Life* was sent to Jack Cranmer-Byng for editing, and in his initial letter to the editor John Murray himself wrote:

As to the author: he writes from India from the Maha Bodhi Society. He writes very friendly, sensible letters and appears to be studying Buddhism the hard way. He is a doctor and a 'Greats' man from Oxford, and he has written poems, and his first Buddhist book was issued by the Society last year. For some reason or other he does not want his Western name known. He has other projects in mind about which he is telling us in due course.

John Murray added in his letter, dated 26 April 1960, that 'Mr Jivaka' had got in touch with the firm because he had so much enjoyed its edition of the Milarepa poems.

The Life of Milarepa, which was so eagerly accepted by John Murray (although the firm only paid what sounds like an extremely low advance of £25 in total), is probably Michael Dillon's best book. It contains an interesting and readable introduction to Buddhism and was last reprinted in 1979. Michael would have been pleased to know that it remained on John Murray's list for so many years.

In his introduction Michael explains the nature of the guru relationship, of which there is no exact counterpart in the West. Nowadays most people are familiar with the notion of gurus and Eastern religions, but in the early 1960s the explosion of interest in meditation, Zen Buddhism and allied subjects had not yet happened. It was set in motion mainly by the books of Lobzang Rampa, which continued to sell well even when he was discredited. Michael Dillon was probably one of the first Westerners to go on the 'hippy trail' in search of the truth – even though he was in his mid-forties by the time he did so and the word 'hippy' had not yet been invented. He also writes in his introduction about the psychic powers of yogis, something which had exercised the West for many years. Are they genuine, or are they faked? A true yogi, Michael wrote, has very definitely developed higher, or psychic, powers, but he will not display these to a curious public for either monetary gain or fame.

'These psychic powers' (he writes in his introduction) 'have been well attested down the centuries by responsible persons. They come with the practice of mind control and are known in very attenuated forms in the West as "natural gifts" in a few men and women, who may make a career for themselves as "mediums", or else are so frightened by their abilities they suppress them and prefer not even to think about them.'

The phenomenon of Vital Heat, whereby Tibetan yogis can sit out in the snow, naked, and melt the snow round them by raising their own body temperature, is well known in the East, as is telepathy. By the time he wrote the introduction to his *Life of Milarepa*, Michael has already accepted most of the tenets of Eastern religions, for which his wide reading of Gurdjieff had prepared him, and in the few years that remained to him he was to embrace all the 'wisdom of the East', including belief in reincarnation, telepathy and psychic powers as matters of fact, not merely aspects of faith.

He also provides a useful explanation of the doctrine of karma, which must have brought much comfort to Michael once he had heard about it and understood it. Briefly, this doctrine, accepted without question by both Buddhists and Hindus in the East, maintains that as you sow, so shall you reap. In the context of many lifetimes, things which may seem unfair in one life, such as disability, poverty or otherwise harsh circumstances, are believed to have been brought on the individual by mistakes made or crimes committed in a previous life or lives. Karma does not imply punishment by God for past misdeeds: simply that the individual's own past actions shape his present situation.

It is easy to see why the doctrine of karma should have appealed so much to Michael once he came to terms with it. It would mean that, somehow, he had been fated to be born into a female body, even though the non-physical part of him felt absolutely male. According to the law of karma, he would have had some 'unfinished business' to work out as a female before he could go on to his next 'incarnation'. The soul is considered to be neuter, and according to the doctrine can occupy any number of both male and female bodies. Usually, of course, individuals keep the same gender during the lifetime of a single body, although some people perceive that they have to change to complete their karma in this life.

The doctrine of karma is by no means accepted by all transsexuals, but it certainly offers an explanation, and one which made complete sense to Michael after he had finally repudiated Christianity, which offered no explanation whatever of his predicament. According to karma, whatever had happened to him was the result of something he had done in a previous life, or lives. Those individuals who are unhappy, ill or poverty-stricken are generally spoken of as having 'bad karma'. It is very often these individuals who turn towards Eastern religions, in the hope of changing their karma, or improving it, by good actions. This was probably a major factor in Michael's behaviour. He had tried to live his present life as a lie, and had been found out. He had therefore accumulated more bad karma, which he now had to work off. The harsh life of the Buddhist monk would, he thought, enable him to do that. All things considered, it is remarkable how much of Buddhism Michael had come to understand in just a year.

Truth, he wrote in his introduction, is received at different levels in accordance with the hearer's own degree of spiritual development. If hearers do not understand what they hear as truth, they may be sure that the fault lies in themselves, not in the doctrine. The four Noble Truths of Buddhism are that suffering is a characteristic of life on Earth; that the cause of suffering is desire; that cessation of desire procures cessation of suffering; and that the means to that cessation is by the noble eightfold path of rightful living.

Certainly Michael wanted an end to his suffering. He perceived that his earnest desire to be male had caused great suffering, for him and for others in his life. In the end it had not brought happiness, only more suffering. In fact, it seemed that the suffering would never end.

The Noble Eightfold Path consists, he tells us, of right viewpoint, right aim, right speech, right conduct, right livelihood, right effort, right mindfulness and right concentration. When an individual manages to live by this eightfold path and achieves enlightenment, the whole cycle of birth and death and rebirth stops. Once there is no more karma to be paid off, there are no more births, according to Buddhism.

After the introduction, there follows a well-written and exciting account of the life of Milarepa, who endured many hardships on his way to becoming enlightened. Michael must have identified strongly with his subject's sufferings, his own having been so great – although, to the minds of many, entirely self-imposed.

While engaged in his literary labours, Michael was becoming increasingly disillusioned with the form of Buddhism he had encountered so far (Hinayana); he was becoming far more attracted to the Tibetan variety, as described in *The Life of Milarepa*. He now began to be interested in the Mahayana, rather than the Hinayana, sect, and wanted to learn all about it. At Sarnath Michael met Lama Lobzang, a Tibetan monk who was later to become a friend, and asked to be re-ordained into the Tibetan form of Buddhism. Surprisingly, this appeared to present no problem.

Michael wrote to the English Buddhist monk who had put him up at Kalimpong asking if he would like to attend the ordination. There was no reply to this invitation; instead, the English monk sent a letter to Lama Lobzang telling him all about Michael and breaking every confidence which had been vouchsafed to him. When confronted, the English monk protested that it was his duty to defend and protect the monkhood, and that Jivaka was not a suitable person for ordination, in his view, as he was a member of the 'third sex' for whom the ban on ordination is absolute.

Michael felt completely betrayed. All other considerations aside, this was the man to whom he had given his most precious possession, his signet ring. His sense of betrayal was heightened by the fact that the Tibetan lama would not now ordain him.

About a month after this accident, the Dalai Lama came to Sarnath for a month and Michael asked Lama Lobzang to tell his whole story to one of the religious leader's senior staff. This resulted in Michael meeting Koshok Bakula, a widely respected lama who came from the Ladakhi royal family and who was later to become his personal guru. Kushok, Michael records, gave him a look of compassion which he could never forget, and said that it was not at all impossible for him to be ordained. He must however wait until the fuss had died down.

The upshot was that Michael was eventually re-ordained a novice monk in the Tibetan order, to be known in future as a *'getsul'*, which means 'Tibetan-ordained-Buddhist-monk', thus becoming the first (perhaps the only) Westerner ever to do this. His name of Jivaka could not now be changed, as he had already become quite well known in Buddhist circles for his writings. So the word 'Lobzang', ordained monk, was added to it, and this became his name for the brief remainder of his life.

11

Imji Getsul

ALMOST as soon as Michael had been ordained, in the summer of 1960, it was suggested that he should pay a visit to a monastery in Ladakh, as he could not go into Tibet. The idea was that he would learn at first hand about life in a Tibetan monastery and would live just like all the other monks. This experience was to form the basis of Michael's next, and best-known, book, *Imji Getsul*, which has for many years been recommended reading for travellers to that part of the world.

Michael Dillon had now been living in Buddhist monasteries of one kind or another for eighteen months, and was slowly coming to the conclusion that he did not want to return to the West at all, but to stay in India as an ordained monk for the rest of his life.

Survival remained a terrible struggle, however. He was now writing prolifically and sending articles off to every Indian and Buddhist publication he could think of. But he faced the problem that all freelance writers face: the long gap between having a piece of writing accepted by a publisher and getting paid for it. Added to that, the payments made by the publications to which he sent his material were extremely low. He wrote:

> When an article was accepted by a paying journal there was a long wait until its publication and the arrival of the cheque. *Indo-Asian Culture* was a good paying proposition, but a quarterly, and so the wait was prolonged. *The Aryan Path* paid on acceptance, though at lesser rate, but the editress was kind, although we had never met, and would send books for review when my need was greatest. The *U.K. Citizens' Monthly* paid fairly quickly but not highly. The best payer was the *Sunday*

Statesman, to which I offered short stories under a secular name, since they might embody things and situations of which novice monks were better ignorant. And so it went on; looking always for new markets, struggling to pay the postage to England or, optimistically, to America, and finally with success to Australia. In the lean weeks I would exist on credit with the char wallah, who also was kind and paid my little milk bill and gave me bread until a remittance came and I could pay him off. But in those days there was no butter, much less jam, no eggs, no fruit, only the bread and milk and roti [Indian bread] and dhal [lentils] for lunch. And then I would rapidly lose weight. And as soon as a remittance came the char wallah would have to be paid, stamps would have to be bought in the hope of earning another cheque, paper and carbon were needed before ever food could be sought. Robes, of course, were supplied free by the ordaining *bhikshu.*

Michael could have easily averted this struggle if he had not divested himself of all his capital and assets by making a 'will' and having it executed while he was still alive. Only two years previously Toto had died leaving him about £12,000, which would have been plenty to live on in luxury in India for many years. But, as he writes in *Imji Getsul,* rather than do this he 'brought a degree of social security to persons who had been lacking it through no fault of their own'.

Most of the time he was pretty near starvation level, as he had to provide his own food. As he was to write in *Imji Getsul,* published a month before his death in May 1962: 'It was food, food and the means by which food was to be acquired, that was the sole and ever-present problem.'

He had already lost over two stone in weight, and was becoming dangerously emaciated. He neither enjoyed nor became used to the vegetarian diet to which his religion bound him, and constantly longed for what he considered a proper meal (he admits to having visions of bacon, eggs and hot buttered toast with coffee). Vegetarianism was in those days generally considered very cranky in the West, and as a doctor he regarded the meatless diet as unhealthy, since it did not contain enough high-quality protein.

Michael wrote about the vegetarian diet in *Imji Getsul:*

To this I never succeeded in becoming accustomed . . . the eternal rice and curried vegetables, all tasting exactly the same, was a hard trial, but one which had to be endured, for I had but little money with which to buy extras after paying for my keep and I was permanently hungry.

From his writings it seems that Michael never understood the doctrinal reason for the vegetarian diet – that of not causing violence to other living creatures or consuming the results of that violence. He merely felt deprived, and could see no harm in eating meat.

For all of his four years in India Michael was never really well; he was always teetering on the edge of starvation and liable to succumb to peculiar illnesses. There is little reference to these illnesses in his published writings, although his letters to John Murray and Simon Young at the time indicate that his health was not good. Michael never makes any mention of the effect of the sudden withdrawal of male hormone, although after so many years of taking it his body must have been affected in some way. The years of taking testosterone may have adversely affected his liver, as it was liver trouble which plagued him most often and one side-effect of too much testosterone is liver damage (however, this may not have been known in Michael's day).

He was now studying at the Sanskrit University of Varanasi, near Sarnath, and being guided by Professor Guenther, an eminent Tibetan scholar there. One day in November 1959, as Michael was having lunch with the Professor, Guenther suggested that he might like to spend some time in a real Tibetan monastery. Tibet itself was closed to visitors, but there were plenty of suitable monasteries in the small neighbouring country of Ladakh. Guenther suggested a particular monastery, Rizong, which was especially strict, honouring all the practices laid down by the Buddha – more than could be said for most of the monasteries in the area. It would, said Guenther, provide excellent training for Michael, who seemed so sincere in his wish to become a proper Buddhist monk and, moreover, seemed to be veering ever closer to the Tibetan form of Buddhism. For Michael's own part, he at last felt that his search for truth was at an end – he had found the one true path.

Until this time Michael had never even heard of the country of Ladakh, which at the time was a disputed territory between India and China occupied by the Indian Army, If he were to go he would have to get a special permit, for Westerners were not normally allowed there at the time. Ladakh was officially opened to tourists in 1974 and is now considered part of India, remaining under army occupation. It has, however, its own language (Ladakhi) and royal family.

Owing to the high altitude and the impassability of the only road, covered in snow for at least half the year, Michael would not be able to go to Ladakh until the following summer. It was suggested to him that before going he might like to spend a couple of months in Kashmir with the guru Kushok Bakula, if a permit could be obtained. Michael knew that it would not be easy, and that he would have to satisfy the authorities that his reasons for wanting to go were absolutely non-political.

So the following spring, after finishing off *The Life of Milarepa* and posting the manuscript to Simon Young at John Murray, Michael set off with some Tibetan monks to Kashmir, where he was to apply for a permit. His guru, Kushok Bakula, was to be his sponsor in this enterprise. In the event, it took two months for the permit to come through. At last, in July 1960, Michael flew alone from Srinagar to Leh, the capital of Ladakh, in a military aeroplane. The other monks who were going to be there with him had already gone, by jeep. By not travelling by jeep, Michael missed the acclimatization, now re-cognized as essential for people who are not used to such high altitudes. The journey by road takes at least two days from Srinagar in Kashmir – longer if there is an army convoy on the road, as in many places the road is single-lane and army vehicles always take preced-ence. Also, dramatic though the views are from the air, he missed seeing one of the wonders of the world, as there is nothing quite so thrilling as the panorama visible from the bumpy and sometimes dangerous road from Srinagar to Leh. Even in July, not all the snow and ice has gone and vehicles have to pass through vast, eerie banks of melting ice on each side of the road.

Although Ladakh now has a thriving tourist industry, it has not basically changed since Michael Dillon landed at Leh's military airport just outside the capital. One of the highest countries in the world, with an altitude of about 4000 metres, Ladakh is a bare, barren, brown, mountainous country, with touches of startling green in the valleys, where apricots and barley are grown. It has about four inches of rainfall (in a good year) and is full of gentle-faced Buddhist monks walking the streets in their dark red, usually dirty and stained, robes.

Most people find that their life is never the same again once they have been to Ladakh, and Michael Dillon was no exception. It is hard to visit the country and not be deeply affected by it. There are monasteries *(gompas)* everywhere, built into the hillside. The houses are little square buildings with tiny square windows, and generally the people still wear their national costume, consisting of a singular high hat with wings on each side, and maroon or brown robes with bright pink or peacock blue sashes. Both men and women have pigtails, and often wool is woven into the hair to make the pigtail longer and more luxuriant. Most of the people are devout Buddhists and go around with their prayer wheels, intoning as they walk. The country also has many *stupas*, or shrines, and it is not uncommon to come across whole fields of them. The whole country exudes spirituality in a way that no other place in the world does.

Ladakh is also one of the few countries in the world to practise polyandry, which permits women to take more than one husband. Because of this, and because so many boys become monks at the age of four or five, the population has hardly increased for centuries. Polyandry is a logical system for a country like Ladakh, which has few natural resources and can support only a very small population.

Michael Dillon's permit was for three months, which he was to spend at Rizong, possibly the most remote monastery in the world, both then and now: even today it features on few tourist maps, and often even experienced guides have never heard of it. For this reason it has kept all its treasures intact, whereas they have mostly disappeared from the more accessible monasteries, which were often rifled by thoughtless tourists before the monks realized what was happening, started to charge admission fees and, rather than giving things away, began selling them. Rizong is full of beautiful *tankas*, or wall hangings, jewels, carvings and paintings; it has an air of lushness. As with all other monasteries, doors are small – only about four feet high – which forces you to bend before going through them. This is supposed to teach monks, and visitors, humility.

Rizong is not an ancient monastery. It was built in 1829 on seven levels on a sheer rock face, 3450 metres high. It takes about one-and-a-half hours of arduous uphill walking to get to the *gompa* from the main road. Down at the bottom, near the road, is a Buddhist nunnery known as Chulie Chen. Rizong is approached through groves of apricot trees and sparkling streams and the walk, for one who is feeling well and strong, is quite magical, almost like stepping on to another planet. The first glimpse of Rizong is spectacular. Large and well-built, it occupies a commanding position in beautiful scenery.

Michael felt that his main reason for coming to Rizong was to break down his '*sahib*' personality – the tendency to judge people by whether they had cultured accents or were good-looking. He was to get plenty of practice at this during his three months in the monastery. He requested that he should not be treated as anybody special (and certainly not regarded as an English doctor) but exactly as all the other newly-ordained monks, who would have been about twelve years of age, and carry out similar duties.

One of the first things Michael discovered in Ladakh was that he had to adjust dramatically his ideas relating to personal hygiene. As the country is so very short of water, washing is a luxury and therefore not something that is indulged in very often. At first he was dismayed when dirt became ingrained in his hands, elbows and knees and he could not wash it off. Occasionally he would go down to the stream and strip down to dark red swimming trunks, to the amusement of the other monks. The head lama at Rizong had never in his life seen bathing trunks before; he stood and stared as Michael washed himself with a bit of soap he had brought with him. This was reasonably pleasant at the height of summer but as it grew colder, towards autumn, the freezing mountain stream held less allure. Michael tried to get used to this, writing, as if to persuade himself:

> For centuries the peoples of Ladakh had lived successfully without the excessive washing that takes place as a matter of course in other parts of the world.

His other cleanliness problem concerned his dark red robe. He, like the other monks, possessed only one. Washing it would have been difficult as the robe consisted of 7½ metres of very heavy wool cloth, and it would have taken several days to dry. In the meantime, he would have had no other clothing to wear. As he was working in the kitchen he soon became extremely dirty and ragged, but had to stay that way.

The kitchen in the *gompa* had no modern appliances. It was (and is) a large blackened room with a cauldron containing the famous yak butter tea bubbling away in the middle. All the cooking was done in huge cauldrons, and was organized to make the least amount of work, so that the monks would have as much time as possible for the services, and their 'real' work of raising their spiritual consciousness. The floor of the kitchen was swept occasionally but never washed – water was far too precious to be wasted on a kitchen floor. The tea kettles were polished with ashes rather than proprietary brass cleaner, and were kept shining.

Michael soon found that at Rizong even the curried rice and vegetables were not available. Rice, which is not grown in Ladakh, is considered a luxury. Instead, everybody eats *tsampa,* a kind of porridge made with barley, the only grain crop the country produces, and whatever vegetables are available, whether grown locally or imported from Kashmir. Radishes are fairly common and Michael was to become very familiar with the boiled version. Also, there were, and are, plenty of apricots in season. But mainly the diet is monotonous in the extreme, as the natural resources of the country are so limited.

At Rizong, famed for its strict adherence to ancient Buddhist rules, none of the monks ate after midday, but they could eat as much as they liked of whatever food was on offer before this time. Michael soon discovered that the food situation was even worse than at Sarnath. He was practically always at starvation point, and this made it difficult for him to get to sleep. He soon lost yet more weight and became very weak. But, according to his book, he seemed to remain cheerful enough. At least here at Rizong everybody accepted him.

The other factor that bothered him was an almost complete lack of privacy. Yet Michael had more than most. While the boy monks slept on the floor in dormitories, Michael was granted his own tiny cell in which to work, translate and have time to himself. But every time Michael tried to work in his room, translating or studying Tibetan, somebody would come in and want to talk. Conversation was fairly limited as few of the monks could speak any English, but Michael was trying to teach himself Tibetan and Ladakhi. One of his tasks while there was to teach the head lama English, too, but both found this extremely difficult. At first Michael wondered how it was that a man who had assimilated huge books of Buddhist doctrine a thousand pages long should have so much trouble with a few simple words of English. It may be that Michael himself was not a very good teacher, however.

Michael's social status at Rizong ranked above the child novices but below that of the youths, who had been ordained for far longer than he (Buddhist monks remain novices even after their initial ordinations, when they become *gelongs;* only after receiving Higher Ordination do they cease to be novices). From the start, he insisted on being regarded exactly as any other novice, although he had brought his stethoscope and other medical instruments with him. The others remained rather in awe of the English doctor. (The name 'Jivaka' had been given to him because it was the name of the Buddha's physician.) He was set to work in the kitchen, to cook and prepare vegetables and *tsampa* for the monks to eat. After the preparation was done, he would have to dole out the food to the other monks before eating himself – and very often, he recalls ruefully in his book, he would find only dirty water instead of soup or any solid edible matter.

The rest of his day, starting long before dawn, was taken up with *pujas,* or temple services. These were held mainly in the early morning or early afternoon, and attendance was compulsory: there was no excuse for missing *puja.* The *pujas* themselves were by no means all the same, and would follow various patterns, according to whether they were non-musical, slightly musical or very musical. Their purpose was to procure an altered state of consciousness by the interaction of mind and body through reacting to musical sounds, different sitting positions and intonations. The non-musical *pujas* were the most tedious and monks often nodded off during these. Yak butter tea was served at every *puja* and was an integral part of the service.

The *puja,* of which there are 108 different types, all bearing some relation to the positions of the moon, is the Buddhist equivalent of prayer. However, Michael was soon to find out that to the Tibetan Buddhist prayer means something very different from what it means to the Christian. For example, worshippers may not ask for anything or plead forgiveness for sins. There is no interventionist god; each human being has to reach salvation individually, by practising self-discipline and thus achieving the required state of mind for understanding the scriptures. Instead of Christ, or the Holy Ghost, each monk has his own guru, and the relationship between them is sacred. Michael's own guru, Kushok Bakula, was not resident for most of Michael's time in Ladakh, but coincidentally the head lama there was also called Kushok.

A practice which Michael found hard at first was the triple obeisance, in which the monk has to fling himself prostrate on the floor of the temple. He records that the Englishman's ingrained sense of dignity does not easily allow him to do this, although it seems perfectly natural to all Orientals. Although Michael had assimilated a vast amount of Buddhist teaching in a very short time, he found his entrenched English aristocratic outlook on life hard to reconcile with the total humility of Buddhism. It was relatively easy to shake off the Christian teachings, once he understood Buddhism, but he realized that other aspects of his personality were less easy to shed. Michael had been brought up to think that white-skinned English people were far superior to Indians and other Eastern races, and his writings at this time reveal that one of the main reasons why he wanted to be a novice monk and work with 12-year-old boys in the kitchen was so that he could get this completely out of his system.

Michael found that the other monks, of which about 30 were in residence during his stay, accepted him quite readily and regarded him as one of themselves (no one at Rizong knew of Michael's secret).

They also, as Michael discovered, loved to laugh and fool around; they enjoyed practical jokes and an occasional rough-and-tumble. They would tip each other into firewood boxes and then roar with laughter. Michael soon found out that each monk had his own individual character. Some of the monks were likeable and intelligent, while others seemed dim and stupid. The identical dress and the fact most of them had never known any other kind of life did not mean that they were identical in their natures. Michael seemed rather surprised to discover that they were all as different from each other as any set of pupils and teachers would be in an English school. They all worked extremely hard, too, as carpenters (they made *tsampa* pots out of tree trunks), tailors, painters, builders, scribes and domestic servants. The nuns from Chulie Chen were not allowed to work for the monks, either in the kitchen or in any other capacity, because women were not, strictly speaking, allowed in the monastery – other than occasional visitors. The strict segregation was intended to remove any possibility of temptation, both monks and nuns having vowed eternal celibacy.

The monks made their own paper, which looked like furry parchment, and produced their own books. They also dyed their own robes dark red but had to buy the dye. This was almost the only thing they did have to buy, and none of the monks, apart from the head lama, had any money.

The life was harsh but not unhappy. Most of the day was taken up with services of one kind or another, and also hard physical labour, as the monastery was entirely self-sufficient. The monks kept the various temples in the monastery clean and also undertook all the other manual work which was needed to keep the place going, including the tending of Rizong's enormous apricot orchard. They spent the rest of the time copying out books by hand. There were no typewriters or printing presses, but there were – and are – literally thousands of books there. Young monks had to learn whole passages of the scriptures off by heart, and were liable to be given a beating if they missed out parts or had not committed the set texts sufficiently well to memory.

Life at Rizong was not boring. It received a continual stream
of visitors; the Ladakhis themselves made pilgrimages to the
monastery, one of the most beautiful in their country. Also, the
monks often made trips to other monasteries, to festivals and to
the local towns and villages. Overall the monastery was, Michael
records, happy and well-disciplined and the monks worked in
harmony with each other.

After Michael had accepted Kushok Bakula as his guru, he owed
him absolute obedience, as between master and servant. In Buddhism
nobody becomes a guru unless they have shown themselves worthy
of the position, so the novice monk can have complete confidence
in his master. However, this ideal situation does not always obtain,
as Michael had discovered when he tried to make the English *bhikshu*
his guru.

The three months he spent at Rizong were largely happy. The
physical deprivations of the lifestyle served to make him forget, or
at least to put to the back of his mind, the nightmare of being 'found
out' on board ship. He threw himself wholeheartedly into learning
the *puja*, cooking, chopping up firewood – in short, doing everything that was asked, including, at times, small medical tasks. He
found it all tremendously exciting, moreover, for he was learning
about a way of life never experienced at first hand by any other
Westerner.

Not all of Michael's time in Ladakh was spent at Rizong. From
time to time the monks would go on visits and excursions, and on
rain-making expeditions. The 'rain-making' lamas were considered to
be extremely important, in a country which had so little rain, and their
abilities were taken very seriously. To his astonishment Michael found
that it really did rain when they were with the rain-making lamas in
Yon Tan, a nearby village. The Rizong monks spent a few days there
and each day, Michael records in *Imji Getsul*, the weather would take
the same course. It started off fine but by eleven o'clock the sky was
overcast, and not long after it would be raining somewhere in the
district. At Yon Tan it rained twice while they were there, and there
were two huge thunderstorms. This meant that the rivers would be full
and the success of that year's barley crop assured. Michael puzzled as
to how the lamas could make rain, and came to the conclusion that
it was achieved by intense concentration of the mind, which could
affect physical events. To this day the power of the rain-making lamas
remains a mystery; nobody really knows whether it would have rained

anyway, or whether they have actually induced the rain to come. (The great eleventh-century yogi Milarepa reputedly had the power to call up hailstorms at will – and these he rained down on his enemies.)

While at Yon Tan Michael was told that a star was going to move across the sky on a certain night – that of 17 August 1960. In the evening, back at Rizong, a *gelong* (a monk who has received Higher Ordination) burst into Michael's room to say that a star was indeed moving across the sky. Michael ran out instantly and saw what looked like a star moving across the mountain range. At first he thought it must be an optical illusion, but then realized that it was definitely moving.

The general opinion of the monks was that it was something dastardly from Russia, but Michael wondered if it could be a flying saucer, or a UFO: he now believed in the existence of such things.

The star was seen the following evening, and Michael was asked by the other monks what it could possibly be. He gave his theory of flying saucers and the speculation went on as the star continued to be visible for more than a week. It was, of course, the Soviet sputnik, and the monks were right, although they never read newspapers nor did they have access to radio or television.

During August Michael noticed a dramatic change in the weather. Suddenly summer disappeared and autumn came, in a single day. The wind became very cold and Michael shivered in his bare-shouldered red robes, by now stained and streaked all over and torn in many places. But there was no wherewithal to get another robe. He also found that his room and several of his books were louse-ridden. He naturally started killing the nits, but the head lama Kushok was horrified when he saw Michael squashing the lice between his finger and thumb and reminded him that killing was contrary to Buddhist doctrine. All the other monks would just flip the lice out of the window, leaving them still alive. To the Buddhist, especially the ordained monk, all life is sacred, but Michael's Western upbringing was all too quick to reassert itself where these unwanted creatures were concerned.

Michael amused all the other monks when he announced one day that he would make an apricot tart. Apricots are the one fruit found in abundance in Ladakh, and they resemble exactly the famous Hunza apricots. The normal ingredients for an apricot tart, which include butter and sugar, were of course not available, and he had to use *tsampa* (barley) flour instead of wheat flour for the pastry.

But he persevered, rolling out the pastry, trimming the edges from the dish, then adding a pastry lid to the boiled apricots and cutting the traditional little slit in the top. As he was doing this, all the other monks watched in amazement. They had never seen anybody cooking fruit before, nor could they see the point when you could just eat the fruit direct from the trees. Michael put the tart to cook on the red ashes in the kitchen range, and when it was ready bore it in triumph to Kushok and the Rimpoche, to give them a quarter each. The dish was supposed to be a treat, but it was not popular. Most of the monks put their portions back on to their plates after taking one bite. Michael, however, did not mind all that much because he scoffed all the leftovers and, for the first time since he had arrived at Rizong, felt his hunger was satisfied.

As he worked in the kitchen he regretted that he knew so much about nutrition, which had been part of his medical course, for it was obvious, when the calories and vitamins in a typical meal were added up, that the food was woefully inadequate. He wrote that he sometimes wondered what the monks' total calorific intake was over the day – and came to the conclusion that it would hardly be considered enough to sustain life in the West.

Michael Dillon had been celibate for the whole of his life, not necessarily from choice, but now for the first time he was among people who had consciously committed themselves to a lifetime of celibacy. The punishment for a monk who indulged in sexual intercourse was instant removal of his status as a monk. Yet Michael was to find few, if any, instances of Buddhist monks becoming sexually frustrated through lack of an outlet. He wrote that there were no 'perverted practices' at all at Rizong, though he does record that one of the older monks tried to stroke him in the wrong way when he first arrived at the monastery. This may have been Michael's interpretation of a completely innocent gesture: one can never know. At any rate, Michael dealt with the problem by hitting the senior monk with his fist, and the incident was not repeated. 'At all events,' he wrote, 'heavy manual labour always helps in this respect, and there was plenty of that for anyone who wanted it, in fetching wood and water up the mountain.' The sparse vegetarian diet, too, did little to promote sexual desire.

The life of Buddhist monks, especially in such a remote place as Ladakh, might be assumed to be monotonous. But as Michael Dillon's account shows the days can be packed with incident and variety. One day the Rizong monks heard that the governor of Kashmir, Karan Singh, was touring Ladakh and would be passing in a jeep, together with Kushok Bakula, Michael's guru. Michael was ordered to get ready and at once go down the hillside to wait for the governor's arrival. He had already met the governor, having been invited to tea when he was staying in Kashmir prior to going to Ladakh. The governor had naturally been intrigued to meet an English 'lama' and had lent Michael a book from his library. Michael surveyed his now black and filthy robe with distaste and wished he had a clean one in which to greet the governor. Even so, he felt excited and there was a holiday atmosphere at the monastery.

But when he got down to the road – a lengthy journey – he was told by two military policemen in another jeep that Karan Singh was ill and would not be passing after all; he had decided not to finish his tour and would be returning directly to Kashmir after resting in Saspola, a village about five miles away from Rizong.

The head monk from Rizong, who had ridden down the mountainside on his own white horse, asked Michael if he would go to see the governor and treat him, in his capacity as an English doctor. Michael quickly summed up the situation: he would have to travel to Saspola by foot, as there was no other means of transport available. But he agreed, and eventually, at about four o'clock in the afternoon, he set out bearing letters for Karan Singh and also for his own guru, Kushok Bakula, who was in the party.

Michael managed to hitch a lift from a passing military truck and arrived at Saspola quickly, only to be told that the party had gone back to Leh, the capital, about thirty miles away. Michael was in a quandary, as he had not received permission to go as far as Leh, but reasoned that he was a doctor and that the governor might need urgent medical help. So he went back to the truck and asked the driver if he was going on to Leh himself. On being told that he was, Michael got back in and was driven there sitting on top of a pile of soldiers' kitbags.

It was now night, quite dark and also cold; by the time he reached Leh Michael was both frozen and starving hungry. The truck stopped at the barracks just outside the capital and Michael had to finish his journey on foot. He decided to spend the night at Lama Lobzang's house, as he had already received an open invitation to stay there at any time. Michael found the house quite easily – Leh is very tiny, consisting of only one main street – and was glad to see a light from an oil lamp in the living room. He knocked and banged on the door, but nobody answered, so he sat down on the step to wait, huddled in his robes. Eventually he took the decision that there was nothing for it but to break in, which he did by climbing through a window. He tried to sleep on the wooden bed inside the house.

When dawn came Michael was away quickly, still shivering with cold as he had been all night, and set off to find Sankar Gompa. He arrived before anybody was up and soon found his guru, Kushok Bakula, who told him that the governor was not really ill at all, but that the constant jolting of the jeep had irritated an old wound he had suffered years previously and made his leg ache badly, so he had had to rest.

As so often before, Michael experienced intense disappointment, having fantasized in the jeep about saving the life of the governor. Moreover, he discovered that even if the governor *had* been seriously ill, there would have been plenty of highly qualified doctors around, attached to the army (currently in Ladakh to prepare for a possible Chinese invasion of the territory).

While Michael was wondering how he would get back to Rizong, Kushok Bakula told him that he was holding a reception that day for the governor, to which Michael was invited. Once more, Michael looked at his torn and dirty robes in utter dismay. He asked for at least hot water to wash in, and was given a basinful, plus some Lux soap, and had a bath far more luxurious than any he had managed for the past two months, when he had to wash in an icy mountain stream using a tiny piece of soap which refused to lather in it. He was also lent a newer outer robe, but there was no other skirt available. None the less, he had managed to spruce himself up quite a bit for the occasion.

At about midday the guests started arriving and the monks moved out to the grounds, where a marquee had been erected and rows of chairs put on the grass outside it. Many army personnel were present. Michael felt desperately ashamed of himself in his dirty clothes and tried to stay in the background; but before long people began to realize who he was and expressed a desire to speak to him. Apart from Kushok Bakula himself Michael was the only monk at the gathering, and his robes made him stand out from the crowd.

Some very important guests were attending, including the Rani of Ladakh, a relative of Kushok Bakula, whom Michael found extremely attractive. He records that she wore a plum-coloured velvet dress and light blue silk trousers – the costume still seen on many Ladakhi women. The Rani would not speak to Michael as she had been taught from birth not to look at men other than those to whom she was related, and was conditioned to casting down her eyes when passing by a strange man.

A band started playing, an archery contest was held and, after that, luncheon was served. It was a wonderful meal, by far the best that Michael had eaten since arriving in this strange country. He was busily eating chips and tomato salad when Kushok signalled for him to come to the 'high table' where all the dignitaries were. So up he went in his streaked and stained robes and ate more magnificent food, including a bowl of canned peaches – unprecedented luxury. He felt, as he filled himself up with good food for the first time in many months, that his decision to take the trip had been highly worthwhile.

When the feast was finished, Michael pondered again on how he would get back to Rizong. He had not been given permission to stay out so long and was now eager to return, as the other monks would be wondering what had happened to him. Michael was offered a lift back to Rizong by one of the frontier guards who was touring Ladakh in a jeep. He promised to return in an hour with his driver.

Michael waited for two hours, then the jeep arrived to pick him up. The guard's name was Yusuf Ali, and he spoke excellent English. This was also a great treat, as Michael had not spoken English since arriving in Ladakh, and conversing in Tibetan and Ladakhi was never less than a struggle for him. Michael learned that the guard had been educated in England – London and Bristol – whereupon he asked immediately whether he had ever come into contact with Canon Millbourn of Bristol Cathedral. Astonishingly, Yusuf Ali had. The rest of the journey passed in pleasant reminiscences.

When Michael arrived at Rizong, in the dark, he found many of the monks still up, excited to learn what he had been doing and what had kept him so long. They were particularly impressed to learn that he had eaten lunch with the governor of Kashmir. The head monk also waived the rules so far as to allow Michael and his guests, Yusuf Ali and the driver, some food before they went to bed, even though the monks were not supposed to eat after midday. Michael was ravenous again, having eaten nothing since lunchtime.

By now Michael's three months in Ladakh were almost up. He had been told by Kushok Bakula that all attempts to renew the permit or to get an extension had failed, and that he would now have to leave the monastery in two weeks' time, at the beginning of October. Michael wrote: 'And I did not want to go at all! I had been happy here, despite the hard, uncomfortable life, and I felt that I had at last found my home.'

He knew he would not be able to stay over the winter, but hoped that by the following spring he would be able to get a new permit and come back again. In the meantime, he should be able to receive the Higher Ordination and become a *gelong* – no longer a novice but a fully-fledged Rizong monk.

On the morning that he had to leave the entire monastery came out to see him off. Some horses had been brought up to take Michael and his belongings down to the road and thence on to Leh. Michael was intrigued at the prospect of travelling into the capital by horse, but soon discovered that there would be only two horses available instead of the promised eight, which meant that for much of the time he would have to walk, with four other lamas who were also making the journey. It would take about three days. 'I welcomed it as a new experience and adventure,' he wrote.

He had a total of four rupees with him, to buy bread, if necessary. The small party was to spend the nights in mountain huts. Eventually he arrived in Leh and, with Kushok Bakula and his attendants, boarded the military plane at Leh airport which was to take him back to Srinagar.

The Rizong interlude was over. In the three months that he had been there, Michael felt that he had really become one of the monks, and he had largely been able to forget the trials and troubles of the previous years. The sheer harshness and activity of the monks' life had driven out all self-pity and negative emotions.

For the next few months Michael's home was to be the Maha Bodhi Society in Sarnath, where the daily struggle for existence had to be resumed. He lost no time in writing an account of his stay at Rizong, and then contacted Simon Young at John Murray to see if he would be interested in publishing it.

In view of the fact that Michael arrived back at Sarnath only at the beginning of October 1960, it is rather astonishing to learn that by 12 October Simon Young was writing from John Murray to say that he had received the first three chapters of Michael's book about life in a Buddhist monastery. Either Michael must have started writing it while in Rizong, or he worked on it feverishly from the moment he returned from Ladakh. Simon Young received the first chapters in handwriting, as Michael had no access to a typewriter, which

175

rather suggests that the script was started while he was at the monastery.

Simon Young was not overwhelmingly enthusiastic. His reply to Michael at Sarnath complained that the style tended to be formal and stilted at the beginning, 'where you were aiming at a legible handwriting', but said that it became more fluent later. He also felt that Michael did not succeed completely in conveying the very special atmosphere of the monastery, or in painting vivid enough portraits of the unusual people he met there. 'It is too much a chronicle of superficial outward events,' Young complained, 'and the life, the humanity, the underlying feelings and motives escape.'

Young ended his letter by asking to see the rest of the manuscript and saying that there were certainly the elements of an unusual and interesting book in the story. He asked particularly for more depth and colour.

By 14 October Michael had written 50,000 words and also sent another manuscript off to John Murray, to be included in the *Wisdom of the East* series. This, called *Shes Rub Dong Bu* (Michael's version, based on a 1919 translation by a Major Campbell, of an ancient text on the wisdom of discipline), Simon Young had no hesitation in turning down instantly. In the meantime, however, the contract for *The Life of Milarepa* had been signed by Canon Millbourn, who was to act as Michael's informal literary executor, and the agent John Johnson had agreed to take Dillon on. A third manuscript, a short life of the Buddha, had also arrived at the John Murray offices in Albemarle Street, and this was given careful consideration; in the end it was turned down.

Simon Young described, in a letter to Jack Cranmer-Byng, general editor of the *Wisdom of the East* series, his reservations about the manuscript of the life of the Buddha:

> After all he has only been a Buddhist for a short time and rather went off on the rebound from Western religion judging by his autobiography, and the Series might look a little foolish if, in a few years, he was back again having changed his mind. Do you agree about this?

Jack Cranmer-Byng had recommended acceptance of the life of the Buddha and felt that the volume 'should prove a useful and saleable addition to the series'. In November, however, Cranmer-Byng agreed with Simon Young that he had come to a 'sensible decision' about Jivaka's latest biography.

Simon Young wrote back to Cranmer-Byng on 21 November 1960 that he would be 'rather intrigued to see Jivaka one of these days and find out what sort of person he really is'. He never did meet him, in fact. He learned about his history only a month or so after Michael had died.

After finishing the *Imji Getsul* manuscript and sending it to the agent John Johnson, Michael became very seriously ill, which was hardly surprising considering the privations he had endured at Rizong. Strangely enough, he did not appear to have become ill while at the monastery, but now the semi-starvation and the harsh way of life had begun to take their toll. In December he succumbed to typhoid fever; he had also sustained liver damage and was suffering from jaundice. He wrote to Simon Young from the Rama Krishna Mission Hospital that the local medical staff did not know how to treat these conditions properly, and could not provide the diet which, ideally, he should have had – jelly, beef, tea, strained soups and so on. Michael sent a member of the hospital staff to find some Heinz baby foods, but he had no idea what to look for and came back with Oxo cubes at the huge price of 9½d (about 4p) a cube.

Michael told Simon Young that he expected to be in the hospital for some time and that when he emerged, 'a yellow skeleton', he was going to convalesce at one of the big Western hotels in Varanasi, where they understood English food. In a previous letter, Simon Young had written to Michael to tell him the rest of the advance for *Milarepa* was on its way; Michael had been overjoyed, believing that his financial problems would now be solved for the time being. The money would enable him to convalesce properly. 'Write to tell me what you did for Xmas,' he ends a letter dated 19 December 1960, adding: 'There won't be any here. Nor would there if I had been up, but still . . .' Self-pity, always Michael's greatest character weakness, still threatened to overcome him at the first opportunity. After all, it was entirely by his own choice that he was now in India and poverty-stricken. He could have had enough money to stay in luxury hotels all the time, if he had not had his 'will' executed while still alive. But it is of course a common practice for people embracing the religious life to give up their worldly possessions, wealth and spirituality being uneasy bedfellows. What is illogical about Michael Dillon is that he did these things and then complained about the inevitable consequences. There is no indication anywhere in his writings that he ever reaped the spiritual rewards of the religious life, however –

177

for example, achieving a state of altered consciousness through the meditation and *pujas*.

Many people who have given up Western life to follow an Eastern guru or to embrace an Eastern religion do so because they have experienced complete and utter bliss in the presence of their master, or while meditating. It is this which enables them to endure all the privation and discipline. This bliss makes all other experiences pale into insignificance. But nowhere at all does Michael state that, for example, he saw a joyous vision, beheld the face of God, or had a sense of being bathed in a sea of rapture. When he heard Buddhist teachings explained properly for the first time, they made complete sense to the logical part of his brain, his intellect; sadly, however, he never seemed to embrace them with his intuition, or with what we should now call the right brain. When, all those years ago, Michael had written in his book *Self* that masculine logic and reasoning were more important and reliable than female intuition, he did not realize that he had seen the wrong quality as taking precedence. All his life, as a philosophy graduate, Michael had worshipped at the shrine of reason, but it let him down when he most needed it.

In order to embrace the religious life fully and be happy in it he was obliged to recall the feminine side of his nature, the one that had been so ruthlessly suppressed over the years and dismissed as unimportant. In order for anyone to be happy as a spiritual person, the feminine side has to come to the fore. As this could never again happen with Michael, he was to be petulant and easily irritated – by bad food, slow-to-arrive cheques and the inconsistencies of other people.

Now came another trial, a delay in the payment of the final stage of the advance for the *Milarepa*. Problems had arisen: the Oxford University Press had informed John Murray that the copyright had not been properly cleared on the original translation for the popularized version to go ahead (despite the fact that OUP had previously written to Michael to say it had no objection to his book going ahead). But now, Young had had to write to Canon Millbourn asking him to return the agreement until the matter was sorted out, and informing him that the rest of the advance could not be paid until this had happened.

He wrote:

This will be sad news to Jivaka because in a letter received from him this morning he says that the promise of the remainder of his advance would have solved all his money problems this winter; and he is now in the Rama

Krishna Hospital in Benares with congestion of the lungs. However, we must accept the facts, and I shall write to tell him the news immediately.

Michael was certainly being tested. His problems seemed never-ending. Here he was, now aged 45, lying ill, alone and penniless in a strange hospital where, to his Western doctor's eyes, the treatment he was was receiving was completely wrong. He was also having to pay for his antibiotics, out of a non-existent income. Added to this, another Christmas in isolation was approaching, and he could not get on with writing, the only means now left to him of earning any money.

One cannot help wondering why this unceasing succession of misfortunes came Michael Dillon's way. Now that he was an ordained, practising Buddhist monk, he himself could see these in terms of karma: for some reason he was attracting these misfortunes to himself, and would continue to attract them until valuable lessons had been learned. Already he was learning not to give into self-pity, that seductive negative emotion which had troubled him since childhood and even now often tended to rise to the surface to ruin his equanimity.

There is no indication that Michael ever became truly spiritual, or that he was able to change his character markedly. He retained all his old power to annoy and irritate people and could rarely empathize with them. This lack of empathy was the main reason why Michael was so isolated all his life. Honest and well-meaning as he was, at heart he was just not interested in other people. This was probably why the manuscript of *Imji Getsul* did not come alive for Simon Young, who was looking forward to dramatic descriptions of the colourful characters Michael must have met in Ladakh. But it was no use expecting these: Michael just did not have the gift of imaginative expression, because he was too bound up in himself ever to be able to put himself in someone else's position or try to see life from another's point of view. He was in no sense a creative writer, although he was able, having worked to develop the logical and rational side of his nature for many years, to describe the main doctrines of Buddhism very clearly.

Michael received the letter from Simon Young saying his advance payment had been held up while he was still in hospital. By 29 December Michael was too weak to write properly; he could only just manage to acknowledge letters, in a very shaky, palsied hand. The news that the copyright on the *Milarepa* translation had not been cleared and that his money had been delayed could hardly have helped his recovery. His condition was steadily worsening.

More protracted to-ing and fro-ing took place, between Oxford University Press, Dr Evans-Wentz (the author of the original translation) in America and Michael in India. It all took months and months – and as there was only the last instalment of a £25 advance at the end of it, Michael must have wondered whether it was all worth the trouble. John Murray would easily have spent over £25 in postage by this stage. The final outcome was that Evans-Wentz granted permission for the use of his translation but asked for half the royalties on the new book. Young wrote to Michael asking if he had any objection. By this time Michael must have been weary indeed of the matter, but he agreed to the half royalty.

He sent some photos of Rizong to Canon Millbourn, to be included in *Imji Getsul* when it was finally published. One is of a group of monks which includes Jivaka, and Millbourn wrote to Simon Young asking that on no account should this photograph be enlarged, in case anybody recognized Jivaka from the picture (he added that this was highly unlikely, and must have been horrified himself at the emaciated appearance of his long-time friend). Michael's own writings reveal no indication that his new friends in India were concerned for his health or welfare. This may well have been the case, for the Buddhist view would have been that if the body was too sick to maintain life it was better to leave it and be reborn in a fresh body, one that might serve the soul better.

In the end, John Murray turned the *Imji Getsul* manuscript down, with the excuse that it would not fit in with the list. John Johnson sent it off immediately to Routledge, Kegan Paul, where it was accepted instantly and an advance of £100 offered.

By March 1961 things were looking up. Michael had recovered from his illness and was back at the Maha Bodhi centre; the copyright matter had been sorted out and the *Milarepa* was going to press; so too was *Imji Getsul*, which Routledge had accepted without requesting alterations.

On 7 March 1961 Michael wrote to Simon Young: 'I'm beginning to feel like an author!' A book he had written for teenagers on Buddhism had been accepted and published by an Indian publisher and was selling very well indeed, he reported to Young. Perhaps his luck was now turning and he really would succeed as a writer.

Routledge did not, any more than John Murray, seek to probe

'Jivaka's' identity but was satisfied with Canon Millbourn's assurance that he was completely genuine and had his own reasons for wanting to remain incognito. Nor did the company enlarge the picture of him with the other monks and put it on the cover, as it might have done. In fact, although Michael had had so much hassle over *Milerapa* he was very lucky to have been dealing with editors such as the late Simon Young of John Murray and Colin Franklin of Routledge, who is now retired. Both men handled the manuscripts sensitively and competently without trying to discover who their author was or why he had decided to disappear. Also, Michael was thrilled with the amount of the Routledge advance, achieved, very probably, through the acumen of John Johnson. Michael had asked for the royalties to be sent straight to Rizong, as he fully expected to be back there within the next two or three months, perhaps permanently this time.

By March 1961 Michael had written at least six books, of which four had been accepted, two by English publishers and two by Indian publishers. In addition, he was still producing a steady stream of articles on aspects of Buddhism and was preparing a Tibetan grammar and dictionary. There seemed no end to his industry, yet he was still not restored to full health. But after the miserable Christmas – always a feature of his life – he had pulled through. His next hurdle was to try to regain admission into Ladakh, for summer was approaching once more.

12

Last Days

ALL his life Michael Dillon had been a prolific correspondent, and still, despite the continuing difficulty of finding the money to pay for postage, he was despatching regular long letters to Simon Young, to his literary agent John Johnson and to Canon Millbourn, as well as composing several articles a week and writing both short stories and more books. Almost as soon as Simon Young introduced him to John Johnson, Michael began deluging the literary agency with manuscripts, synopses and ideas.

John Johnson, who died in 1987, made heroic efforts to sell Michael's *Life of the Buddha,* a book of short stories called *Bell, Book and Dorge* and *External Forms of Tibetan Buddhism,* all of which John Murray rejected; however, even Johnson drew the line at the Tibetan grammar, writing to tell Michael that he could not see any possible market in the United Kingdom.

While this prodigious effort was going on, Michael's health had steadily deteriorated. He had realized long before, when still in Ladakh, that he had become shockingly weak. This was brought home to him when, one day, he tried to pick up a bale of wool and failed. His humiliation was complete when the same bale was picked up easily by a small boy – and when, later, he saw nuns from the nearby nunnery carrying far larger bales without any apparent difficulty. He also found it impossible to carry a sack of *tsampa.* 'After managing to get it on my back I was unable to raise it and myself up the first steep step, try as I would, although I had been a rowing man at Oxford and had several cups to my credit,' he recalled in *Imji Getsul.* Michael put this physical weakness down to 'two years of malnutrition'. Now, in March 1961, he broke his arm and had to have it set in plaster, which meant he had to write letters with his left hand.

Soon after his arm mended, Michael set about trying to get a new permit to enter Ladakh. He went to Kashmir once more to stay with Kushok Bakula, his guru, and was assured that there would be no difficulty. But although he tried repeatedly, the permit was absolutely refused this time.

It seems that the Indian government harboured ideas that he might be a spy in disguise. By this time Michael was writing regularly for the *Hindustani Times* on aspects of Buddhism. For one of these articles the editor had requested a few lines of autobiography to explain who Jivaka was and why he should be writing these articles with, apparently, so much inside knowledge. Michael mentioned that he had stayed during the previous year in a Ladakhi monastery, to which he hoped to return. A communist weekly paper called *The Blitz* had noticed this and written a column charging Michael with being in the British Intelligence, an ex-Royal Navy Officer and a spy hired by Nehru to spy on the Chinese in Ladakh.

Michael records that this idea was so fantastic that nobody could possibly have believed it. But they did. The matter of Michael's permit blew up into quite an issue, with Indian communist MPs asking about his visit to the defence area of Ladakh and questioning whether he was in fact trying to discover strategic or otherwise sensitive information. Nehru himself intervened and declared that Jivaka was a genuine Buddhist, not a spy at all. Some of the other MPs alleged that he was only posing as a monk and was really one of those Oxbridge spies, like Burgess and Maclean. Michael wrote that the idea of him being a spy was fantastic, but for many Indians the notion of a British doctor being an ordained Buddhist monk, and wanting to live in a remote Ladakhi monastery, must have seemed far more fantastic and unbelievable than the spy theory.

One Indian newspaper also published a garbled story of how Michael had once been a lady doctor but had changed sex and was now a Buddhist monk. Michael never discovered the source of this story, but suspected one of the Indian *bhikshus* in Sarnath. Perhaps they had been talking amongst themselves when the story leaked out. One way and another, therefore, Michael Dillon was now regarded as a highly peculiar character, and one who should not on any account be allowed into a politically sensitive area such as Ladakh. Nobody tried to find out the truth from Michael, but of course he was himself very evasive: he had no wish to reveal to anybody in India who he really was.

At any rate, he was not given permission to return to Ladakh and there seemed no chance whatever that he would be able to go back to Rizong. It was, in all probability, this refusal which hastened his death, even though he was by now leading a very full life in the Buddhist community, writing several articles a week for Indian and Buddhist publications, teaching English at the Sanskrit University of Varanasi and preparing for his own Higher Ordination.

He was, however, very excited about his forthcoming publications. The work on *Imji Getsul*, scheduled for publication in spring 1962, was going well, and Michael compared this book's swift and easy passage unfavourably with the slow progress of *Milarepa* in a rather muddled letter to Simon Young:

> Your letter re Milarepa proofs received last night and filled me with horror. I though you would have had them corrected in England. Apart from the good chances of their getting lost in the post, awful as it is out here, the return postage is going to wreck my carefully planned budget which is to get me back to Sarnath and get in a small initial supply of food and no more. [When Michael received the proofs he was still in Kashmir with Kushok Bakula.] Routledge's have had everything done in the UK, paying a bloke [to read the proofs], the money to come out of royalties in the future, except the pictures which they sent over.

Simon Young replied:

> Sorry to hear that the news of the proofs being on the way has filled you with dismay. You must be one of the very few authors who does not like to see their work again at this late stage, but it is understandable with your tight budget. John Murray are pleased to advance you the postage for the single copy you have to return.

Simon Young also mentioned the manuscript of yet another book, about Nanak, the fifteenth-century teacher and founder of the Sikh religion, which Michael had wondered about for the *Wisdom of the East* series, but which John Murray turned down. Although Young's many letters to Michael are unfailingly polite and good-humoured, it could be that this strange Jivaka, who in spite of a constant lack of money kept writing and sending manuscripts by almost every post, was beginning to get on his nerves. Michael did have this effect on many people, after all.

In a later letter to Simon Young, dated 5 November, Michael again complains about the firm of John Murray:

I am amazed at publishers. You throw over my Imji Getsul which will undoubtedly sell well, and then reject the Nanak book which is a gem for the Wisdom of the East. Have you anything on his teaching in your series? I have never seen anything. Very strange. In fact – nuts!

Despite Michael's own deep imbibing of the Wisdom of the East, he had not learned to be tactful.

While staying in Kashmir he started working part-time as a doctor at a hospital in Srinagar, although he does not say whether he was paid for this work. Most probably he was not; he wrote in a letter to Simon Young in October 1961 that he would miss his weekly operating session when he returned to Sarnath, but whether for financial reasons or reasons of self-fulfilment is not known.

Michael was now plagued with constant colds, influenza and other illnesses, not always easily diagnosable, throughout which he continued his writing and his teaching work at the Sanskrit University of Varanasi.

This Christmas, 1961, he had a much better time, as he went to Delhi to the home of his Indian publisher friends Mr and Mrs Bedi. Mrs Bedi was an Englishwoman and her husband, educated at Oxford, was a half-blue, so Michael reckoned they had plenty in common. They had a real 'English' Christmas, with a Christmas tree, one of the other guests (an American lady) dressing up as Father Christmas. But, Michael being Michael, there were of course disasters to offset the pleasure of having a proper Christmas. On the train journey to the Bedis he had his bag and coveted Tibetan boots stolen – he had no hope of getting any more – and the Christmas pudding which Canon Millbourn had sent him simply failed to arrive. As ever, he had plenty of cause to be miserable. He had to keep reminding himself that, according to Buddhist teaching, nothing material is permanent and so nothing material really matters. But he could never feel this, although rationally he had accepted it as a good attitude to take.

He was also complaining to Simon Young that the promised money from John Murray, to cover postage and the rest of his advance from *Milarepa*, had still not arrived, even though the agreement had been drawn up and finalized many months previously. In January 1962 Michael wrote to Young:

> I am eating my lunch with one hand and writing with the other. Boiled veg, potato, carrot, onion and cauliflower, only half the pot today and half tomorrow. Bread and butter and jam to follow. But if you think this is rather meagre fare please get on to Coutts to see what they are doing about the draft: is it registered?

He complained endlessly to Simon Young about having to eat the same tedious vegetables for lunch day after day, and that the banker's draft had not arrived, although none of this was Young's fault. Eventually the money did arrive, just before Michael was making plans to leave Varanasi for Kashmir, and to renew his efforts to get back into Ladakh. Perhaps the troubles of the previous year would not reassert themselves, and everybody would have forgotten the story about his being a communist spy. He was now suffering from eye trouble, a recurring problems since Oxford days, and had to see a surgeon in Benares.

He had now received a copy of the dust jacket of *Milarepa* and was horrified at the picture of the monks on the cover. 'They are shockingly long-haired,' he complained to Simon Young, but grudgingly admitted that the rest of the cover was 'OK'. Simon Young good-humouredly replied that as they did not really know what monks looked like in Tibet in the eleventh century, perhaps they could be allowed to get away with this one.

In April 1962 both *Milarepa* and *Imji Getsul* were published, and Michael waited hopefully for news of reviews. Both John Murray and Routledge had sent him the six free copies to which he was entitled as an author.

But suddenly the voluminous correspondence which Simon Young, Canon Millbourn and John Johnson had come to expect from Jivaka stopped. On 22 April Canon Millbourn wrote to Simon Young saying that he had not received a copy of *Milarepa* from Jivaka or heard from him at all for several weeks. He wrote to ask whether Simon Young had received any word from him recently, and the answer was no. Canon Millbourn had now retired from Bristol Cathedral and gone to live in Dorset, where he had married an old friend, his first wife having died the previous year. As Canon Millbourn was responsible for Michael's literary affairs in England a friendship had grown up between him and Simon Young, and the two now regularly corresponded, and even met on occasion.

But neither of them had heard a word from Michael, either to acknowledge receipt of the complimentary copies or to register excitement at having two books issued by major publishers in the same month.

On 21 May Simon Young wrote to Canon Millbourn saying he had heard from John Johnson that there had been a notice in *The Times* the previous Saturday announcing that Jivaka had died. 'Apparently it was a very brief paragraph from Reuter's giving no details. I wonder if you saw it or have already had news from India?' Young asked.

He had not, but on 30 May Simon Young received the following letter from a Sister Vajira in Darjeeling:

Dear Sir,
In case the following news has not reached you, I have to report that Lobzang Jivaka died at the Civil Hospital, Dalhousie [Punjab], India, on May 15th.

You recently published a book by him on the Life of Milarepa, Tibet's Great Yogi.

Yours truly,
Vajira.

The announcement in *The Times* on 20 May read simply:

DELHI. Lobzang Jivaka, formerly Dr Laurence M. Dillon, of Britain, who became a Buddhist, is reported to have died in the Himalayan town of Dalhousie after a short illness.

None of the monks ever wrote from India to any of Michael's contacts in London to say what he had been doing in Dalhousie, or what the mysterious illness was which finally killed him at the age of 47, fifteen days after his birthday. No letters were received by his guru Kushok Bakula or any of the other monks with whom Michael had lived and worked over the past four years. But a few weeks later a story appeared in the Buddhist journal *The Middle Way* recounting how, while on his way to Kashmir to join Kushok Bakula, Jivaka had suddenly become very ill; after being taken to the Dalhousie Hospital he had died within two days and was cremated according to Mahayana rites, the lamas officiating. This journal, which printed a full obituary, stated that Michael was a prolific writer of books and articles, and also of letters to friends. It did not reveal what illness he had died of, or what treatment he had been given in hospital. It all sounded very sudden indeed, and to this day the exact cause of Michael's death remains a mystery. It might have been a heart attack, typhoid or even some kind of poisoning . . . The hospital sent no more details, just the cryptic letter from the nurse, Sister Vajira.

The article in *The Middle Way* contained a tribute from Professor Guenther, who had first aroused Michael's interest in Ladakh and Rizong Gompa. Guenther said:

> Our mutual friend Jivaka is dead. I am very sad, as not only did I like him very much, he also was seriously trying to find access to a little-known world of inner experience. We hope this seeking will be carried on in a future life, and that his path may be made more easy of pursuit.

Some weeks after reading about the death of Jivaka, John Johnson received the manuscript of his autobiography, which had been completed just 15 days before his death. The manuscript, well typed on very thin foolscap sheets, provided details of his early life, the sex change, the years on board ship and in India. It is a very full, honest and factual autobiography, but John Johnson was unable to find a publisher for it. Despite having so recently published *Imji Getsul*, which was attracting highly favourable reviews, Routledge turned this one down as being 'quite unpublishable'.

Norman Franklin of Routledge, cousin of Colin Franklin, remembers the manuscript as being 'very serious and sad' and retained a vivid picture of Michael's miserable years as a garage hand in Bristol, while he was attempting to change roles. He says now that he wished Routledge had decided to publish the manuscript, but it was felt at the time that the sex-change story was too sensational and not suitable for their list. John Johnson was certain that somebody would be interested in publishing the book, especially now that Michael Dillon's story had come out and everybody knew who this mysterious 'Jivaka' was, but there were complications. Michael had sighed the manuscript 'Michael Dillon' as well as Lobzang Jivaka, indicating that he now wished his true identity to be revealed. Perhaps, when writing the autobiography, which was compiled from personal notes and journals he had kept all his adult life and could not have taken him more than a month, he realized that the end was near. There is, however, no hint of impending death and no mention of illness on 1 May 1962 (his 47th birthday), when he finished the typescript and sent it off, which indicates that death was very sudden. Michael enclosed with the manuscript a hand-coloured photograph of himself as a Buddhist monk, a further indication that he did not wish to remain incognito any more.

The autobiography begins by complaining that if men and women had a right sense of values, there would have been no need for this book to be written and published: all the hurt and upset he had suffered four years previously when his story leaked out was intact, resurfacing as he went about his daily life in India. The autobiography is not bitter in any way – except where he describes the attitude of the *Sunday Express* – and is very factual and detailed. Several publishers who read it pronounced it 'boring'. Even so, it is surprising that Johnson could not find a home for it, for the story is so very unusual and remarkable that it would surely have aroused a lot of interest.

In his foreword to the autobiography Michael expresses a hope that the book will bring to the public a greater understanding of those with gender problems. With understanding, he says, comes an improved sense of values, and this is the first step on the path to emancipation 'from the fetters of materialism and all that is driving man insanely to his own destruction'. The rather priggish and humourless tone of this foreword may have been a factor in publishers' lack of enthusiasm for the work.

A story appeared in the *Sunday Telegraph* on 24 June 1962 describing Michael's life and carrying some quotes from his brother Sir Robert, who told the reporter that after Michael's story had come out, years earlier, in the *Sunday Express,* 'there was nothing for him to do but to go into some sort of privacy.'

The report added that Sir Robert had given instructions to his Dublin solicitors to have the manuscript of Michael's autobiography burned, as he did not want it to be published, but John Johnson was quoted as saying: 'Dr Dillon felt there was no reason why, finally, his story should not be told. He wanted to tell it in his own way, in his own time.'

The *Sunday Telegraph* story mentioned that Michael had studied at the Sanskrit University of Varanasi and had made a 'will' just before he died. He was cremated as a Buddhist. This 'will', which left everything to Kushok Bakula and various Buddhist organizations in India, was later found to be invalid, as it was merely a deathbed scrawl which left Michael's closest friends in a quandary: it did not clarify what was to happen to the royalties from his books, and it failed to nominate a literary executor.

The day after the article appeared Sir Robert contacted his solicitors to say that he would not be prepared to give any more quotes to newspapers, and that if anybody asked questions of the sort that the *Sunday Telegraph* had asked, he or she should be referred immediately to Michael's solicitors. As far as the press was concerned, Sir Robert considered the matter had been aired and wanted it dropped. In the event, no more newspaper stories appeared.

Johnson contacted John Duff of Orpen and Co., Michael's solicitor in Dublin, to ask what was to be done about the manuscript of the autobiography, the royalties and any other literary matters pertaining to Michael. They had no real answer and simply advised Johnson to wait and see what happened. In the event, the autobiography, plus many other Dillon manuscripts and letters, mouldered in John Johnson's offices for a quarter of a century, untouched by anybody. After Michael's death, nobody wanted to take responsibility for the unpublished manuscripts, or for handling the royalties. Sir Robert had quickly made it clear that he did not want to be involved in any way with his brother's affairs. John Johnson sent the royalties as they came in to John Duff; maybe they went to the Maha Bodhi Society in Sarnath, as Michael had requested: the facts have proved impossible to clarify. John Duff, Canon Millbourn, John Johnson, Sir Robert Dillon and Simon Young are all dead, and no correspondence concerning Michael is dated later than the middle of 1963. It seems, from a letter Simon Young wrote to Millbourn, that the canon had some idea of publishing Michael's letters to him – which cover the years of the sex change and which, unfortunately, appear to have been lost – and also of reconstructing the 'unpublishable' autobiography. On 25 July 1963 Canon Millbourn wrote to Simon Young, who had asked whether he would be acting as Jivaka's literary executor:

> There was no formal arrangement between Jivaka and me, and I very much doubt if anybody stands confirmed, so to say, as his literary executor. He may have mentioned the point in the will he attempted to draw up in hospital, and perhaps Duff will sooner or later know what is in that document, as evidence of Jivaka's intentions. The will itself is, I gather, invalid in British law.
>
> What I had more immediately in mind when we were talking was the large collection of letters written to me by Jivaka. These would go

far towards reconstructing his autobiography, and I am wondering if the reconstruction at some future date would be of real interest and value.

But the matter of legal copyright arose at once. Simon Young informed Millbourn that he (the canon) head no legal copyright in the letters, or anything else, but the question of who did own the copyright was never settled. As John Duff is dead and his firm no longer in existence, it has proved impossible to discover whether Duff ever had received the hastily written deathbed 'will'. Not one person from those years, apart from the nurse at the Dalhousie Hospital, ever contacted Michael's agent or friends in England, even though he had told Canon Millbourn in a letter that he wanted to bequeath what was left of his worldly goods to his Buddhist friends.

Meanwhile, reviews of *Imji Getsul* were appearing. The first came out in the *Western Morning News* (Bristol) on 2 April 1962, before anybody knew who Jivaka really was, and says simply that the book throws further light on an utterly different way of life from most people's. Christopher Wordsworth of *The Guardian* recommended the book for its 'glimpses of the ardours and ordures of a rude medieval commensality [sic] and of a dedicated man. Serenely, he attests the prowess of the rain-making lamas.' Cecil Northcott of *The Sunday Times* felt that the book had 'the ring of truth and is well told', but not all reviews were so favourable. Those from religious publications felt that there was a decided lack of spirituality in the book, and wished there was more to indicate where the appeal of this way of life lay; everybody, however, felt that the account was absolutely authentic.

H.W. Ponder, writing in *The Age Literary Supplement*, opined:

There is nothing in his account to indicate what useful purpose such a monastery serves; and still less to attract other Western professional men to follow his example. If, indeed, Rizong Gompa is a fair sample, it is difficult to feel that the suppression of its counterparts in Tibet by the Chinese will be any great loss. . . . For all his philosophical musings, he never reveals an inkling of 'The Truth' he found that was so much more satisfying than one of the noblest and most unselfish vocations that can be practised by man – i.e., medicine.

This attitude was echoed by a review in *The Month*, which declared:

The author's resolution, enterprise and endurance in pursuit of his aim claim respect, but from a Christian standpoint he appears curiously lacking in self-knowledge and spiritual insight.

But in *The Daily Telegraph* on 22 June 1962 George Evans wrote:

Imji Getsul, whom we now know to have been Dr Laurence Michael Dillon, died, unhappily, in India last month, his mission unfulfilled. The fervour and sincerity of his final testimony of faith, strikes a clear and authoritative note of almost medieval piety. It is in every respect a worthy addition to the great literature of religious experience and thought of all ages and creeds.

The most common complaints were that the autobiographical element was too slight. Writing in the *Church of England* newspaper, K.N. Kibblewhite observes that: 'In all there are less than fifteen pages which tell us about this undoubtedly remarkable fellow who from Oxford in turn was theologian, doctor, deck-hand and then religious novice in distant Asia.'

The reviewers who complained that the autobiography lacks spiritual insight and self-knowledge were in fact right. Although interesting, it remains, like Michael's other books, a curiosity rather than a true work of literature or insight, and compares very badly with, for example, Andrew Harvey's *A Journey in Ladakh*, which is full of spiritual insights and reveals a high degree of self-knowledge on the part of its author. Harvey, a young poet from Oxford, also reached a crisis in his life, and felt that some greater understanding of life would be vouchsafed to him in Ladakh. It was.

No such revelations came to poor Michael. Although he struggled constantly to attain Truth, he never succeeded either in coming to terms with life or in getting to know himself. *Imji Getsul*, like so many of Michael's letters, is full of petty complaints, even about the *pujas*, or daily services, which he found boring, and the privations of the monks' way of life. He compares his breakfast of boiled radishes with the hot bacon and scrambled egg served at his London club, but never gives any indication that he has achieved spiritual insight or uplifting of the soul as a result of his three months at the monastery. He seems not to recognize that it is pointless to compare the two ways of life, ordinary Western and Eastern religious, as they have nothing whatever in common. He also reveals a distinct lack of empathy with the people. Although he states in the book that he does not want to leave Rizong, the reader cannot feel that Michael was ever at one with the life there. More generally, he never adapted to the sheer culture shock of India, which can be difficult even for those who do empathize with people from another culture.

The other book of his that was published at this time, *The Life of Milarepa,* is well written and surprisingly enjoyable, possibly because in this one Michael could lose himself in the story of another human being. But wherever he writes about himself the all-too-familiar self-pity tends to intrude. By the time he went to India the habit of this negative emotion had become so ingrained that he could not overcome it, even though he understood logically and rationally that self-pity was destructive. This emotion may indeed have helped to undermine his health and hasten his end.

Along with the self-pity went considerable foolhardiness. There was no need for Michael to have been so poor in India. Whenever he did have any money, such as when he received his naval pay, he gave it away instantly. Michael seemed to have a wish to live life always on the edge, at as harsh and uncomfortable a level as possible.

He could easily have been more sensible about his health, and made sure he ate and slept properly. But for some reason he did not want to: he became, in his own way, as silly as Daisy and Toto, who lived like paupers when they had a large amount of capital in the bank. Michael lived as a pauper in India because he would not hang on to money. He asked for some of the advance from Routledge to go straight to Rizong, for the monks there, even though he could hardly buy himself lunch in Sarnath. He could at least have made sure he was able to eat properly. Nor was there any need for him to have walked from Sarnath to Mussoorie, a distance of almost 600 miles, which he did six months after his ordination – an ordeal which is graphically described in *Imji Getsul.* For this pilgrimage Michael set out without money or belongings, just like a real Indian pilgrim. He soon found that nobody would give him either money or food, and he went for 27 hours on foot without receiving any food at all. He eventually reached Mussoorie eight days later, having completed the journey by truck, thanks to the kindness of a Sikh driver.

This experience undoubtedly contributed to his illnesses and continuing malnutrition. One thing Michael never learned in all his years was common sense.

His unpublished autobiography is divided into two parts, 'Conquest of the Body' and 'Conquest of the Mind'. He reckoned that once he had been made, cosmetically, into a male, he had conquered his own body, but in terms of his general health this was not the case at all. Similarly, though he tried to train his mind and though he tried his utmost to find his true self, through extensive reading of Gurdjieff and of Buddhist works, he never really succeeded, possibly because he tried too hard to obliterate the feminine, intuitive side of himself. He genuinely believed, as is evidenced in his book *Self,* that logical, step-by-step, more 'masculine' thinking was superior.

Although Michael struggled so hard and so valiantly to become a 'real' man, he never truly achieved this. He did not feel at home in female company, as he realized only too clearly at Oxford, but neither was he ever one of the boys. As a female and as a male, he was marked out to be a loner. He was not at ease in company and never lost the shyness which set in during his adolescence.

But finally, what kind of person was he? He was a fighter – somebody who all his life strove to overcome enormous odds. Although he never became famous, and never sought fame, he was in fact one of the more remarkable people of the twentieth century. From childhood, he exhibited a questioning, analytical spirit and would not simply do what was conventional. He did not ever set out to be unconventional – merely, as he so often said, to be himself. It was just unfortunate that in the struggle to become himself he had to fight, singlehandedly, such formidable battles.

The first major test of his inner strength came with his determination to secure a good education and get to Oxford, in spite of tremendous opposition from the aunts and also his elder brother. The aunts could not see the point of Oxford, or indeed of further education, and did their utmost to turn their tomboy niece into a quiet, obedient and ordinary young lady. Michael never had a single role model in his life, and was forced to be a pioneer in just about everything he did.

He had a remarkably good, and original, brain. Despite rather indifferent schooling, and no proper grounding in the classics, he managed to get an honours degree in the most difficult of university courses. Although he did not manage to attain the first-class honours that would have enabled him to carve out an academic career – which would surely have suited him perfectly – he did himself more than justice.

As a teenager, while still Laura, he found to his dismay that he did not fit in at all at Oxford. He could not wear ballgowns and go to dances, as the other young ladies did, and he was naturally excluded from many men's activities. But he took up rowing – and it is largely thanks to his efforts that women's rowing became a seriously acceptable university sport.

After Oxford he had endured the long, dreadful years of working in the garage, years when, unbeknown to anybody except one or two doctors, Michael was quietly changing his sex and preparing to face life as a surgically constructed man – something no woman had ever done before. Although there had been instances throughout history of women living as men, never before had a biological woman taken hormones and undergone surgery to effect a physical sex change.

Working in the garage and living among uneducated, low-class people meant a repudiation of all Michael's genteel upbringing. Although not personally snobbish, he had been brought up to consider himself a member of the upper classes, and certainly working in a garage was not something that could be deemed fit employment for a Dillon. The garage period was a time of almost intolerable loneliness, pain and anguish. No wonder Michael made a friend of the little orphan boy Gilbert Barrow – the only human being to show any kindness or understanding throughout that terrible time.

Even when Michael did eventually manage to re-register as a male, his troubles were far from over. There was the question of what to do with his life. Again, it was hardly an obvious or an easy solution to train to be a doctor. He had no grounding in science and therefore none of the normal qualifications which would enable him to enter medical school, and when he finally did so he was about ten years older than most of the other students. As with Oxford, he did it the hard way. During every vacation he underwent searingly painful surgery to achieve, from his own living flesh, a semblance of male organs. He returned from vacations weak and ill – something which the other medical students found extremely odd.

He not only passed all his examinations, but had a book published and a scientific paper accepted by the Irish Medical Society; in addition to this, he rowed for Trinity College. During his spare time, he wrote plays which he hoped might be staged in London. He also fell in love for the first time.

Although Michael was by nature a shy person, and many people thought him gruff and aloof, he had a great capacity for friendship. Even through the darkest, gloomiest years, he was sustained by friendships which lasted the whole of his life. He maintained contact with Gilbert Barrow until almost the day he died – and would have been thrilled to learn that Gilbert's son won a place at Brasenose College, Oxford. Michael also kept in regular contact with Canon Millbourn and with his philosophy tutor Jimmy McKie. It is often said that in order to have a friend you must be one, and Michael certainly fulfilled that criterion. He was extremely kind and generous, and more than one of his contemporaries at medical school has said that he was a 'lovely person', although always rather remote and difficult to get to know.

After medical school Michael could have settled down into the life of a country GP or a hospital doctor. But even in this instance he chose an unusual path. In a letter to Roberta Cowell, discussing their wedding plans, he had mentioned that at their wedding he wanted the hymn 'Father, hear the prayer we offer! Not for ease that prayer shall be. . .'

He considered that the lines

Not for ever in green pastures
Do we ask our way to be:
But by steep and rugged pathways
Would we strive to climb to Thee

could have been written expressly for him. His own life was never to be led in green pastures. The years as a ship's surgeon were hardly comfortable and secure. After each voyage ended he did not know when or whether he would be taken on again, and during that time he had no home base. In fact, he spent most of his shore leave staying at the Mission to Seamen.

Michael considered that he had found his true home when he became ordained a Buddhist monk. Here, again, he was a remarkable pioneer. No Westerner before him had ever been ordained a Buddhist monk in Tibet and certainly nobody from the West had ever lived in a Ladakhi monastery as one of the monks. Michael's literary output during the Buddhist years in India is astonishing. Although often ill, frequently lonely and almost always destitute by now, he turned out at least eight full-length manuscripts, as well as numerous articles for Buddhist and other Indian journals, and wrote hundreds of letters to friends. He referred to the little circle of friends who kept his true identity secret after his disappearance in India as 'The Jivaka Club'. Michael managed to remain cheerful in his letters, and there is no bitterness apparent in his writing, although he coped with a fair degree of rejection from publishers.

Ever since childhood, Michael had been determined never to have the same attitude towards money as his penny-pinching aunts. He was completely unmaterialistic and possessed no desire to make money at all. He inherited quite large sums at intervals throughout his life but gave most of the money away. He saw money as a means to do good, using spare cash to send Gilbert Barrow's son to a private school, to make funds available for struggling university students, and to support his fellow Buddhists. He may have been foolish to divest himself of so much of his worldly wealth on becoming a Buddhist monk – there is no doubt that his extreme poverty contributed to his early death – but, as ever, Michael wanted to do things properly. If he was going to be a monk, he must embrace the vows of poverty, chastity and obedience (as binding in Buddhist enclosed life as in Christian orders) completely and absolutely.

All his life Michael had a strong religious streak. He wanted to find out the truth – about himself, about the world around him, about God, and about different religions. He had quite a few qualms about abandoning his native religion but, again, was not afraid to be a pioneer. Nowadays many Westerners are Buddhists, but in Dillon's day it was still extremely unusual. Yet Michael seems to have gained little comfort from religion. There is no evidence from his writings that he ever felt himself close to God, or that he experienced the state of ecstasy and bliss which many religious people find is achieved by deep meditation.

But, gifted as Michael was, he grew up without two qualities which would have made life far easier for him – charm and tact. It was probably his painfully scrupulous honesty which accounted for his lack of tact. While in the employ of the De La Warr Laboratories, he accused the principal of cheating on his experiments. It is more than likely that he was right, but such an observation would hardly have made for good working relations. He informed Simon Young of John Murray that Routledge was an excellent publisher, and paying him very well – hardly the kind of comment one publisher is anxious to hear from his author about another. Michael's greatest failing – and surely one reason why his writings did not achieve more widespread success – was an inability to put himself in somebody else's position.

Given his own history, this may be understandable, but it led to Michael being accused of being selfish, of never taking anybody else's views into consideration, and of riding roughshod over the feelings of others. He did not really behave like this, but for him it was simply impossible to understand the thought processes of others. He was also somewhat short on humour – a quality which would surely have prolonged his life, had he possessed it. He could never laugh at himself or see the funny side of what he was doing. Perhaps he would have argued that there *was* no funny side, but laughter is a time-honoured release from pain and tension which seems to have been notably lacking in Michael's life. A good laugh would have enabled him to become more detached from himself, to see incidents such as that of the *Daily Express* cable in their true perspective rather than allowing them virtually to destroy him.

Although he readily made friends, Michael could not find many soulmates, which for him would have meant, essentially, someone who had been through a similar experience to himself. The only person with whom he ever felt a true affinity was Roberta Cowell, whose situation he saw as parallel to his own. He felt that he could confide to Roberta all the thoughts and longings that nobody else would understand. By this time desperate for love, Michael poured out love and affection in letters and gifts in a way that he had never before been able to do. The aunts had always repudiated his attempts to give them gifts, or show love, and he never had any real rapport with his brother.

After Michael finally realized that Roberta did not return his love, he adopted for the rest of his life the doctrine that the greatest love is that which is conferred unconditionally, without any expectation of return. He gave his love, his time, his money, to those who were materially worse off than himself, and who could not repay him in kind. Indeed, in many cases, the recipients did not even know who their benefactor was.

Michael was one of those unfortunate people whose views and beliefs were many years ahead of their time. He championed greater tolerance of homosexuality, lesbianism and sexual inversion at a time when people were far more rigidly confined to stereotyped gender roles than they are today. He argued for 'mutilation' of the body as the only real solution to the transsexual's problems decades before this method of treatment became generally acceptable. He embraced Buddhism many years before it became a trendy religion in the West, and before the 'counter-culture', with its antipathy towards materialism, established itself as a major force. Both in his life and in his beliefs Michael anticipated a great deal.

In attempting so valiantly to change himself for the better, he undertook a struggle which never ended and which was a factor in his early death. He attempted to 'conquer', as he put it, both his body and his mind.

His real tragedy was that, despite his unceasing search for truth, he felt compelled to live a lie – to pretend to the world he was something other than he was. Perhaps, however, by writing his memoirs with the intention that they should be published, and thus proclaiming to the world who and what he was, he finally achieved a kind of victory – and one which, after the trials and tribulations of his comparatively short life, he richly deserved.

Acknowledgements

Many people were kind enough to help with this book. I should particularly like to thank John G. Murray, of John Murray, the publishers, who discovered a huge pile of correspondence from and to Michael Dillon and allowed me access to this.

Andrew Hewson, of John Johnson, authors' agents, managed to unearth several unpublished manuscripts by Michael Dillon, which had languished in a dark corner for more than a quarter of a century, and also gave me access to a large number of Michael Dillon's letters. It was really the exciting discovery of this material which made the biography possible, for I should have had a hard job without it.

Norman Franklin of Routledge, Kegan Paul and his cousin, Colin Franklin, also of Routledge, and now retired, were both extremely helpful in making available reviews, newspaper cuttings and letters.

Thanks are also due to Gilbert Barrow, Michael's friend since 1941, who provided reminiscences as well as copies of *Imji Getsul* and *The Life of Milarepa*, Dillon's last works to be published in Britain and long out of print.

Several doctors who were medical students at Trinity College, Dublin at the same time as Michael Dillon provided me with additional material covering these years. Especial thanks to Dr Patricia Leeson, Dr James Morrow, Dr Hillas Smith, Dr Brendan Judge, Dr Doreen Mallagh, Dr John Meldrum and Dr Ruth Ransom.

Mr and Mrs Moncrieff, the present owners of the house in Folkestone where Michael Dillon was brought up, kindly took the trouble to show me round.

I am grateful to Hanif Boktoo, of Kolahoi Trekking and Travels, who arranged a special trip to Rizong Monastery, greatly off the beaten track, when I was travelling in Ladakh. I am very glad I was able to see for myself the Buddhist monastery where Michael Dillon lived as a novice monk. My thanks are due, too, to travel journalist Christopher Portway who struggled up the mountainside with a heavy camera to take pictures of Rizong while suffering badly from altitude sickness.

My greatest debt, however, is to Roberta Cowell, who knew Michael Dillon well between 1950 and 1951. It was she who first told me about him, about 17 years ago, and showed me many pictures of him as well as letters he had written. For this, and for our enduring friendship, thanks, Betty.

No help was provided by any member of Michael Dillon's family.

L. H.